Writing from the Trenches

Success-proven tips from 10 award-winning and bestselling authors

Connie Almony, Lynnette Bonner,
Hallee Bridgeman, Louise M. Gouge,
Michelle Griep, Julie Lessman,
Elizabeth Ludwig, Ane Mulligan,
MaryLu Tyndall, and Erica Vetsch

Writing from the Trenches

Success-proven tips from 10 award-winning and bestselling authors

© 2018 by Olivia Kimbrell Press, Inc.

ISBN-13: 978-1-68190-125-1 (Trade) | 978-1-68190-124-4 (POD) | 978-1-68190-123-7 (ebk)

Library of Congress Cataloging-in-Publication Data is on file at the Library of Congress, Washington, D.C.

Cover Design by Connie Almony
Editor: Louise M. Gouge

Dedication

To American Christian Fiction Writers, we thank you for being there for us when we were just starting out, providing support, connections, answers, and prayers.

Table of Contents

Section 5 – Finishing Touches

Connie Almony
Lynnette Bonner
Hallee Bridgeman
Louise M. Gouge
Michelle Griep
Julie Lessman
Elizabeth Ludwig
Ane Mulligan
MaryLu Tyndall
Erica Vetsch

SECTION 1

Getting Organized

Chapter 1
Plotting Techniques

You've heard the terms "plotter" and "seat of the pants" bounced around the industry. But what if you fall somewhere in between? What if you're the crazy oddball who doesn't start yours from the beginning but somewhere else?

This book has ten multi-published authors contributors. Each one of us has a different method of plotting ... or not. The purpose of this chapter is to help you find the best way for *you*. You may glean a few points from more than one and put those together for your own style. Bravo! You've found a way to plot.

Why is that even important? Because one day every writer will:

- Run into a brick wall and stall out,
- Have to produce a synopsis for their publisher before they write the book,
- Have to find out where to go or what is wrong.

All those problems can be solved by some creative plotting, brainstorming with a buddy or alone for the storyline. You can have some real breakthrough ah-ha moments while brainstorming a plot.

Connie Almony

It was the year before I began writing novels in earnest. I'd had one story swimming in my head for nearly two decades, but I had never believed I could finish an entire novel, complete with adventures, descriptions, and details. Then, I found a biography on one of my favorite Regency Romance authors, *The Private World of Georgette Heyer*, by Jane Aiken Hodge, and read the words that instilled the confidence to give it a whirl ...

And all sorts of things happen – though exactly what, I don't know.

You may wonder how these words could change me. They were the words of an author I'd admired as she outlined to a friend a story I'd read, and of which I knew the details, but at the time she wrote them, she had no clue how it would come together. Ms. Heyer had the characters. She had a hook. She had an ending. However, all the stuff in between remained a mystery. Knowing this was how she began, another mystery had been solved for me—the question of how I could begin to write a novel when I didn't have all the details. The answer? I didn't need them ... yet.

Then another exciting thing happened. I googled something about writing and found a description of *The Snowflake Method,* by Randy Ingermanson—a means of plotting a book not from beginning to end, but from global to specific. And the rest is history. I've never looked back and wonder how I'd ever been stuck before.

In his *Snowflake Method,* Mr. Ingermanson uses a metaphor that comes from an important mathematical object, the shape of a snowflake. Given he is a physicist, it makes sense he'd use it. However, not being a physicist—my careers include counseling, teaching, and motherhood—I like to think of this method as analogous to one of those children's biology books with clear overlays showing the total workings of the body. If you start at the front, you see a picture of a child. Turn the page, which is the top overlay, and you'll see the same child from underneath the skin. In other words, the muscle tissue. The next page turned reveals the organs, and the following shows the skeletal system. This visual of the child's body starts at the whole and digs a little deeper into more details as each page is turned.

This is how I construct a novel. I start with a general idea, maybe a sentence or two, then flesh it out into paragraphs, and then a lengthy description. After I have a several-page summary, I map scene ideas onto a calendar spanning the time period I project the story may take. Then I write detailed notes on the various scenes.

Because I start with a general idea of the story, sometimes I don't even write my scenes in order. I've been known to write the climax first, then go back in time to carry my characters to the finish line. If another scene interests me on a particular day, I'll write that scene even if I don't know what's going to happen before it.

I've found this unshackling from order to be liberating. Because I write what energizes me at the moment, I'm less likely to suffer writer's block. It also makes sense to me in that I first define my goal, then I figure out how to get there. Additionally, this method lends itself to creating foreshadowing, since when I add foreshadowing to earlier scenes, it's with a greater understanding of what will happen later.

In my first completed novel, *One Among Men*, I kept getting a visual of the hero running barefoot toward the heroine as if her life depended on it. Up to that point, I was writing a simple romance. Why would he need to run to her, and what kind of trouble could she be in? Suddenly, that story needed a drug dealer who'd once been a friend, and an old abandoned mill to lend an eerie quality. Now I had to redefine my hero's reason for going back to college. No biggie. I had not begun to write that part yet.

After I complete the first draft of the novel, each scene will need a little nuancing: more sensory detail, description of the character and his or her physical responses, memories, thoughts, metaphors, etc. It's like adding flesh to bone. This fleshing-in embellishes the story and grows it from the inside out, giving it character and substance the earlier structure did not have. It's my favorite part of writing.

Then, once I have gotten the general artistry of the work added, I begin the polishing stage—cleaning up and tightening the awkward sentences, finding better word choices that are more meaningful, and ensuring my punctuation is as accurate as I know how to make it. Lastly, I give it a few "final" read-throughs (often out loud) to make sure the story flows as it should, and to ensure the wording is clear.

That is the Connie Almony style of global-to-specific plotting and writing a novel. Give it a whirl … if you dare!

Lynnette Bonner

When I was asked to contribute to the chapter in this book on how I plot, I just laughed. Because you see, I DON'T plot. I'm what many people call a "seat of the pantser" or just "pantser" for short.

When I start a project I generally have a pretty good idea about my main character(s). And I have a blip of an idea for the inciting incident. But from there I just start typing and sort of discover the story as it comes to me.

This can be a bit scary. And it can result in writing yourself into a corner, if you don't pause to reassess now and then. This happened to me with one of my early manuscripts, and I had to backtrack and get the story back into a proper arc. So you DO need to know about plotting and the basic points of story structure, even if you are a seat of the pantser.

My general practice is to write about one third of the story. Then I go back to the beginning of the book and reread and edit as I go. Then I write the next third, and then again, go back to the beginning and read it through from the start. Finally, I write the last third, and then once more read the book all the way through. This helps me make sure I have a good through-line and arc to the story.

I remember struggling through classes like creative writing and trying to master plotting. But it wasn't until I set myself free to just write the story without trying to think through all those details that I finally completed my first book. That's it for me. I can't tell you how I come up with the story or how I figure out the dark moment, etc. It just comes as I write. And I know there are many more of you "pantsers" out there, because I run into people like me all the time. And how freeing it is to realize "Ah! I don't have to do it the *hard* way!" I do believe that as pantsers we must do a lot of reading. Most pantsers I've met have sort of an innate sense of story, but those who have the best sense of it are avid readers.

I know this has been short, but if you are just discovering that you are a pantser like I am, I hope this will be helpful to you!

Hallee Bridgeman

When I first started writing, I woke up from a dream and sat down at my first ever personal computer and started typing. I was 27 years old and never had any aspirations to ever write anything, much less a book. However, six weeks later, I had finished the first draft of my book, *A Melody for James.*

I didn't plot anything out, but in my mind I had a specific scene toward which I was writing. There's a car chase scene in it, and four chapters before it happened, I knew I would get to that scene.

I wrote that way for several books, but more than once, I discovered that I had written myself into a corner and had to back out of it. To me, that is a little counter productive. Plus, I tend to "know" the story before I start, so I tried plotting it out.

I'd heard of outlining a story, like with Roman numerals and such; however, that felt very tedious and much too formal for me. So I basically sat down and said, "Chapter 1: This happens." I'd write out a brief description of what I wanted to happen in chapter 1, then went on to do chapter 2, etc.

Because I was still "writing to a scene", just like with that car chase scene, I just synopsized my way to the scene. Then I'd synopsize my way to another scene.

Once I discovered Scrivener, a word processor written by writers for writers, I found a way that fed my creative brain visually as well as intellectually. I still do "chapter 1, this happens," only now I used the Scrivener corkboard. This is what it looks like:

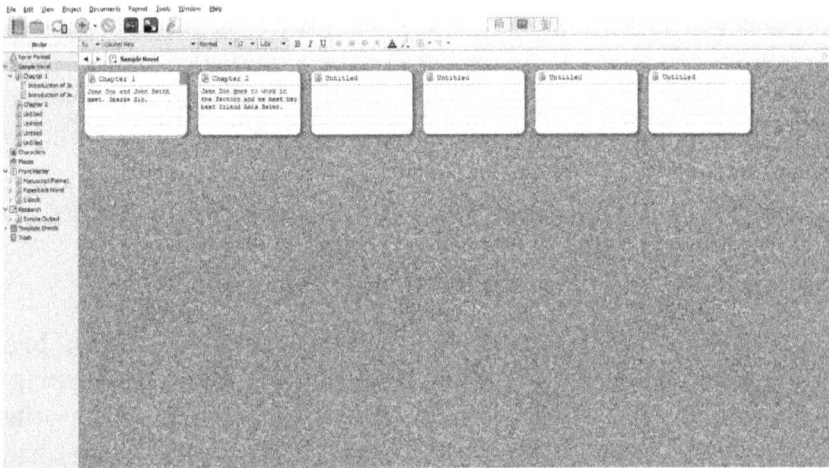

I actually created a video showing the entire process for my plotting. You can view it here: https://youtu.be/FjkinaKrRW4

Once I get the main scenes and plot points into the outline I've created, I see where I can add more to the story, filler scenes for stronger characterization, and needed scenes for bigger emotional or spiritual impact. When the whole thing is laid out in front of me like a series of notecards, I am able to visualize the three acts of the story, make sure the dark moment is in a good place, and that the romance arc, the suspense arc, and the spiritual arc are solid and ready for writing.

Once it's plotted out that way, it's a simple matter of expanding the chapter synopses into action, dialogue, setting, thoughts, and feelings. Because the hard part, the telling of the story, is already done.

Louise M. Gouge

I write historical romances, but my stories include more than my heroine and hero meeting in some historical setting, falling in love, and living happily ever after (HEA). To create a compelling story to capture and hold the reader's interest, an author must weave together three threads.

The **Plot** thread: this is the storyline, of course, and in any book, regardless of genre, this must be strong and interesting, with plenty of conflict to keep the reader guessing how everything will turn out. In romance stories, the conflict often involves the hero and heroine being at odds with each other over some external issue in a way that suggests they could never be romantically involved with each other.

The **Emotional** thread: the protagonists grow and mature or learn something about themselves. Again, the heroine and hero are at odds, this time over an internal issue such as fear of commitment or lack of trust.

The **Romance** thread: Despite both external and internal issues keeping them apart, the heroine and hero risk everything to fall in love, whether early or late in the story, and by the end have overcome the barriers and have made a lifetime commitment of marriage to each other...with a promise of that HEA.

Because I write novels with Christian themes, I always include a fourth thread: The **Spiritual** thread, which describes the characters' growing relationships with God. Just as with their romance, the hero and heroine each have some issue that keeps him/her from trusting God, either for salvation or as the guiding hand of his/her life. Just as in real life when a person learns to trust Jesus Christ as Savior and Guide, my characters experience transforming encounters with God that break down the barriers to their faith.

Weaving these four strands together, I pace the internal and external events so that each one comes to a satisfying conclusion for both heroine and hero at about the same time.

Michelle Griep

Are you a pantser or a plotter? Let's clear this little saying up right away, shall we? You're not being asked about your taste in trousers. Here's what it means: if you don't plot at all, if you don't plan one little thing for your story but just start writing whatever you feel like, that's known as "writing by the seat of your pants."

My first published book was a story I created using the pantser method. *Gallimore* is a time travel tale that takes the heroine back to the medieval age. At the time I wrote it, I was a mother of small children and, boy howdy, did I ever want to time travel out of that crazy chaos! So I did. I went to the library one night a week and made up an entire novel from beginning to end simply on a whim.

Just putting down whatever comes into your head is a fun way to write, but it also makes for a LOT of rewriting. Why? Because when you write on a whim without thinking ahead to the consequences of where that might lead your story or characters, there's a good chance you'll hit a wall. Something won't be plausible. Something might not work, especially in the case of having to keep historical details accurate. More often than not, you'll have to go back to the drawing board. And that takes a lot of time. I'm not saying you can't plot this way. I'm just saying you should be aware of the cons of this method.

If you're serious about getting a manuscript finished and sent off to an agent or publisher in a timely manner, I don't recommend the seat-of-your-pants route. Which, then, begs the question, what do I recommend?

I use a technique called Freytag's Triangle or the dramatic arc. It's pretty simple. There are only five basic steps to it.

#1. Exposition

Exposition is the opening curtain on your drama. It's where readers are introduced to your characters and find out what the world is like for them. Your goal at this stage is to draw the reader into your story world and make him *feel* like that's where he is at the time.

#2. Rising Action

Every true narrative needs conflict to make it interesting, to make the reader into wonder what's going to happen next. This is the part of your story where you figure out the three progressively bad things that are going to happen to your hero to thwart him from attaining what he wants.

#3. Climax

The climax is the point where your characters face their biggest threat, their biggest fear, the moment when all will potentially be lost. The tension is palpable. It's the yikes-what-will-happen-next moment for your reader when they'll wonder how your hero or heroine will get through this horrific event.

#4. Falling Action

What comes next in your plot is known as the falling action. In this stage you begin to clean up all the mess and solve the big problem. The falling action ties up loose ends and moves the story toward closure. Something to note about this stage: it's relatively short. This should take up only the last several chapters of your book. Aim for being three-quarters of the way done before you start tying up your loose ends.

#5. Resolution

This is where you write the satisfying end of your story. The story world you created and then muddled up is made right again, although it now looks different than when the story began. This is the time in your novel where you give the reader a cause for a great sigh of contentment because everything has finally worked out.

Julie Lessman

To plot or not to plot—that is the question!

And if you had asked me that when I was writing my debut book, *A Passion Most Pure*, I would have modeled my newbie "pants" for you. Because I was definitely what they call a "pantster"—a writer who doesn't plot anything out on paper but has it all in her head. Shocking, I know, but the first line I literally ever wrote was the first line of the book!

It wasn't until my first book was written and published that I learned there are two kinds of writers: a *pantster*, who writes by sheer emotion, feelings, and imagination, and a *plotter*, a more organized individual who carefully plots out his or her story ahead of time with a detailed synopsis, a chapter-by-chapter outline, character development outline, etc.

So, what am I now, after writing twenty-one books? Ha! A definite plotter with strong pantster tendencies, because I quickly learned when you have fifteen main characters in a continuing family saga like my Daughters of Boston and Winds of Change series, you darn well better have a timeline for birthdays, weddings, anniversaries, children's names, etc., as well as a pretty good idea where you're going with the family story.

When you write a series, it's critical to lay the groundwork for future series novels in the first book, because the storyline always builds on the past. It didn't take long for me to discover that I was always going back to Book One to either change something I needed to gel with the next two books or just flat-out locked into a scenario that didn't work as well for Books Two and Three. That alone is reason enough to be a plotter!

But another good reason is that thinking ahead on a book by outlining and delving into character personalities ahead of time not only makes it a smoother writing process, but it most definitely enriches and deepens the story.

For me, the plotting tool that works the best is a very *in-depth synopsis* because I can play the entire story out from start to finish to give me a better idea of how to proceed and how to shape the characters. In fact, my synopses are *so* detailed and embellished with bits of dialogue I eventually use in the book, that both my agent and editor said my synopses read like short novels.

Once the synopsis is done, I write *the first line of Chapter One*, and that one line usually gives me enough clues about the heroine and the story that I'm off like a shot. As a side note, first lines are critical to the story for so many reasons as MaryLu Tyndall outlines in Section 4, "Going Deeper, Hook your Reader in the First Chapter."

Usually the first and second chapters come easily after that, and since that's really all you need for a proposal, I always polish those to give me a good start.

Next, I begin a *scene-by-scene timeline/outline*, which I dash out in a free-flow manner to give myself an idea whose POV (point of view) the scene will be in, the date and time it takes place, and the general gist of the scene. I generally only outline five or six scenes at a time because, as a pantster, I never know if the characters are going to change something that I didn't see coming! When I finish a scene, I highlight it in yellow to tell myself it's done.

Because I am still a pantster at heart, nothing is etched in stone in my outline, and I can always change in the blink of a character's eye. Whether it's a character who moves me in a different direction than I planned, edits from my editor or agent, or just an innate sense that something isn't right with the story, my plot is always fluid rather than etched in stone.

15

So, in summation, here's my plotting style:

1. I write an in-depth and very detailed synopsis, including bits of dialogue I will later use in the book.
2. I write the first line of Chapter One.
3. I write the first two chapters or so.
4. Finally, I write a scene-by-scene timeline/outline from that point on.

Whether you are inclined to be a fly-by-the-seat-of-your-pants pantster *or* an organized and detailed plotter, your best bet is to be a little of both, going with the flow of your natural tendency. Plotting needs to feel comfortable and satisfying in order to help make writing a joy.

With that in mind, happy plotting!

Elizabeth Ludwig

Plotting mysteries is vastly different from plotting my historical novels. This is mainly due to the difference in the way these two genres progress. Historicals tend to be character driven. Mysteries, on the other hand, are plot driven and, as such, they are crafted to answer one simple question: Whodunit?

My process for plotting a mystery is quite simple, but it does require quite a bit of initial legwork. I begin with a diagram, a sort of wagon wheel, if you will. In the center is the crime. It can be as sordid as murder or as whimsical as a message sheared into the side of a sheep. (Yes, that is the plot of my current mystery. LOL!)

After determining the crime, I create all of my secondary characters, or in other words, the suspects. For each suspect, I draw a line tying them to the crime. Remember, in a mystery, all of the secondary characters must serve some sort of purpose—either they are helping to solve the case, or they are hindering it. Also, for every suspect, there must be ample opportunity and motive tying them to the crime. There must also be one or two red herrings—things that make the reader believe one thing, while hiding the true answer.

Once these key components are in place, I write a lengthy, detailed synopsis of everything that the protagonist will encounter in their quest to solve the mystery. This includes the clues they will use, the red herrings they will stumble over, and finally, the information that will help them to figure out whodunit. Though this final step can feel tedious, it does prevent me from failing to tie up any loose ends—a trap that I have found can be very easy to fall into due to the complexity of the storylines. I've also found this method to be quite a powerful weapon in avoiding the dreaded writer's block *and* in meeting that fearsome Grim Reaper of publishing...deadlines!

Ane Mulligan

In the writer's world, there are plotters (those who make a detailed outline) and pantsters (those who write by the seat of their pants). The plotters boggle my mind. I can't sit down and write a detailed outline, because I don't fully know what will happen yet. And the seat-of-the-pants writer? I mean, who can sit down with not much more than a "what if this happened" and end up with a good story that works?

Quite a few it seems. But I'm not one of them. I'm neither. I've discovered I'm somewhere in between. Author Rachel Hauck calls it a Planster. It fits me. I need a plan. A map of sorts. And my map is a storyboard.

Story-boarding is a trick I learned from my husband. His company hired an ad agency for campaigns. He told me how they would develop ideas by posting sticky notes on a board, moving them around, keeping some and tossing others until they arrived at "the" idea.

I tried it and it worked well for me. After spending time getting to know my characters, their backstory, their main problem, the lie they believe along with their goals and motivation, I can see the conflict that needs to obstruct them. I get ideas of how to make that happen and start my storyboard.

I like to use multicolored sticky notes for the hero and heroine (or my protagonist and secondary lead if it's women's fiction without romance) and another for main conflict points. After I have several, I move them around. I have hot pink notes for the inciting incident and the black moment, two of the main plot elements. I know where they need to go in the timeline.

In *Chapel Springs Revival*, I had two protagonists, Claire and Patsy. They each have a plot line, and there was a town plot line. I used three colors of sticky notes. Each plot line has a goal, a conflict, and an outcome. After I had several chapters worth of sticky notes, I began writing.

About 12,000 to 15,000 words in, I need to go back to the storyboard and brainstorm some more. By this time, the Pantster part of me has come out and my characters have changed some of what I planned. Since they're nearly always right, I follow them, adjusting the story line as needed, weaving the plot lines together in a way that makes sense.

After I'd written several novels, I tried another method. I suppose we all do that sometimes. But I realized after a bout of writer's block that I needed to go back to my tried-and-true method.

So, I can legitimately say, "Back to the drawing board—uh storyboard."

MaryLu Tyndall

Seeing how different authors plot their novels should prove that there is no one right way to do it. We are all unique. Our writings styles are different, our stories, our backgrounds, talents, and skills. So why would we all plot our novels the same way? That's why I get upset when some instructors tell you that there is only one way to plot effectively. Plotting your novel is as much a creative activity as writing is. Yes, there are certain elements of plot you need to include, such as a great beginning, at least two major crises, and a fabulous ending, but everything in between is up to you. Basically, you want to tell a great story with fabulous characters, lots of conflict and tension, a great character arc, an impacting theme, and an ending that makes your reader sigh. If you can only accomplish that by plotting out each scene in great detail, then by all means plot away. If you can only create your best story by letting your creative imagination fly with the wind, then go for it!

Here's how I plot. I've been doing this for over twenty books now, and it seems to be working for me. I guess you might say my method is a bit of both detailed plotting and SOTP--writing by the seat of my pants. Before I start writing, the main things I focus on are characters and character arcs for the main two characters. (Two because I write romance!) I also incorporate a theme in each novel, so I spend some time deciding how best to convey the theme or moral through the story.

I typically have very detailed character sheets for the main characters, complete with pictures I've chosen to represent them. I'm very visual that way. Included in these charts are tons of background information that I may never use in the actual story, but which help me know the character well. I also draw their character arcs in a semi-circle on a blank sheet of paper. I list where they are spiritually and morally at the beginning of the arc (story) and then where I need them to end up, spiritually and morally, at the other end. In between, I list various incidents and influences related to the plot that help change the character. As I said, this is where I focus my plotting, if you could even call it plotting. Where does the character begin spiritually and emotionally? What internal problems do they have? And where does the character end up in these areas at the end of the novel? The theme is the vehicle for their change. The plot is what changes them. I may spend several weeks on characters, arc, and theme.

For the actual plot, I have a general idea of the main points of the story before I begin. I know the beginning, at least two, often three, major crises that will happen to the main characters, and then the ending. That's it! Since plot, theme, and characters are all tied together, I also have an idea of what sorts of things I need to happen in the story to move my characters along in their arcs and also toward the grand finale where I want them to end up. As far as specific scenes and details, I have no idea! This is where I let my imagination and creativity flow and write by the seat of my pants. I love it when the story and characters begin to take off on their own! Try it. You might like it.

Erica Vetsch

I began my writing life as a "pantser" making things up as I went, discovering where the story was going as I wrote it. After I received my first contract, however, the publisher asked for chapter by chapter outlines for the next several stories, and I needed to learn how to plot in a hurry!

Enter, The Plot Board. I first learned about The Plot Board method of plotting in a post on www.Seekerville.blogspot.com (You can find the post by searching the archives on the

Seekerville Blog.) You can also view a simple how-to video at: https://www.youtube.com/watch?v=Yu7v3C5YIk8 for creating your own plot board.

The basic upshot is that I use a cardboard science fair display board, easily found at an office supply store, and a pile of colored sticky notes to plot my stories. Since most of my stories have about 20 chapters, I draw 20 numbered boxes. I also create a small chart for the hero and for the heroine that outlines their internal and external goals, motivation, and conflict in the story. What do they want, why do they want it, and what keeps them from getting it? The plot board gives me a visual representation of the chapters and scenes, characters and goals, and I find it much easier to manipulate the ideas and summaries by moving the sticky notes around rather than working in a Word document on my computer.

Here are my easy-peasy steps to plotting with a plot board:

1. Select a sticky note color for each Point-of-view character. (I write romance, so I usually have only two POV characters per book, but you can have more.)
2. Write out as many scenes and moments as you can think of, as fast as you can. You've been envisioning scenes and characters in the run-up to plotting the story for a long time, so spill all these ideas out onto the sticky notes. You don't have to go into much detail, just get a line or two on the sticky note to hold that idea in place.
3. Once you have about 20-30 scene ideas written out, arrange them on the plot board by chapter into a logical order. You can tell quickly what needs to be moved around, what needs fleshing out, and what needs to be discarded. Check for a balance of POVs, for the approximate location of the major story beats, and whether you've left enough time for a satisfactory resolution.

4. When everything has been filled in and manipulated and organized, find someone to TELL the story to and get their feedback. This person should be great at asking questions and pulling on plot threads to see what unravels. (This step isn't mandatory, but I find it very helpful.)

5. The final stage is to take the sticky notes, one by one, and type of a brief account of the scene in a synopsis. Try to leave a bit of wiggle room for any serendipitous ideas or twists that might occur in the story as you write, but for the most part, stick to the script. When you're done with the transcribing, read through the synopsis, tweaking it as needed, and then you're ready to write!

SECTION 2

Research

Chapter 2
The Basics of Research for Fiction
By Erica Vetsch

Research! For some authors it's an agony, a drudge, a torture they must endure before they can write the story of their heart. For others (and I suspect most historical fiction authors) it is a joy, a journey of discovery, and the very foundation from which story ideas spring.

Wherever you fall on this scale of love/hate for research, know that whether you write contemporary, mystery, historical, or suspense, you're going to have to do *some* research. I know some writers say 'It's fiction. I'm going to make everything up.' But if you choose to go that route, be prepared in this world of social media and everyone expressing their opinions on everything from sushi to snowshoes, for a maelstrom of criticism to come your way.

Today's readers, particularly those who read a lot of historical fiction and/or police and military fiction, are well-informed. They want authenticity, they want to be confident that the author has done his or her homework, and that if they learn something new while reading your story, it is based in fact.

I, personally, fall into the "LOVE to Research" Camp, and I could talk for hours on the subject, but for the sake of brevity and your sanity, I'll keep it to just three topics:

- Where Do I Look?
- How Do I Stay Organized?
- What are the Pitfalls?

Where Do I Look?

Diving into research can be daunting, especially when you aren't sure exactly what you need. Our go-to these days tends to be Google. "I'll just Google that."

As a card-carrying (Literally, my library card) bibliophile, you might expect me to say stay away from online research, but you'd be wrong. By all means, start with Google. Search engines are great tools for getting a broad overview of a topic. Online resources are similar to the old "Encyclopedia Britannica." Great for basic information and a jumping off point for where to look next.

The Internet is loaded with great information, and in some unlikely places, too. Google Maps' satellite feature is a wonderful resource for learning distances and topography. Historical Society and museum sites will have photographs, quick bios, and overviews of historical events specific to a location and era. Sites maintained by authors and aficionados often have historical research they've come across when investigating their passions. Regency terms, Victorian clothing, Gilded Age architecture…the possibilities are endless!

One caveat: *__just because you find it online doesn't make it trustworthy information__*. Wikipedia is created and edited by volunteers. Anything you find on that site should be verified either by a primary source or a reliable secondary source. Fan sites, hobby sites, and collaborative sites can start you on the road to good information, but check. Treat online info like Reagan did the Russians. "Trust, but verify."

So what is considered a reliable source? How can you know if a tidbit you uncover is true? Some authors follow the 'Rule of Three.' If they find an item repeated in three separate sources, they count it as reliable. This isn't a bad rule to follow, understanding that sometimes it can be hard enough to find out a fact in one source, let alone three.

I try to find primary sources first when doing historical research. Primary sources include diaries, letters, autobiographies, first-hand newspaper accounts, and the like. Eye-witness, written accounts of an event or person can be eye-opening. Primary sources are fairly reliable, but keep in mind personal viewpoints and sensationalistic journalism when basing your fiction on these sources. The diary of Mary Chestnut, a Confederate sympathizer during the Civil War, will read much differently than the wartime diary of Louisa May Alcott, who was a Union nurse during the same war. Their individual biases will show and should be taken into account.

If you cannot find a primary source on a particular topic or person, secondary sources can be mined for some rich information. Secondary sources include scholarly works, biographies, history books, and documentaries. When consulting secondary sources, *be mindful of the publisher*. The most reliable and well-researched history books are published by university presses and historical societies. There are some publishers who specialize in historical research books. The more academic the source, the more likely the research has been verified before publication.

Another great place to research is through interviews with specialists and experts. First-person interviews are especially helpful when writing contemporary fiction where you might not be familiar with the inner workings of the FBI, or a hospital emergency room, or a racehorse stable. You can often find someone with experience in a given area who is more than willing to share that information with you. You can also conduct interviews with experts in historical matters. Museum curators and docents, professors, or historical re-enactors are good sources, too.

So, where do you start with research? By all means, start online to get a broad overview. Then find primary and secondary sources. Consult experts when possible. And verify! Confirm your information with more than one source.

How do I Stay Organized?

Now that you have a ton of impeccable research and facts, how do you keep it organized so you can refer to it without having to find it all over again in the flow of your story? Different authors organize their research in different ways, so I'll give you a few methods, and you can choose the one that works best for you...or you can combine and manipulate parts of all of these and create the method that works best for you.

Some authors (myself included) create a separate research document on the computer. Into this document go my character sketches, photographs, maps, calendars, timelines, historical tidbits, and most importantly of all, the bibliographical information I need, whether the web address, or the title and page of the book where I found the research I want to include. If I have that information all in one place, it is easy to go back and look at something again, and, if an editor queries your research, you can easily access the source. This document, depending upon how detailed you want to get, can run to ten to twenty pages in some cases.

If you're a tactile person, you may want to create a binder or notebook with your research. This tends to satisfy the 'I love office supplies' gene of most writers. Page protectors, highlighters, colored paper, pockets and dividers. Fill them up with your research, label your sections, keep everything tidy. You might want to keep a pad of paper handy when you are researching, then you can jot down your notes to type and print them out later for your notebook.

Perhaps you treasure print books. I have an extensive library of history books, and I love using them to research my fiction. I also NEVER write in books, even books I own. I use bookmarks, and especially Post-It notes to flag pages I will need to reference. For me, there's just something about turning the pages, holding the book, being able to flip from one section to another, to the glossary, to the index, to the table of contents, that makes research so satisfying. I tend to write a line or two on the Post-It to jog my memory, and sometimes I color-code the notes based upon topic.

Whatever method of organization you use, a computer document, a binder, or stack of books, the key is to be able to find what you need without having to replicate your research. Keep track of your sources in case you have to prove where your information came from.

What Are the Pitfalls?

Sometimes research can be the reason we can't get our story written. We can get so immersed in the history we never quite get to the story. Don't let this be you! There are enough other pitfalls that can stall us out, don't fall down the rabbit hole of research and never start writing your fictional tale.

So, what if, in spite of your best efforts, you cannot find what you're looking for, even though you've tapped every resource you can find? You have a couple of options. You can make your best, educated guess. You can forge ahead with what you feel is a plausible solution to the research gap. If you cannot find out what color the chamber pots were in King Charlemagne's palace, you can make an educated guess (I would think white?) Or, your other choice is to leave out the specifics. Be general in your description, or don't mention the chamber pots at all. This can apply to just about any research item.

If you're like me and love diving into research, you can be faced with the temptation to include simply ALL of it in your story. You find it all fascinating, so won't the reader? Um, mostly, no. Today's readers want the flavor of research, but they want it included in a way that doesn't read like a dissertation. I like to keep in mind what I call *"The Iceberg Rule"* when it comes to how much to include. Only 10% of an iceberg shows above the waterline with 90% hidden beneath the surface. Only about 10% of your research should show up in your fiction. The other 90% is yours to cherish, revel in, and hopefully supply blog post fodder when you market your book later! None of your research is wasted, but resist the temptation to chuck it all into the story via the dump-truck method.

Sometimes you have an amazing story in your head, and as you begin your research, you realize that historically or factually, the story can't possibly unfold the way you had hoped. You wanted to have Abraham Lincoln make a cameo in your story set in July of 1865, only to realize he was assassinated in April of that year. Or, you want your hero to take the train from New Orleans to El Paso in 1845, only to find that the railroad didn't cross West Texas for two more decades.

When historical research means your storyline is impossible…change your story. There are some things you just can't alter, even for the sake of story. That being said, you are given some creative license when using historical facts and people. If you want an historical figure to make a cameo in your story, great! Just make sure they couldn't demonstrably be somewhere else. Don't have Eisenhower at a baseball game in the Bronx during the D-Day invasion, or King John at a jousting tournament on the date when he was forced to sign the Magna Carta.

You will encounter roadblocks in research, whether it's being unable to track down the information you seek, or having too much information and not knowing how much to include. Or you might find that reality clashes with your initial story idea. But don't panic. Use your imagination to fit your story to the facts, keep the research included to a minimum of around 10%, and know your topic well enough that you can make some educated guesses when you can't find a specific answer to a research question. There are ways around roadblocks, and your story will be the better for it!

Find out more about Erica Vetsch at the back of the book

Chapter 3
Planning a Research Trip
By Michelle Griep

Just because you write fiction doesn't mean you can make up everything. But other than dozing off in dry non-fiction research books, how else can you discover the information you need to know to make your story come alive? A research trip. And here's how to put one together. . .

If you fail to plan, you plan to fail. But you can't even formulate a plan until you figure out some basic information. It's worth it in the long run to ask yourself several important questions.

What do you want to find out?

Your entire trip hinges on the answer to this question. Let's use my research trip for *The Captive Heart* as an example. I wanted to know what life was like in the late 18th century in the rural South, especially for an outsider (as was my heroine). Pinpoint what it is that will be important for you to know in writing your story. Don't gloss over this because your entire trip orbits around the answer to this question. This is your prime objective.

Where are you going?

It's a big world out there. You can't tromp around all of it for the sake of a story. Unless you're Warren Buffet and have gobs of disposable cash. You have to decide exactly what geographical location will best suit your trip. Going back to my previous example, *The Captive Heart*, the rural South is a large area. Even South Carolina, where my story takes place, covers a lot of ground. So I narrowed the area down to about a hundred-mile stretch that included where my characters would've roamed.

How are you going to find out what you want to know?

Once you've decided why you're going and where, it's time to figure out exactly how to discover the information you need. Remember to keep your prime objective in mind while doing this. On my previously mentioned research trip, I brainstormed a list of ways that this could be accomplished, like hiking the area, hitting up museums, visiting reenactment historical sites, making an appointment with a curator, stopping at an Indian reservation. Yeah, that's quite a big list, because at this point in the research trip stage, the sky's the limit. Dream big. You might not get to do everything you'd like, but at least you'll have a plan.

So now you have an idea of what, where and how, but what comes next? How exactly do you pull it all together into one coherent research trip? This is where pre-trip preparation comes in. Yeah, I know, all you spontaneous types out there just flinched. The thing is, though, that if you want to make the most of your time and money, you've got to figure out the best regimen and that involves three pre-trip preparations: budgeting, planning, and praying.

Budgeting

I'm not gonna lie. This is my least favorite thing to do. I'm great with words, but money? Not so much. Okay, not at all, unless it comes to spending it. Still, budgeting is a necessary evil if you don't have unlimited funds. You're going to have to crunch numbers sooner or later, and the first number you need to figure out is how much money you have to invest. This will often determine the other thing you need to budget: your time. How long you stay on a research trip hinges on how long you *can* stay—and you won't know that until you have a dollar amount. Just a little heads up: it will never be as much as you want, and you'll never get to stay as long as you want. But don't panic, even if all you can manage is a weekend jaunt or just a day trip, whatever you can do is totally worth it.

Planning

Once I'm done with the numbers, I party by planning. I love to plan. I adore lining ducks up in row upon row upon row. And with a research trip, there are oh-so-many-ducks. Let's talk about them in depth.

After you know where you're going and how long you're going to stay, the next thing to figure out is transportation. If it's close enough to drive to the place, then go for it. But if you need to fly, here are a few money-saving tips:

Tip #1: Fly on Tuesdays, Wednesdays, Saturdays
Tip #2: Book on Tuesdays
Tip #3: Purchase tickets 3 to 30 days in advance for domestic flights
Tip #4: Purchase tickets 5½ to 1½ months in advance for international

Don't forget to plan ahead on how you'll get around once you arrive at your destination. In urban areas, public transportation is usually the cheapest choice. And often if you go online, you can find advance sales of day-trip tickets at a discount. If you need to rent a car and you're a Sam's Club or Costco member, check into their deals. AAA or AARP also offer discounts.

Once you're there and you can get around, you're going to get tired at some point. Where will you sleep? The obvious choices are a hotel or a bed and breakfast. Both valid choices. But one of the best ways to really get to know an area and the culture in an all-encompassing way is to stay with people in the area. Last time I traveled England, my husband and I stayed exclusively at Air BnB's.

This next planning tip might seem a little over the top—an oh-my-gosh-woman-are-you-crazy kind of a suggestion, but it could end up being worth your while. Figuring out ahead of time the restaurants that are in the area can be a big part of your research trip. How? Well, besides eating the local cuisine and getting a taste for what your characters might be nibbling on, you could discover a place that would be a perfect setting for one of your scenes.

Once you've got all these little details ironed out, it's handy to put it all in one computer file and print out an itinerary.

Prayer

The last thing you need to prepare ahead of time is prayer. I know. Sounds a little holier than thou, but this is an important step. Not that you'll be calling down the heavens to bless your trip, though that's not a bad idea, but think about asking God to prepare the way ahead of time to bring people across your path that you can be a blessing to. There's no reason in the world your research trip can't also be a mission trip. It's not all about you or your story all the time. Pray that you'd be mindful to see opportunities to be the hands and feet of Christ while you're in a different place.

Well, I've just gone on and on about traveling to a research destination, but some of you might be a little pouty faced because of a lack of funds or time. I totally get it if you flat out don't have the cash to go anywhere. Traveling, even on a shoestring, still costs money. But please don't feel discouraged. There are other ways to go on a research "trip" without boring yourself to death in the nonfiction section. Here are a few:

Pinterest

Pinterest isn't just for women or crafters or foodies. It's a wealth of information and inspiration for authors, too. Type in an area in the search bar, and you'll find gobs of images and material to inspire and educate you.

YouTube

Don't write off YouTube as a lame source of viral time-wasters, though it is that. Still, you can find tutorials and travelogues on just about anything or for any destination.

Netflix/Amazon Prime

Watching documentaries, historically accurate period pieces, or travel shows like Rick Steve's travelogues can be research trips in and of themselves. And there's a bonus! You don't even have to deal with groping TSA agents.

Google Streetview

By accessing Google Streetview, you can virtually walk down almost any street anywhere in the world. You'll see people, cars, storefronts, plants, trees that are native to the area, and many other interesting tidbits. Even if you're writing about a fictional town, you can base it off a real place and use Google Streetview for inspiration.

Another note: Remember that taking research trips is one of the perks of being a writer, especially because you can write them off on your taxes!

Find out more about Michelle Griep at the back of the book!

Chapter 4
Transporting a Reader into the Past
By Erica Vetsch

Have you ever read a story that picked you up from your life and dropped you smack into the past, so vivid and detailed that you felt as if you were there? Have you ever read a story so richly written that you feel as if, should you wake up in that setting, you could function with familiarity?

We all love those kinds of stories and long to write them, but how do we translate that into our historical fiction? I'd like to share four tips that I use to create a realistic fictional world set in the past that will, hopefully, aid you in your writing and creating those unforgettable settings that have readers transported to another time and place.

1. Do Your Research!

The first responsibility of an historical writer is to get the research right. Since I cover the basics of historical research in another chapter in this book, I won't go into detail here, but remember that there are many areas of research to cover if you really want to immerse your reader in the history of a particular era. Clothing, architecture, transportation, communication, customs, vocabulary, food, politics. Read, read, read! Delve deeply into the era you want to cover. Read fiction and non-fiction from and about the time period, find out who the artists of the era were, the authors, the musicians, the orators, and actors. Know what made the social classes distinct, what polite society considered polite, and what vices were common. All these details will create a rich landscape for your story.

When writing historical fiction, become immersed in your chosen setting and time period. Learn what made the era unique, the challenges people of that time faced, both physical and moral, and use what you learn to create realistic conflict for your characters.

As mentioned in the chapter on research tips, only about 10% of what you discover should make it onto the page. Trust your reader to fill in gaps with what they know about the era. You are not responsible for educating every reader on everything that happened in the Victorian Era or during the Civil War or the Crusades. You're responsible for telling an entertaining story that is historically accurate. Use your research sparingly, allow the reader to bring some of their own knowledge to the table, and let them invest in the reading process. Draw them in and make them a part of the experience by allowing them to fill in some of the details in their minds as they read.

2. Use Real World Events and People to Ground Your Story

To lend veracity to your tale, sprinkle in some real-world events and people. Have a character mention the current President or Monarch, any wars or events that would be common knowledge at the time that the reader is probably familiar with. Does your story take place at the same time as a natural disaster like the Johnstown Flood? Or a newsworthy event like the Chicago World's Fair? Put that in your story. It can be as simple as having a character notice a headline on a newspaper or overhearing two people arguing a point of politics like women's suffrage or taxes on tea. Just as your life does not take place in a vacuum, neither should your characters' lives. Make them interested in the greater world around them, give your story some context, and your reader will dive right into the believability pool!

3. Make the Characters Interact with the Setting

In years gone by, establishing a setting was done with great gouts of description at the beginning of every chapter. (James Fenimore Cooper anyone?) Taking three pages to detail a sunset won't win you many reader-friends these days, nor will clobbering a reader over the head with an avalanche of historical facts. While your research may be impeccable, readers don't crave fiction for the factual learning experience. Fiction is about the characters and what is happening to them. So how can you get your reader grounded in the proper era without tons of description or going on at great length about the setting?

Use your characters. Rather than paint the setting around them and then dropping them into it, have them interact with the world they inhabit to create it for the reader. And be specific with a few details to clue the reader in. If you say the heroine eased aside the curtain, it doesn't tell you very much, but if you say the heroine eased aside the silk, brocade drapes, immediately you know she isn't in a shack on the Nebraska prairie—or if she is, your story just got a whole lot more interesting. If your hero looks at his watch, he could be in many eras, even present day Pittsburg, but if he slips his pocket watch from his waistcoat, you've not only established a rough era, but also his wardrobe choices.

The next time you're reading historical fiction, note how the author has the characters interact with their surroundings to create a realistic and rich setting. Also note how much your mind fills in what the author has hinted at but never said. You might be surprised at how light a touch can be employed and still give the impression of a rich tapestry of setting details.

4. Slay Anachronisms and Sprinkle in Period-appropriate Words

Have you ever been jerked out of a story when the author used a word you knew was wrong for the era the story was set in? The term for a word used out of historical context is anachronism, and they are the bane of every historical writer. Some anachronisms are glaringly obvious. To have your Civil War general whip out his cell phone...yeah, you'd know that was way off, but did you know that every time a heroine of a story set before 1895 is described as feisty, that's anachronistic? Not the behavior, but the word. Feisty wasn't used before 1895. Some authors say that you should only worry about anachronisms used in dialogue, but I believe that if you want to create an accurate portrayal of an historical era, you should slay anachronistic words wherever they arise.

Anachronisms don't just pop up in word usage, but also in the actions and mindsets of the characters. Too often, historical fiction writers are guilty of "revisionist history" when it comes to our characters world-views. To have a medieval character concerned about the environment or animal rights or the nutritional content of their food is anachronistic. It is fine for your characters to fight for social justice, but make sure it is in the context of the historical period of your story. Try not to overlay current world-views onto your characters. This is where your research is invaluable. Find out what the artists, orators, and preachers of the era were talking about, concerned about, trying to change. Read diaries and newspapers and historical accounts from the era to understand what people were thinking, their views on life and the social issues of the day, and bring those into your story.

In addition to taking out words and mindsets that are not appropriate to the historical setting of your story, be sure to sprinkle in words that were common for the time period. The past is rife with words we no longer use, but would have been easily understood during Regency or Victorian or American Westward Expansion times. Be specific when speaking of wardrobe and household items. In dialogue, throw in the occasional slang term that a person would've used, giving a hint as to the meaning without explaining it in detail. The reader will figure it out, or they will look it up, and they'll feel brilliant, will have learned something new, and they'll really believe in the setting of your story. What more could a writer ask of their target audience?

Writing fiction is about world-building, and historical fiction requires a deft hand to ground the reader in a real-to-life setting that they've never lived in but feel as if they have by the time they finish your story. Research carefully, include some actual historical events and people to give your story context, have your characters interact with their surroundings to give the reader clues as to the setting that allow them to fill in the details as they like, and be vigilant about your word usage by eradicating anachronistic language while scattering in some period-appropriate terms that will add an interesting flavor to your fiction.

SECTION 3

Characters, Characters, It's all about the Characters!

Chapter 5
Character Development
By Hallee Bridgeman

In fiction storytelling, there are only three basic conflicts:

1. Man Versus Man
2. Man Versus Nature (or God)
3. Man Versus Technology

Man Versus Man

This is when a character is pitted against another character. Think *Rocky*, *Star Wars*, *Cinderella*. Some writing guides will tell you that there are five conflicts, and separate Man versus Man with Man versus Society and Man versus Self—but that is still Man versus Man, just with a plural antagonist or a singular antagonist.

Basically, you have protagonist(s) versus antagonist(s), with both character motivations working against each other. Rocky's antagonist was Apollo Creed. It was also himself—he had to work through some inner conflict. *Star Wars* on a broad scope was the Rebels against the Republic. On smaller scales, you had Obi Wan Kanobi against Darth Vadar and various other plots and conflicts. In *Cinderella*, we have Cinderella up against the wicked stepmother. In the recent Avengers films, two heroes with what each felt was the right thing to do end up facing off. This could also be considered CHARACTER VERSUS CHARACTER, because in science fiction stories, characters aren't always human, but they still fall under this conflict.

Man Versus Nature (or God)

This is when a character battles against the forces of God and/or nature. Think *Moby Dick, Master and Commander: The Far Side of the World, Six Below: Hero on the Mountain.* In *Moby Dick*, Ishmael witnesses Captain Ahab as he battles against the whale (and, as a side conflict of man vs. man, he also battled against himself). *Master and Commander*, Jack Aubrey battles against the raging sea. In *6 Degrees Below*, Eric LeMarque battles against frigid temperatures while he's lost on a mountain during a blizzard.

Man Versus Technology

Think *The Terminator, iRobot, Outbreak.*

In *The Terminator*, we're battling the machines of the future who have become sentient. In *iRobot*, again, we're battling robots that have decided what's best for humanity. *Outbreak* is a little harder to see as man versus technology, but medical advancements are considered technological advancements, and in that story, an airborne virus is killing people.

Seven Basic Plots

With three basic conflicts (or five if you separate Man Versus Man into three separate conflicts), we also have seven basic plots:

1. Overcoming the Monster
2. Rags to Riches
3. The Quest
4. Voyage and Return
5. Rebirth
6. Comedy

7.   Tragedy

Overcoming the Monster

Again, we're going to look at *Star Wars*. In this example, the monster is Darth Vadar, and in a larger picture, the Republic. The characters must overcome the monster that is Darth Vadar, destroy the Death Star, and live to fight another day.

Rags to Riches

When I teach the class, the image I use to explain this plot is the king placing a crown on Cinderella's head at the end of the Disney movie. There are even a couple of movies with the title *Rags to Riches*.

The Quest

Quest is defined as the long and arduous search for something. *Indiana Jones* immediately comes to mind when talking about quest stories. Another great one would be *National Treasure*.

Voyage and Return

Think *Wizard of Oz*. In a good voyage and return, the protagonist is drastically changed during the process of the voyage.

Rebirth

To me the best example of this is *A Christmas Carol*. By the end of the book, Ebeneezer Scrooge is radically changed, reborn, if you will.

Comedy

There are so many great examples of comedy. My kids just recently belly laughed their way through *Daddy Daycare*. One of my husband's favorite comedies is *Uncle Buck*. My personal taste runs more toward *Raising Arizona*, but I tend to be weird with comedy.

Tragedy

Immediately coming to mind is *The Fault in Our Stars*. My daughter was reading that on her Kindle during lunch at school one day at the height of the popularity of the book. She was sobbing and sniffling but couldn't stop reading. A friend walked by and glanced at her (unable to see the book because it was a Kindle and not a paperback) and asked, "*Fault in our Stars?*"

Set Apart

Some stories have multiple conflicts and more than one basic plot. That's completely fine. Look at just the examples, and you can see different plot categories and more than one conflict. That's okay.

So, with only three (or five) basic conflicts and seven basic plots, how can you take your "Once upon a time, this happened, then this happened, then this happened, and they all lived happily ever after," and breathe life into it so that it pulls away from the herd? What will set your story apart?

Have you ever read a book that had you crying the way my daughter did when she read *The Fault in Our Stars*? Have you ever gasped with surprise when something happened in a suspense novel? Has your own heart swelled with love when the hero goes to one knee to profess his undying love for the heroine? What causes this kind of reaction or emotion from the reader? It can't be the plot; there are only so many plots out there.

"The characters are so *true to life*."

In my experience as an author, I've observed that one of the things setting my books apart from all the others is really good characterization. Over and over throughout my reviews and letters from readers, my realistic characters are brought up.

So often, I hear from a reader who was thinking about how my characters are doing right now before she remembers that they're fictional characters and not really doing anything at all right now. Recently, I had a reader tell me she found herself thinking about the circumstances one of my main characters was in and got so very angry at the antagonist—away from reading the book; just thinking about it while doing another task.

"This series is very honest. The characters are real and don't make you feel like you are *less than*. The topics covered in the series cause you to look deeply into your own personal life and send you straight to the Father to have a one-on-one conversation with Him. Makes you deal with the issues we sometimes bury deep in our souls."

The thing is, readers *want* to know your characters. They want to connect with them, to find a way to relate to them. They want to feel their pain and their joy and their love. It's why readers read. The plots are important, but really only in a way that it creates the circumstances around which the reader connects with the characters.

What makes good characterization?

When a popular young adult series was turned into a movie, my daughter was thrilled. She bought the magazines that contained character interviews, behind-the-scenes images, and snapshots of costumes. I remember her excitement as she poured through the magazines over and over again, waiting for the movie release. We went on opening night, and I watched the joy on her face as this beloved book unfolded in front of her eyes.

After reading several reviews by fans all over the place, all containing great praise for the sets and casting and costumes, I was filled with intense curiosity. I wanted to know what the author had written that would create such a reaction from people worldwide who went to the movie. The sets were fantastical, the costumes extraordinary. What words did she write that produced such imagery?

I borrowed the books from my daughter and spent a weekend reading them. Gratefully, the books were superbly written so I could let the editor in my head take a break. I enjoyed the first book tremendously, the second I thought was just okay, and by the end of the third, I felt strangely disconnected from the story. I no longer cared what happened or how it would end. After I finished it, I spent the next couple of weeks mulling over my response and why I thought I felt that way.

As I said, the books were well written. The descriptions put the reader firmly into every scene seeing light or dark and luxury or squalor with equal literary flare. For descriptive characterization, the narrative had me feeling cold or hot, hungry or full, healthy or in pain right along with the protagonists. The story line was just as plausible as any dystopian novel could be, and there was a genuine struggle with bad people that needed to be overcome for the common good. For nearly half a month I wrestled with the ambivalence I felt for the story by the final book. Finally, it occurred to me.

There was a complete absence of **faith** in the story.

It wasn't just not there, it was like it was stripped completely away. As Christian authors, we know that our souls seek out God, even when we don't know what we're seeking. I understand the oppressive regime post-apocalyptic environment in which the series was set; however, there wasn't even an underground religion, or a remembering of what used to be as far as religion goes. There was simply nothing, which isn't realistic.

Once I realized what was missing, I thought about it further. What happened was that, subconsciously, the characters became less real to me. Characters I'd felt invested in while reading the first book were so two dimensional by the end of the third book that I could no longer find a way in which to relate to them. I no longer cared what happened to them because I didn't think of them as real people anymore. It didn't matter how it ended, because they were "just" characters on a page. They were not real to me.

Three Dimensional Characters

Any main character in your story, and many secondary characters as well, must be three dimensional. There are three dimensions we can explore in the narrative.

1. Physical/Material
2. Intellectual/Worldview
3. Emotional/Spiritual

Physical/Material

What physical traits are displayed? What do they look like? What kind of physical ailments do they live with? What kind of clothes do they wear? What kind of shoes do they like? What mannerisms do they possess? What is the character's physical appearance, and what are his physical traits?

What materialistic concerns or environmental attributes are communicated? Where are they in the world? How is the weather? Is it day or night? Are they on a mountain peak, a beach, or the ocean floor? Is it raining, snowing, a sun-bathed beach or desert? Do they feel wet, cold, hot? What colors surround them? What sounds come to them? What fragrances do they detect? What do the character's senses tell him about the world?

Intellectual/Worldview

What do they know? How did they learn it? Does the character possess a worldview based on indoctrination? Does he subscribe to a particular political affiliation? What are his assumptions about mankind, life, the current conflict, other characters, his nation state, the world at large, or the universe?

How does he think? How does he learn? How does he reason? How perceptive is he or she? How do the characters filter information that comes to them? What kind of special knowledge do they have? What kind of mental deficiencies might they possess? How does the character's brain process information? Does this character demonstrate deductive, reductive, or inductive reasoning? What do they do with information they receive?

Spiritual/Emotional

How are their feelings filtered through spiritual understanding? What do they believe in spiritually? What is their faith? Why is there a lack of faith? How much of their faith affects their processing of the world around them? How much does their faith affect their emotions? What is their history with deep emotional moments in their lives? What deity do they claim? What is the basis of that belief?

What do they feel emotionally? How do they feel it? Why do they feel it? How do these emotions affect them?

Character Shapes

If you think of the three dimensions as circles or rings and inside each circle are all of the characteristics that make up that component, now imagine that these rings can overlap and intersect. That point of intersection will describe your character.

A one-dimensional character will demonstrate traits from only one circle. Let's say your main character spies a man wearing a red bowler hat and carrying a blue umbrella. That man is a one-dimensional character demonstrating only physical traits and arguably environmental traits since he is carrying an umbrella. Just like a circle only has one side, the outside, that character is going to have one side. The reader has no insight into the man's thoughts or worldview and no insight into the man's emotions or spiritual temperature. Thus, that man is a one-dimensional character.

A two-dimensional character is going to display characteristics from two circles. Say that same man takes a seat in the diner near your main character and quietly blesses his meal before eating, ending his blessing with, "In Jesus's name I pray. Amen." Now you have a character who displays some physical traits: a male with a red bowler and blue umbrella who is hungry. He is also displaying some spiritual traits. Clearly, he is a Christ follower who has enough devotion that he blesses his meals. Those two rings intersect and make a two-sided shape. Thus, that man is now a two-dimensional character.

In many popular secular romance novels, you find nothing but two-dimensional characters. In these stories, there is an abundance of the physical and enough of the intellectual to drive the plot. Likewise, in a lot of mainstream Christian fiction, there is an overabundance of spiritual and emotional content and enough intellectual content to drive the plot with nearly an absence of anything physical.

What Shape Is Your Character?

While every main character should portray all three spheres, not every single character in the book must display all three dimensions all the time. With a peripheral character (the hotel bellman, the taxi driver, the waiter), one or two dimensions are usually all you need. Unless the waiter in the restaurant reappears as a new character in this book or maybe later in a series, then knowing that he's wearing an ill-fitting cheap suit with a mustard stain on the shirt might be all we need to know. We don't even need to know HOW that stain got there.

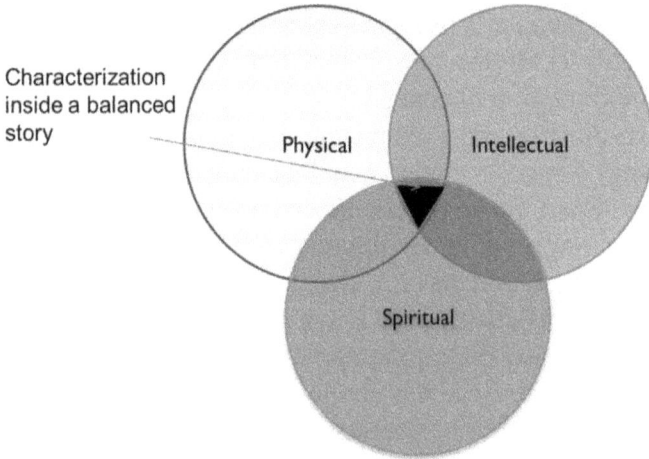

Characterization inside a balanced story

Physical

Intellectual

Spiritual

However, with main characters and most secondary characters, you need to divulge all three dimensions to the reader in some way or form. In order to do that, you need to KNOW your characters as if you raised them—which, in an odd way, you do.

There are many different ways to do this. One way is to create a character worksheet. I have included one at the end of this section to give you an idea of what it may look like. There is a lot of information to fill out in such a character sketch, especially if you're working on your current book right now and know your characters like you know your own kids.

However, when you're writing multiple books in a series, you will be so thankful to yourself if you take the time to fill out something like this and keep it handy. While you may think that your current characters will always have priority in your mind, the fact is they will not. As you go from project to project, your current characters are the most important characters, and what you know about the characters from previous books starts to fade away.

I'm a very visual person. I think better when things are laid out for me. Consequently, when I'm working through a character, I do a lot of my work in Pinterest. I create a board for each book, and as I pin images of characters, clothes, tattoos, houses, cars, the character comes vividly to life in my mind.

There is no right or wrong way to sketch out a character. Do it the way that works best for the way your mind works; however, do it. Try to bring the character to life before you try to bring the book to life. MOST of the information you come up with about your character might not make it to the page.

That's okay. It's important that you know as much about your character as possible, because then what you do bring to the page will be whole and complete, three dimensional, instead of just a shell.

Sample   Form: Character Sketch

CHARACTERIZATION
WORKSHEET

CHARACTER NAME: _____

_____

PHYSICAL DESCRIPTION:

Male/female	
Age	
Height	
Weight	
Shape/build of body	
Skin color	
Shape of face	
Eye color	
Hair color	
Scars	
Tattoos	
Freckles	
Moles	
Left or right handed?	
Distinguishing limp or other physical ailment	
Mannerisms	
Taste in clothing	
Wedding ring?	
Glasses or contacts?	
ANYTHING else?	

BACKGROUND

Success-proven tips from 10 award-wining authors

Ethnicity	
Location of birth	
Regional area where raised	
Raised by whom?	
Siblings	
Abuse?	
Pertinent young years information	
Education	
Any arrests or trouble with the law?	
Dark secret	
Biggest regret	
Biggest accomplishment	

CURRENT

Lives where?	
Type of home	
Type of vehicle	
Marital status	
How many children?	
Job	
State of mind	
Financial status	
Emotional	

Success-proven tips from 10 award-wining authors

status	
Health status	
Name of best friend Details about relationship with best friend	
Favorite color	
Favorite music	
Favorite movie	
Favorite book	
Habits	
Addictions	
Faith	
Goals	
Priorities	
Skills	

PERSONALITY

Pet peeves	
Idea of an enjoyable evening	
What is a day off like?	
What does a work day look like?	
Dreams	
Optimist or pessimist	
Introvert	

or extrovert	
Internal motivations	
External motivations	
Favorite place to travel	

RELEVANT   LIFE
EXPERIENCES

Motivations

What exactly does "character motivation" mean? It's a simple definition for a deep and complex concept: Character motivation is what the character wants and why he or she wants it. Or, more simply put, it's the reason a character acts a certain way.

In reality, character motivation is created when you create that three-dimensional character we talked about. It doesn't do any good for a character to make a certain decision or act a certain way if the motivation isn't established and the reader can't figure it out.

MOTIVATION

- Motivations reveal characterization.
- Motivations distinguish characters.
- Motivations drive action.
- Motivations spawn character growth.
- Motivations create drama.

Motivations Reveal Characterization.

You are really unlimited in the number of different motivations you can give your characters. The motivations reveal who your character currently is or who your character currently strives to become. Through motivations, we see personality, desire, choices, reactions and actions, and everything else that defines us individually. Having motivations come clear in your writing gives your readers a chance to truly know your character.

They Distinguish Characters.

Motivations also distinguish good versus bad characters. A great example is found in the movie *Raiders of the Lost Ark*. Indiana Jones's motivation when it came to the priceless artifacts he found was to preserve them in a museum. Rene Belloq's motivation was to sell them to the highest bidder. Thus the protagonist and antagonist were formed, and the motivations revealed who was the good guy and who was the bad guy. When you have two characters with such opposing motivations, it helps create tension. This is an effective way to keep readers on edge, wanting to keep reading to see how this tension, this conflict, this opposition will be resolved.

Your character's actions and reactions to internal and external motivations need to ring true. Even in incredible situations that are fantastical and amazing, your reader can get lost in a "suspension of disbelief"—but only if the characters act and react in a realistic way.

Motivation Helps Drive the Action.

Motivation helps drive the action. While Indiana is seeking the lost ark, he is having to do it clandestinely, knowing Belloq is looking for the same thing. Protecting the ark from the Nazis who steal it drives him to commandeer one of the military trucks and chase it down.

Motivations Spawn Character Growth.

Motivations spawn character growth. Since one of the main things that readers are seeking in the story is a way to connect with the characters, then the journey a character makes through the story is a journey that the reader will experience and feel as well. A great example of this shown in the character Dorothy in *The Wizard of Oz*. She begins the story unable to stand up to the mean woman who took her dog from her. Through her adventures in Oz, motivated by a desire to go home and motivated by a desire to help people around her who are in trouble, she grows in courage and compassion, so that by the time she makes it back home, her journey is something that the reader (or viewer) has felt deep in his or her soul.

Internal motivations are forged inside of a character and come from the character's personality combined with his or her life experiences. Dorothy is motivated by compassion for her fellow man, or lion. External motivations are those that generate a required response from the character, either from circumstances that occur during the course of the story or from the actions or reactions of the characters around them. Dorothy's home is blown away by a tornado, taking her to a land over the rainbow. She desires to return home.

As you are writing, you need to make the motivations clear to the reader. You can see Dorothy's heart in the way that she interacts with the farm hands, then with the characters in the Land of Oz. You also know her external motivation because she plainly states it, "I want to go home." If a character just acts without the author making the motivation clear, then the reader is not going to be drawn into the story in quite the same way and will have a harder time connecting with the character.

How does motivation reveal characterization? The truth is that actions speak louder than words. You can say that Dorothy is compassionate, or you can show her crying over hurting the tail of Lion. Actions driven by motivation reveal more about the character than anything the character says or anything you may say in the narrative. By using reactions to motivations in the story, then you're "showing not telling," and the reaction to motivations will organically and naturally reveal the character's personality and likely even his or her backstory.

In the list of Pixar's 22 rules for storytelling, number 19 is:
Coincidences to get characters into trouble are GREAT.
Coincidences to get them out of it is CHEATING.

If your character is in trouble, his or her motivation is going to be to get out of trouble. Waving a magic wand, having a fairy godmother grant a wish, introducing a *dues ex machina*, or having the character wake up to realize "it was all just a dream" is not going to be something readers appreciate. They want to go through the thoughts and feelings and actions of the character to be a part of the struggle that results in the resolution. It's a rare story indeed when a character can just click her heels together and chant, "There's no place like home!"

Motivations Create Drama.

The realistic motivation of the character is going to create drama. Dorothy's motivation to return safely home is going to motivate her to face a lion, oil a tin man, stuff a scarecrow, and battle a witch who has an army of flying monkeys. That's very dramatic. She learns so many lessons along the way, such as the negative consequences of straying from the path before you or putting too much stock in the words of a supposedly all-knowing wizard.

Also, consider that actions have consequences. When you have a main character react to a motivation, be it internal or external, there are going to be consequences, which can reveal the motivations and characteristics of other primary or even secondary characters. However it works out, your characters' motivations will affect those people around them. If they don't, then there's a hole in the development of your characters. When other characters are affected, drama soon follows.

How do you determine your character's motivations? The best way is to flesh it out. I like to write it down on a big white board, with my character in the center and actions/reactions/consequences drawn all the way around, with lines connecting one action to another reaction to another motivation, connecting to a previous action/reaction. When I'm finished, it ends up looking like a complex flow chart.

Your character's actions and reactions to internal and external motivations need to ring true. Even in incredible situations that are fantastical and amazing, your reader can get lost in a "suspension of disbelief"—but only if the characters act and react in a realistic way.

Readers need the completeness of the characters. They crave that as they're reading. The fact that so many of my reviews bring up how much readers relate to my characters tells me that it is something that is lacking in Christian fiction today.

Find out more about Hallee Bridgeman at the back of the book!

Chapter 6
Adding Color to your Cast
By Connie Almony

A Work of Art

A number of years ago I attended a graduate-level Psychological Assessment course. The entire curriculum consisted of taking various tests and analyzing what we learned about ourselves from the results. Though a majority of the tests were the typical forced-choice survey style, the most interesting one involved an analysis of our artwork.

My professor, who'd been a professional nightclub singer in a previous career (and quite a "colorful character" herself), gave us paper, brushes, and a set of paints with which to reveal the depths of our personality. The palette only included the primary colors: red, yellow, and blue. Now, you probably know that most other colors can be made from the primary hues. However, though white is the existence of all color in light, and black is the lack thereof, you cannot make these colors with only a primary palette. Nor can you create shades of the others. Therefore, your artwork will miss two imperative elements: light and depth. Being a lover of muted and mixed hues, my bones practically shook with frustration as I pondered an incomplete visual expression of my being. I voiced my concern to the professor. She responded, "I'll make a note of that for my assessment."

Uh-Oh. What did *that* mean?

Though I can't remember the results of her analysis—or maybe I'm not willing to share them—it turns out I haven't changed. I still love a mix of color, light, and depth in my life.

Without the full array (metaphorically speaking), your fiction will be missing not just light and depth, but all the emotional hues in between. Painting these shades into your prose starts with the most basic and critical element of your story—the cast of characters. For this reason, I'd like to encourage you to go beyond creating nice people who lie flat across your page, and instead develop characters who leap off, steal your reader's heart, and travel in her thoughts for weeks (and longer) after her first introduction to them. Ones that not only stand out among a crowded cast within a single novel, but shine among the shelves of books consumed by the avid reader.

In order to do this, I will be focusing on two main goals in cast creation. 1) How to distinguish each character from other members of the ensemble; and 2) How to include characters that stick with your reader long after he's closed the book for the final time (that is, until he reads it again … and again).

Reading as a Personal Investment

Why are the above-stated goals imperative? First, a cast with a breadth of personality allows the reader to find one with whom she can relate. The more breadth an author puts into the cast, the greater the probability the reader will come alongside one "like them" or like someone they know and love. I have one fan who gushes over my novel, *Flee from Evil*, because the former dirt-track, race-car driving, "lovable curmudgeon," Archibald Lewis, reminds her of an older man for whom she's spent a lot of time in prayer. In a way, experiencing that character gives her hope to continue. She's read that story several times and can't wait to find out what happens to him in future books of that series. Relating to characters, such as this one, pulls us into their worlds, prodding us to take the time to invest in their stories more intimately.

Adding color to characters helps the reader distinguish one from the other. Have you ever read a novel in which, inside your head, all the men looked exactly the same and so did all the women? I've had this monochrome visual when authors have taken great pains to describe one with long blond hair and the other with a raven-colored pixie cut. The cadence of speech, choice of words, lack of personal quirks and mannerisms made them all *feel* the same. So in my mind's eye, they looked the same too. I'd forget the extensive description from the beginning of the novel and fill in carbon-copied visuals of the other guy.

Colorful characters can also make your book the one readers buy even after returning it to the library or borrowing it from a subscription service (i.e., Kindle Unlimited). Once a reader has consumed a story, discovered the secrets, and knows the resolution, he or she is done with it. They will remember its contents but, knowing what happens, don't feel the need to read it again. Compelling personalities change that dynamic. The reader returns not to only relearn the story, she comes back to embark on an intriguing journey down a familiar path with her old friends. At each reading, she knows them better and loves them even more because there are details yet to discover about them in the folds. These are the people who made her laugh, awed her to tears, and opened her heart to something new. She shares in their joy again and again. When the reader closes a book and moves on to another, she may forget the title of the last novel or the author's name, but the colorful character should fill her thoughts and speak into her days, making her wonder what he'd do in this or that situation—If he were real, that is—because that's what colorful characters do.

So how do we go from black and white to living technicolor? You start with lots of paint and an understanding of what happens when you mix it.

Examples of Great Ensemble Casts

If you've read my section on plotting, you'll know I tend to think global-to-specific. I like to know where I'm headed before I decide how to get there. So let's look at our destination, great ensemble casts, through an array of classic and contemporary movies and literature. We'll start with the scariest.

Jaws (the movie)

You can hear the music now, can't you? But I digress. Let's look at the three men who embarked on the sea vessel that brought the big shark down. Can you get a more diverse group of men?

First, there is Chief Martin Brody, a former New York City cop who moved his family to the little island of Amity (which means "friendship") in order to find peace. Already the irony is rich. He's a family man, a devoted father, and ... deathly afraid of the water. Hmm. We wonder why, but it's never revealed, at least not in the first film. The audience can only question, with this particular aversion, why would he choose Amity as the place to settle his wife and children?

Next, there is Matt Hooper, from a family wealthy enough that the young man doesn't really need a profession. Yet he chooses one that repeatedly puts him in danger of being injured by a scary fish. You can feel his zeal, respect and, dare I say it, love for the water-born beasts whenever he unloads his knowledge about them. This information is academic, offered in scientist lingo that stands in stark contrast to the last of the ensemble—Quint.

When I looked up the cast of *Jaws* online, the movie site didn't even list a last name for the sea boat captain. Or is Quint his last name, and we really don't know his first? Either way, that's exactly what one might expect from a character such as he—a longtime man of the sea who speaks with what I'd call a maritime brogue. Crusty, crotchety, sunbaked and deeply worn around the edges, just like the boat he sails. We first meet Quint at the town meeting, attached to a set of fingernails scratching the blackboard as the townsfolk argue about how to catch the shark. Silence descends before the old seadog lays out his terms for slaying the enemy. He doubles the bounty, again contrasting Hooper, who would not only capture the shark for free, he'd spend additional money on equipment to gain the privilege. Quint differs from Sheriff Brody in that he is the opposite of a family man. This contrast is exquisitely displayed in a scene in which the three men prepare to board the boat. Chief Brody kisses his wife goodbye, then she asks if he took his Dramamine and packed his extra pair of glasses, all while in the background, the hardened sailor is singing a scandalous ditty about loose women.

When a story has a great cast, a memorable moment that reveals their depths is sure to be present. *Jaws* has such a moment. The evening rolls in as the three men relax after having tangled once with the shark. Hooper and Quint compare scars. The young scientist's scars come from his academic research with wild sea creatures. The captain's scars are from his experience on the high seas—most, involving alcohol and rowdy associations. As the two men expound on their bravery—or recklessness—Chief Brody lifts his shirt to look at something on his own abdomen. Is it the reason he's afraid of the water, or something so small the grown man would feel inferior to the other two in the telling? We will never know because the chief decides not to share. He's a quieter man who desires a quieter life. And here he is with these other two fellows whose life goals include seeking danger.

Then Brody asks about the etching on Quint's wrist. A deadly silence follows. The scar is from the removal of a tattoo he once had from when he sailed on the USS *Indianapolis*—the ship that delivered the atom bomb. Here is where he unlocks the horrifying tale of being among the sailors dumped into the ocean when a Japanese submarine torpedoed the ship. Being among the few survivors in the water, for weeks he watched the local sharks devour his buddies.

This is a memorable scene not just because it surrounds an actual historical event, nor because its drama and tragedy are unmatched. It is memorable because you see it through three separate pairs of eyes: the scientist who's studied the predatory creatures and is in awe of the survivor before him; the man afraid of water whose fear is only heightened by the tale; and the captain who'd witnessed the savage carnage up close and lived. Suddenly, you sense the longtime seaman's need for vengeance that was not previously evident in the story. Somehow this multiplies the emotional intensity three times what it would have been had we only read the facts in a newspaper. Would you believe this scene wasn't even in the book?

Big Hero 6

Another great ensemble cast comes from an animated superhero film *Big Hero 6*. I wanted to use this movie for a number of reasons: 1) Marvel does a fantastic job developing characters, and this one beautifully fits the large ensemble into a whole. 2) Since this is a superhero story marketed to youth, the characters can be slightly over the top, which is a great place to begin in colorful character creation. You can pare them down later. 3) It's a perfect example of how to make each member of an ensemble cast distinct. And, 4) There are additional resources available from this movie on the DVD (i.e., the Bonus Feature section on character creation). You can also find what the creators call *The Cafe experiment* video on You Tube. The animators developed this video in order to get to know the cast better (Big Hero 6 - CHARACTER STUDY). I'll elaborate on its use later in the chapter.

Big Hero 6 is the origin story of a group of superheroes who combined their disparate skills and abilities to avenge the death of the youngest's college-age brother and save the boy's invention. Though we meet the main character, Hiro, alone at a bot fight at the opening, the audience is introduced to the remainder of the team at the same time young Hiro is. One by one, we learn who they are, as they describe their latest inventions, and reveal a bit of their personalities as they share them. Go-Go is working on a speed bike that is very fast, but "not fast enough." She carelessly tosses the *relatively* slow wheel in the trash. Wasabi demonstrates his lasers with precision and freaks out when Go-Go touches his tools. Honey-Lemon blows up a pink metal ball with exuberance.

Even their names tell us something about them (Wasabi, that he once spilled the spicy sauce on his impeccably groomed shirt). These are the nicknames given to them by Fred—the non-student, school mascot, and avid reader of comic books, who describes himself as a "science enthusiast." Fred is the one who encourages the team to create things like shrink-rays and invisible sandwiches.

A pivotal scene in which all these personalities play out in one effortless entertainment machine surrounds the soon-to-be-heroes trying to escape the masked bad guy. They all jump into a teeny car, the dead brother's medical-companion robot sitting on top, and speed off. Wasabi, OCD neat-freak who is known to be afraid of everything, takes the wheel, his eyes wide with terror. Hiro, the pubescent boy in all his young bravado, tells them the robot, Baymax (whom he'd perfected), can fight the evil dude. Fred presses his face to the window, a mixture of awe, concern, and elation running across it, watches the predator, and says, "We're under attack from a super villain! How cool is that? I mean, scary—obviously—but how cool?!"

Wasabi stops the car at a red light while Go-Go screams, "There are no red lights in a car chase!" She later takes the wheel when Wasabi argues he needs to put his blinker on to indicate his turns, shouting, "It's the law!" While all this is going on, now in a speeding vehicle narrowly escaping death, Honey-Lemon is spouting positive thoughts, and Baymax, the personal healthcare companion robot, is educating the team on vehicle safety. It's an intense scene, not just due to the brushes with death, but because we experience it from six points of view with a myriad of emotions. We are either breathless with fear or bursting out in laughter. The contrast of all of the emotions playing against one another only heightens each further!

Alec Forbes of Howglen

Another great ensemble cast is from the mid-19th-century Christian novel, *Alec Forbes of Howglen*, by George MacDonald. What I specifically love about this group of characters is how the manifestation of each person's faith in God is unique from the others, demonstrating the apostle Paul's idea of the Body of Christ—each different part contributing to the whole.

In this novel, we have Alec Forbes, a fatherless young man, whose values falter once he moves away from home. His Creator has placed an array of helpers in the young man's midst who speak to all the parts of God that cannot be completely revealed through one witness alone.

Alec is a noble youth whose sense of right and wrong endear him to the reader. His duty does not stem from a faith but from a position he and his family hold in the town. The story follows this young man into a maturity of faith as he interacts with the townsfolk. But what makes the recounting of his life such a wonderful tale? The townsfolk themselves. None perfect, but all important in the task of the Creator.

There is Thomas Crann, the stonemason, who the townsfolk regard as religious, more respected than liked. Whenever someone meets him on the street, he asks after their "immortal parts" and uses every opportunity as an analogy for faith in an all-powerful, loving Father. The reader could imagine this man is not easy to be around unless they want to think much on their last days. Yet it's clear George MacDonald is fond of him, for he takes us into the character's mind and his concern that is not born of judgment but of hope for his neighbors' eternities.

Thomas's counterpart is Mr. Cowie, the clergyman, who is regarded as worthy, kindhearted, and gentle. We learn a bit of his character when young Annie Anderson comes to him in fear after she hears a sermon from another church on the wrath of God. He talks her through God's love but falls short on explaining doctrine. Instead, Mr. Cowie gives her a sixpence and sends her home. You can almost feel George MacDonald chuckling as he ponders the little girl challenging the minister to clarify his theology, while at the same time he is demonstrating the loving kindness of our Creator, for Annie went home relieved of her fear, and Mr. Cowie dropped to his knees in humble prayer.

Other characters that round out the cast include the shopkeeper who goes from one church to another in the hopes of gaining customers, the schoolmaster who whips his students out of "duty" and later repents before dying in an attempt to save a child from drowning. There is also an old blind woman whose wisdom comes from what she cannot see, and a drunken scholar whose morality stems from a debauched experience.

One Among Men

When one has a large ensemble cast, it's essential to use methods for distinguishing them early on. In the novel, *One Among Men*, my main character, Samantha Hart, has a six-member, all-male, resident-assistant staff. Because this story focuses on a woman who runs an all-male dorm, moments with all of her employees were a critical part of the telling, so it was important to differentiate each of the six from the beginning. A few techniques helped me do this. First, while approaching the conference room before her first official meeting, Samantha overhears her employees' comments on having a woman take the job. Terrell, the ladies' man, ponders his chances of dating her. Todd, the lovable ne'er-do-well, is grateful she doesn't have a hairy wart on her face and look like a hag. Rico worries she'll make them behave professionally. Kadhi, the serious student, reprimands the others' behavior. Kwan takes a casual, "we'll find out soon enough" attitude, and Preacher, the religious dude-from-the-hood, warns, "She's asking for trouble." In a matter of only a couple of pages, we are given a sense of how different these young men are. Later, these personalities will be fleshed out further when we learn the music they like, how they dress, and other pertinent details.

Getting to Know Your Characters

Character Archetypes
Now that you know what a great ensemble should look like, how do you create your own? A good place to start is to consider the many archetypes that often play roles in story. I will not bore you here with an exhaustive list of the myriad of different types. You can find them in a number of places online. However, here are a few to get you started: Yoda/mentor, benefactor, bully, bureaucrat, caretaker, coward, curmudgeon, explorer, guardian, loner, judge/mediator, manipulator, perfectionist, scholar, trickster ... and the list goes on. I caution, however, that though there are predictable characteristics that often come with these types, what makes an extraordinary character is that one small part of them goes against the grain. When this attribute is revealed, the reader will gasp from surprise and delight. It is what makes the character memorable and somehow more human at the same time because none of us is a perfect caricature of type.

Have fun with these complex beings. My two favorite characters to write were Todd, my lovable ne'er-do-well, in *One Among Men* and *An Insignificant Life*, and Lew, my lovable curmudgeon, in *Flee from Evil*. Their manners were unique and their dialogue lively. It was a lot of fun to be in their heads (writing from their points-of-view) as they stumbled along in their journey through the books.

Personality Tests
A number of novelists take personality tests *as* the character, or they choose a Myers-Briggs test profile and develop a character based on it. These results can give the author a beginning framework, but I have two cautions. First, if you take a test *as* the character, there is a good chance it will come up invalid, making the type not as realistic. Second, be careful not to turn your character into a poster-child for that type. It can make them feel two-dimensional and cartoonish.

Most of us have elements of our personalities that veer from the usual. It's what makes us human. Give your character some humanity and a reason to slip out of her personality-trait box at points.

People Watching

My husband and I love people watching even when we aren't writing. How does a writer make this activity worthwhile? Plop yourself down in the middle of a mall food court on a busy day and take notes. Ask yourself questions about the people you see. Watch the groups moving in and out of the stores across the way. Did they find what they came for? How can you guess? What features are contributing to your assessment? Watch the groups at the tables. Do they get along with each other? How can you tell? What expressions are on their faces that tell you how they feel? Does one's expression change dramatically when no one is looking (other than you, that is)? Why do you think so? Are they hiding something from their friends? What are they wearing? What does it say about them? Do you think it's an accurate portrayal of who they really are, or are they trying to be someone they aren't? What clues tell you these things?

In other words, make up a scenario in your head that would fit the visual cues from the people around you. Use these cues with the characters you write.

In your own social environment, consider the details of the people you know. Do they have favorite sayings, an unusual style of hair, a way of dress, a manner of speech? How do these things mesh with their personality? Do they fit, or are they shockingly out of character? When out of character, why do you think they choose to step out of that particular box?

People watching is the inspiration of The Cafe Experiment (found on You Tube) that I mentioned earlier when talking about the character development for *Big Hero 6*. The animators created a basic "cafe" environment and drew out a scene with each character engaging in it using ideas they'd accumulated from watching people they knew who were similar to the characters they were creating. Hiro, the adolescent boy, enters the cafe, tosses his backpack on the table while staring at his cell phone, drags a chair to where he wants to sit, and kicks it into place before he flops into it and leans back on two chair legs. His college-age brother comes in, waves as if to acknowledge others, neatly pulls out the chair, sits and scoots it forward before taking off his cap and reading his menu. In these few movements, we get a sense of the contrasting level of tidiness between the two characters as well as their respect for others around them. Hiro is engrossed in his own world everywhere he goes, while his brother is consistently considerate of others.

Authors can use their own version of The Cafe Experiment before writing the story. One example of this would be to take a historical event (like September 11) and write out how each character would respond differently to it, using that character's vocabulary, style of speech, and personality traits.

Journaling

One of the best ways I've found to get to know a character from the inside is to journal as if I were that character. I might have them catalog a day or even tell their life story under my pencil. Yes, I often do this with pencil and notebook because I want it to feel very personal. However, I might choose a laptop or even a tablet if I know that character would do the same.

When I write, I *am* that person. I use the words she would use (big, small, academic, colorful). I write the phrasing he would think (full sentences, fragments, with and without subjects). I describe the scene with the tone that fits how he or she feels about the topic. Journaling is one of the best things I can do, not just to get a sense of the character, but as a means of getting unstuck when I'm hitting a writer's block.

Other ways of getting to know your characters include the following:

1) Acting them out. If you've ever had a chance to take an acting class, this can help you tremendously as a writer. I sometimes find myself standing up and acting out a scene as a character before putting it on paper. I've been known to take on characteristics of the cast member *least like me* while writing a novel, as in the months my daughter called me "Rock 'n' Roll Mom" because of the way I dressed, spoke, and even smiled, during the time I was writing a southern-rock musician.

2) Choosing an animal to inspire (and get a feel for) the personality. I once heard Robert De Niro did this with the roles he played. I think he'd chosen a crab for one of them because he thought the character's movements should be shaky and awkward. I know I have some characters who I think of in terms of dog breeds.

3) Select a music muse for the story or even individual characters. I usually choose a recording artist to listen to while writing each novel and at least a couple of songs that speak to the characters in the tale. Music helps me get a feel or tone for the people in the cast.

Character Worksheets

As Hallee mentioned in her chapter on developing characters and their motivations, it's often a good idea to fill out a worksheet on your character. You can start with a template that lists typical characteristics like age, weight, height, political leanings, education, eye color. But then you'll want to add what makes this person unique: a phrase he uses a lot, a philosophy of life, a physical quirk or nervous habit. Keep this handy because you'll refer to it often and you don't want to be caught by a reader who'll find the inconsistencies.

Putting Your Characters on the Page

Thread the Details

If you've read much on writing, you've likely seen the phrase "show, don't tell." I'm going to add another word to this mantra—*thread*. I mean the verb form of that word and not the twisted string. After you have gotten to know your character and his backstory through the methods mentioned above, thread this information into the story bit by bit. Introduce us to them in a scene that will explore their most basic facets, then drop more hints of it along the way. Weaving the information throughout helps us in three ways. First, we don't have an unnatural information dump at the beginning, making the story feel imbalanced and plodding at the front end. Second, the bits scattered throughout remind us who they are and how they tick. This is most helpful to those readers who are memory challenged. I, especially, appreciate it. Third, the slow unfolding of the character can lead to an emotional suspense causing us to read on in order to answer the questions dropped in the initial phases of character introduction.

How do you thread these in? Through thoughts, memories, actions and descriptive action tags.

Earlier in this chapter, I described ensemble scenes that helped us distinguish various members of a cast from each other. Now let's look at some *individual* introductions.

In the novel *Alec Forbes of Howglen* (excerpts taken from the Bethany House edition, entitled *The Maiden's Bequest,* edited by Michael R. Phillips), when we first learn of Mr. Cupples's existence, the landlady tells Alec, "Only ye mustn't be frightened at him." Hmm, this leaves a question about the man that needs an answer. Alec goes to the scholar's room and finds him …

...almost invisible in the thick fumes of genuine pigtail tobacco from his pipe ...

This visual gives him an eerie, mysterious quality. If he is not to be feared, why would the landlady suggest we might think so without her warning?

As the narrative moves on, we learn more about his appearance not in the description of it but from the descriptive actions he takes.

His hand, small and dirty, grasped a tumbler of toddy, while his feet, in unmatched slippers, balanced themselves on a table.

See how the description is woven in without pulling us out of the action to tell us what he looked like and what clothes he wore. Suppose the author said only, "He had small and dirty hands, drank toddy, and wore unmatched shoes." This draws up the image of a man posing for a picture rather than a living, breathing character in the midst of his daily routine.

Alec asks the man to help him with his *Homer*, so Mr. Cupples directs him to his collection of books in a locked cabinet with a "dusky glimmer of splendid bindings" filling the space. Obviously, this character, though given to a couple of forms of debauchery, still holds a reverence for knowledge and the means through which to gain it. He cares for his books enough to lock them away and keep them in good condition. And that is not all he holds in reverence. Alec visits again on the Sabbath and finds there is a "certain Sunday" look about the room even though everything is the same, including "the circles from the bottoms of wet glasses." It isn't until a few moments in that Alec realizes the man is wearing a clean white shirt and collar. What is this act in honor of? Is there a vague awe for his Creator? Dare we hope for redemption of this lost soul? None of this is said, but it is surely felt by the reader.

Nowhere does George MacDonald tell us Mr. Cupples is a drunk. We figure this out on our own from the actions seen through the eyes of the point-of-view character. Mr. Cupples is disheveled and drinking. We find him that way again the next day. The reader gets it, unless the author decides to throw her for a loop later, which is sometimes fun to do.

Once we've established underlying character traits—or at least what we want the reader to believe they are—It's important to add more detail as we go and remind the reader with additional evidence. You can do this through his or her thoughts and memories. Sometimes a memory will take you a little deeper into who they are, as we saw in the example of the sea captain from *Jaws* who'd survived the shark attacks after the USS *Indianapolis* had sunk. Another example comes from my novel *The Long View*. In this story, two of the main characters, Destiny Long and J.T. MacGregor, knew each other as children. This history is challenged by Destiny's concern that J.T. is working for her father's enemies. I wanted to draw a contrast between these two time periods, so I interspersed lots of memories from their youth, when J.T. protects Destiny, both physically and emotionally. At one point, she's done something potentially very dangerous, and J.T. wants her to tell him what it is. She says she won't talk about it. His mind draws up the following …

History told him that's what she always said when she needed someone the most. Like the time she hid in the fort after losing the part of Maria Von Trapp in the high school rendition of Sound of Music. *He'd sat in the grass outside the fort's door as she'd spilled her guts in her efforts* not *to talk about it.*

From this, we see he was a loyal friend as a child, and Destiny trusted him. The reader is left to hope he is still loyal today.

The author can also throw in tiny reminders about the character by using action tags rather than dialogue tags. Instead of writing "she said" attached to dialogue, use that opportunity to thread in a visual of the character that reminds us of who she is and what she looks like.

> *"Don't look at me that way." Sandra twirled a strand of her long blond hair so tightly around her finger the tip of it turned red.*

This example does many things. It lets us know Sandra is the one speaking without stopping to tell us so. It reminds us this character has long blond hair. It also shows us that her request not to be stared at is done with some trepidation.

Taking Your Characters from Black and White to Full, Living Color

It's the Little Things

As we plan our stories with grand themes and extraordinary ideas, we need to understand that though a reader may not remember every detail, the combination of them—or the lack thereof—will surely impact the *feel* of the tale. You may not know *why* something didn't seem true or felt off. You just know it did … unless you have the details to back it up or add to the tone you are trying to achieve in the story.

Remember this as you develop your characters. In fact, many great authors have created descriptive worksheets and extensive backstories, eighty percent of which is not even used in the book. However, the author's knowing all those details informs how the character will think, act, speak, and dress. The reader is not aware of the details collected but feels the authenticity of the persona more because of them.

In the Bonus Features from the extended collection of *Lord of the Rings,* there are many videos on *the making of* the movie that can inspire an author, even the one on costume design. Each character's raiment was developed considering his personality, his heritage, and his own personal history.

When creating Aragorn's garb, the designer took into account the fabric and weave that spoke of his family's royal line. But it was worn out in places and created in such a way that the man could easily repair it throughout his adventures. It was dark and blends well in the forest. The movie audience does not know these thoughts went into the design of the costume. However, what they do see is a man with a regal bearing, though dirty and burdened by trials. He is strong and capable but lurks in the shadows and is not at first readily trusted. These kinds of details help us know the character better, though we may not precisely acknowledge how.

Sometimes a small action can make a character trait explode with light. For instance, in the Christian Medieval Romantic Suspense, *The Unveiling,* by Tamara Leigh, there is a moment where Lady Annyn overhears Baron Wulfrith giving knightly instruction to a squire. At this time, she is disguised as a boy in order to infiltrate the castle and receive training herself. For this reason, she is accustomed to the baron's constant challenge to the student to remember his lessons in order. "What is lesson seven?" Wulfrith asks the other student. Annyn recounts that numbered lesson in her head, then is shocked to find this young man's "lesson seven" is different from hers. Does Baron Wulfrith know his pupils well enough that he creates and memorizes individualized lesson plans for each? We are not only astounded by the master's memory but his care for his students. He does not consider them as nameless numbers. They will receive the best from him as he expects to receive from them. I gasped when I first read this scene because it was analogous to how God works with us. He knows each of us intimately and designs our lives (and lessons) accordingly. This quality in Baron Wulfrith, though taking up very few words in the narrative, endeared him to me in ways well beyond what he would have been otherwise.

As writers, our tools are words. Use them powerfully! Sometimes one well-chosen word can tell you more than an entire paragraph. Take a look at this letter from the opening scene of the light, contemporary Christian Romance, *Manila Marriage App*, by Jan Elder. The book opens with the point-of-view character, Shay Callahan, rereading the letter she received from a prospective fiancé as she waits for the plane that will take her to meet him for the very first time. Shay's "voice" has a light and breezy feel. Though she is highly educated, the reader gets the sense she is seeking something that might shake up her otherwise mundane existence. Contrast that with Timothy Flynn, who writes:

> *Miss Callahan,*
> *The marriage application you submitted has been approved. You will be happy to know you passed scrutiny on all five sections with commendable marks. I am particularly pleased with the informative answers you furnished on the essay questions (section four), and the fact that you have read numerous books in the past year—even if most of them were fiction—has unquestionably placed you ahead of the rest of the applicants.*

There are lots of gems in here. Most due only to a single word choice or an aside set off by parentheses or dashes. Dr. Flynn doesn't *assess* Shay's qualities, he *scrutinizes* them, giving an image of the man scanning the fabric fibers of her sweater sleeve with a magnifying glass. We don't just learn that she had to answer essay questions, but that they were only section four. The answers are not just acceptable. They received *commendable marks.* Can you see him looking down his nose now? And of course, he snubs reading fiction, but at least the books moved her ahead of all the other prospects.

I almost don't want to like him at all, but you'd better believe I must see this icon of arrogance with my own eyes … er, or at least those of the main character, Shay.

His letter continues …

I feel a period of two weeks would be a good length of time for us to evaluate each other.

Evaluate? For some reason, I'm still expecting the words "get to know each other." But no. Not from Dr. Timothy Flynn. Again, he will come with magnifying glass in hand. However, this time he will be gracious enough to gift Shay with one in return.

And if all that isn't enough, he adds a postscript ...

P.S. The photograph you attached of yourself is satisfactory, although as per the application instructions, I will also require a picture of your mother.

Satisfactory! Just the word every woman wants to hear from her future husband. But at least he'll give her another chance by likely *scrutinizing* a picture of her mom. How generous. One wonders what Shay is thinking by accepting his gift of round-trip tickets to Manila. But there is a sense of curiosity about Timothy Flynn that makes you want to check him out and hope Shay will put him in his place (or pop him in the nose). Either way, I'm intrigued and must read on.

Up the Ante
The best way to make your character more memorable, and therefore your book, is to take the character up a notch. One of my favorite examples of this is in MaryLu Tyndall's pirate adventure, *The Ransom.* I have always loved MaryLu's swaggering heroes, but she takes this character to a new high ... or low ... or whatever it is. He is not just the most feared pirate of the seas. He is something entirely different during the daylight hours. I would have been satisfied had the character been just a charming, wealthy philanthropist by day and enjoyed the book very much. But I will *never ever **ever*** forget "Munny," the name his socialite friends have given the pirate's

alter-ego, who is a shallow, frippery sort of dandy, who wears powder, wigs, and patches on his face in order to lead the fashionable set with his trite stories and high-pitched laughter, while waving a lacy handkerchief in his ebullience. I'm smiling now just thinking of his antics, contrasted by what he becomes in the dark of night in the seediest parts of town or sailing the high seas.

As is evident from the ensemble cast section of this chapter, there are a number of excellent examples of upping-the-ante in the movie *Jaws*. Sheriff Brodie is not just the head of the island law enforcement. He is a former New York City cop who is looking for a quieter life ... *and* he's afraid of the water! Hooper isn't just a scientist. He's young, enthusiastic and rich enough not to need the job. Quint isn't just a boatman. He's a longtime sailor who's had a brush with sharks rising to historic proportions. Not only does each character's traits push the envelope, but the contrast between the men enhances the tension while telling the tale.

One of my favorite characters from my own novels is the undergraduate university resident assistant from *One Among Men*, nicknamed Preacher. He is a six-foot-four, broadly built African-American man who scares most people he meets—not because he's actually from the roughest part of the 'hood, but because his ardent faith in an all-powerful God seems to simmer with brimstone, making him seriously intense. In some ways, he's like a darker-skinned version of the stone mason, Thomas Crann, from *Alec Forbes of Howglen*. He grew up immersed in the decadence of his crime-ridden surroundings, watching the result of sin ruin lives while being taught by his grandmother of a loving God who knows all and wants more for His children. When I picture Preacher walking the streets of his hometown, I often imagine him responding to the sight of a couple of young dudes dealing drugs by taking the two by the scruff of their necks and cracking their heads together while quoting scripture. It's a different sort of evangelism, but maybe it gets the job done there. No, he doesn't actually crack any young men's heads together in *One Among Men*, but this visual informed his tone as I wrote him. He is the opposite of his boss, who is the heroine of the story. Samantha grew up in a nice suburb but is currently recovering from the less-than-stellar life choices of her past. Together they make a good team overseeing the behavior of the wayward students who live in the dorm Samantha runs.

Kids and Dogs

Too often, fiction avoids the use of children and pets. This is probably because they are so unpredictable and therefore hard to manage. However, it is this quality that adds color to your story. When done well, these two elements can bring out some surprising characteristics in your main cast and add a few laughs along the way.

In the Regency Romance novel, *Arabella* by Georgette Heyer, we have Mr. Beaumaris, the epitome of the ton (Britain's high society), begrudgingly taking the practically penniless Miss Tallant under his wing as a form of entertainment, a diversion from the ordinary. She is unaware of his schemes and believes his attentions merely stem from a desire to help another wealthy (as she has led everyone to believe) socialite wade through the shallow prospects for husbands. After all, Mr. Beaumaris, himself, is not the type ever to marry. His attentions to Arabella can be considered only along either of these two veins until the kids and dogs enter the scene. First, Arabella rescues a mongrel dog from a beating by a couple of urchins on the streets of London. She pleads for Mr. Beaumaris to take him in and the man, incredulous at his own actions, accepts the challenge. Thereafter we have scene after scene of this icon of fashion being followed by the misbegotten creature, close upon his highly polished Hessians. With each passing moment, the grand gentleman begins to unload more of his thoughts and feelings to the little mutt. Ulysses, for this is the name his master gave him, responds by flattening his uneven ears, stirring his disgraceful tail, and snuggling close to the master's feet. At some point, Mr. Beaumaris wonders what Arabella will saddle him with next. It turns out to be a grimy little chimney boy who is not too keen on baths.

The simple introduction of the dog colors this story as nothing else could. The contrast between the impeccably groomed man of fashion and the wiry-haired mongrel, tromping through London together, gives us new perspective on the man. He is willing to reach into the depths of humility to do Arabella's bidding, yet he still finds ways to make it part of the game. Eventually, another member of the ton buys a mongrel dog in order to be as fashionable as he. However, the conversations with the little beast are most informative, for though Mr. Beaumaris withholds his inner workings from the closest of his acquaintances, Ulysses is the recipient of the gentleman's most heart-revealing truths. We love the icon more for the vulnerability unveiled only to his new furry friend. Without the character of Ulysses, Mr. Beaumaris would be only another arrogant man.

In general, kids and dogs are a wonderful addition to any story. They add an extra layer of vulnerability to the tale. Not just in their own innocence, but in the added responsibility of the caretaker. Additionally, they weave in an element of surprise, because a youthful character has not been sculpted into *the expected* quite yet, meaning just about anything can happen. Not only is it a given they will be colorful in and of themselves, but they will also draw the color out from the other characters they touch.

Mixing Pigment into Your Character's Skin Tone

If you want to have a colorful cast, why not make it literally colorful? You not only can have an ensemble whose members look completely different from each other, but they could have contrasting cultural upbringings.

Jenny B. Jones does this in her young adult novel *In Between*. And as usual, she writes it with extra flair. The main character's best friend's name is Zhen Mei Vega, but she goes by "Frances." Her father is Mexican, and her mother is Chinese. Frances is an American-born, trendy teen, with very little evidence, other than her given name, that her parents were not born in this country. However, when the reader enters her home, it is no-holds-barred Mexican-Chinese, from the dragon statue in the corner to the graphic bullfight painting on the wall. There are flags and knickknacks scattered everywhere, proclaiming both parents' heritages. It's a sensory explosion of cultural overload. Again, we have a contrast of characters, lending a breadth and texture to the story, because Katie Parker, the main character, is a foster child whose mother is in prison, and Katie doesn't know much about her father at all. She has no heritage—at least not one she knows. No layers of family pride. We see the extremes of the two worlds and have an opportunity to wade through the idea of defining self among family. Though the best friend character does not have a lot of air-time within the novel, I've had a clear visual of Zhen Mei Vega (Frances), as well as her family home, in my head years after I read this book. That is great characterization!

In my novel, *One Among Men*, I used different cultural backgrounds to help differentiate the main character's employees. Among them is a rich white boy, a dreadlock-wearing African American guy from the 'burbs, an intensely religious African American from the 'hood, one Jewish-Mexican mix, one of Korean descent, and one very studious student from India.

Having grown up with a mixed bag of nationalities in my own friend group, I love to have a little fun with stereotypes here. Usually, my characters are a mingling of *on* and *off* type (like in real life). The guy from the 'hood is not the caricatured gang-banger. He is disciplined and religious. The rich boy, though struggling with alcohol, is hard-working. The Jewish-Mexican loves country music, and though the Korean-American is proud of his heritage, he's probably more culturally "American" than the average American. Knowing how these characters' traits interact against their backgrounds gives them a new layer of texture, making them more three-dimensional and lively.

Another great example of broadening the cultural heritage of your cast is in the *A Murder in the Mountains* series, by Heather Day Gilbert, starting with the Cozy Mystery *Miranda Warning*. Heather has a way of endearing me to all of her characters. They are warm, at least *slightly* quirky, yet infinitely real. Amidst this backdrop of a West Virginian ensemble cast, stands Axel Becker, the very large, very blond, heavily accented, German-born ... florist. Axel is a beautiful mix of stoic German stereotype—think Dolph Lundgren in *Rocky IV*—and quirky hero. Or is he an anti-hero? You'll have to read the series to decide for yourself.

Tess, the main character of the series, first met him in college when he seemed to show up in all her classes. Was he stalking her? Lots of questions surround the Mammoth-sized cast member, and his behavior constantly puzzles. He is a man of few words, and the ones he does speak are subtly alarming. His gaze roams the pregnant Tess as he utters, "You are with child?" Was that a statement or a question? How should Tess answer him? "Yes, I am." or "Oh? I didn't know that." Either way, she finds a way to remind him she is a happily married woman, and that maybe her husband can take him if he must ... even though he probably couldn't.

Axel often frames his questions as statements. Earlier, while staring at her as she scans a clue he's given her, he says, "You are having thoughts on this?" Though Heather throws in a German word here and there, his *manner* of English feels accented without them. Additionally, the mix of his forward statements, his gruff nature, and his uncensored perusals of Tess's person, make us wonder. Is he socially awkward, a not-very-sneaky stalker, or are his abrupt ways due to his cultural upbringing in another country?

But Heather Day Gilbert doesn't stop there. Instead of leaving him marinating in this uniform type, she does something shocking. She makes the large, lumbering man a florist. Not just a man who sells flowers, but he's good at designing elegant bouquets. Really good. And his shop resembles something from a Beatrix Potter picture book. He's also known for walking along the river every day. Could he be pondering poetry? Who knows? But the questions surrounding him make me want to read more.

As I mentioned before, Ms. Gilbert does an excellent job endearing me to her characters. She threads in so many wonderful little details along the way that allow me to know them well. The married couple is realistic in both natural conflict and cozy resolution. The mother-in-law is warm and lovable as she flaps her hands to dry her nail polish. The youngest brother-in-law is rambunctious and fun. The older brother-in-law is a charming, man-bun-wearing, dater-of-models. I love them all. But … Axel grabs me in such a way that I remember him in greater detail than all the rest. I am grateful he is threaded into the later novels as well because I suspect there is a bigger story behind the big German dude … even if the author doesn't know it yet.

That is All

While writing this chapter on colorful characters, somewhere along the way I realized how often I needed synonyms for the words *different* and *contrast*. Then it dawned on me, *that* is the quality that makes a great story. A varied cast brings breadth, not just in the characters, but in the ways the action can be perceived by the reader. It heightens the experience much like how the drama of a tragic scene is accentuated when trailing a light-hearted, humorous one. These differences ramp up the tension, as though they are pulling a bungee cord from both ends of a larger space.

Also, when your characters *differ* from the *ordinary*, they are more memorable. They are unexpected and exciting even if their differentness comes in the form of the mundane—like an international spy who loves to bake cookies while wearing a ruffled apron. It's that jolt or gasp that sears the image of them in our mind's eye.

So have fun with your characters. Understand how and why they do the things they do, then spice them up with a pop of color here and there, and *voila!* You have an extraordinary work of art!

Find out more about Connie Almony at the back of the book!

Chapter 7
Villains we Love to Hate
By Elizabeth Ludwig

I've always been fascinated by strong characters, especially really good, creepy, nightmare inspiring bad guys (insert evil laughter here). But aside from posing a threat to the hero of the story, what are the marks of a good villain? What qualities must they possess in order to birth a sliver of fear in a reader when they appear on the page?

Developing a complex, multi-dimensional villain takes time and a bit of skill that can be developed with the right tools. It is well the worth the effort, however, if the goal is to keep from having boring, predictable villains who are quickly forgotten when the final scene ends.

So let's look at what it takes to create vibrant, bone-chilling villains, whose demise encourages a feeling of victory...or even better yet, a stirring of compassion.

Developing Memorable Villains through Qualities, Quirks, and Motives

Just like the hero, the villain of a gripping story needs to have qualities that set him or her apart and make them an even greater threat to the outcome of the story.

Are they exceptionally smart? Lethal? Do they exhibit a ruthlessness or dogged determination that compels them to keep going after the hero, no matter the cost (think Terminator here)?

Ponder carefully the qualities the villain of the story will possess. **Aside from making the character more interesting, it must also be something that, once learned, can become a tool in the hero's hand.**

Let's look at the example mentioned above. The villain in the first Terminator movie was, of course, the machine himself. Devoid of feelings or emotions, he can not be appealed to, or bargained with, or dissuaded from his one task—to go back in time and destroy Sarah Connor, the woman who would give birth to the human who would spell disaster for the machines. This dogged determination, this unstoppable, inevitable pursuit, makes the character of the Terminator even more chilling. And yet...

The heroine leads the Terminator to his doom simply by using what she learned about him—that he would continue to pursue her until he accomplished his purpose. Of course, she tries everything else first, like blowing him up, crushing him, and battering him to bits. In other words, she struggles against his strengths until she (and the viewer) realized that doing so is hopeless. Finally, in a moment of desperation, she turns from fighting against his strengths and instead uses them to lure the machine into a fiery vat of molten metal.

Voila! No more Terminator...at least, not until the next five movies came out. But hey, isn't that what a writer should strive toward? This character was so compelling, producers knew they could keep churning out similar movies until viewers lost interest!

Okay, so we've examined the need to give villains qualities that make them exceptional. Now let's look at a device that, while much less complex, is still necessary if we desire to create characters with depth. Namely...quirks. To illustrate this, I could, of course, mention the Terminator's sunglasses. But I prefer to examine a much more sinister villain, one who, by his nature should perfectly demonstrate what I mean.

His name is Dr. Hannibal Lecter.

Did you shiver reading that name? Did the mention of it conjure scenes in your head—visions of piercing eyes, and frightening masks, and chianti? Those who have seen the movie will know what I mean. Those who haven't...well, I won't ruin the film. Instead, let's look at the quirks of this very frightening and memorable villain.

Dr. Hannibal Lecter was a forensic psychiatrist turned serial killer who...ahem...ate his victims. Adding to his threatening demeanor is the fact that he is incredibly brilliant. He is also vicious and, of course, psychotic. Yet he has a soft spot for an FBI trainee named Clarice Starling. When another prisoner threatens her, Hannibal kills him. Why? Because, like any other human being, Hannibal has a weakness, an Achilles Heel, if you will. He can't kick a puppy or stand it when someone else does.

This is the most daring of the characteristics a writer can give a villain—something that actually makes them likable. More examples include Thor's brother Loki, who is handsome and funny; Norman Bates, who is socially awkward and shy; and Darth Vader, who is powerful yet tragic—plus he has really cool music. Each one is twisted and chilling in their own way, yet they stand out in our memories not because of their evil deeds but, perhaps, in spite of them.

Finally, writers must be careful to give their villains powerful motivations for the things they do throughout the course of the novel. Just as the hero has a goal he is working toward, the villain must have a counter goal that works against what the hero is trying to accomplish. In other words, the writer must orchestrate a battle of good versus evil, right versus wrong, good guy versus bad guy.

But...in order for the battle to become epic, the villain must be somewhat justified.

You read that correctly. The *villain* must be somewhat justified. For example, a cattle rancher who is tearing down the hero's fences may just be trying to keep his cattle alive by allowing them to free range. Or, possibly, a villain seeking revenge may have lost someone they truly loved. Their death may have been an accident, but all they see is their loss. Let's look at this last example a little closer.

One of my favorite movies of all time is *Last of the Mohicans*. I mean...Hawkeye. Need I say more? Yes, actually, because the villain of this tale also had a most intriguing backstory. His name...was Magua.

(Just a side note here—the book ending is quite different from the movie version. I won't spoil it, but please note that the comparisons I will be drawing refer to the 1992 film adaptation.)

So, the character, Magua, brilliantly portrayed by Wes Studi in the 1992 movie adaptation, carries a burning hatred for the English—specifically a colonel named Edmund Munro, whom he holds responsible for the destruction of his village and the death of his children. Magua's wife, though spared in the battle, eventually remarries. Stripped of everything he held dear, Magua waits patiently for the moment when he can return the pain inflicted upon him to his archenemy. All of his decisions, all of his actions, pivot on this one burning desire, this goal which runs so perfectly counter to the hero's goal.

Now, were we to turn this story on its head and make Magua the hero, we would think him justified for his actions, right? That is what makes the battle between him and Hawkeye so incredibly compelling. Love won versus love lost. What more excruciating a paradox?

Avoiding cardboard cutouts or two-dimensional villains.

While it can be tempting to invest the most time and energy into crafting an engaging hero or heroine, it is important to remember that neglecting the villain can leave a novel with a flat, two-dimensional quality that robs it of its appeal. Instead of being great, a book will only be good.

Ultimately, it will not be received as well as it might have been had the author taken time to properly get to know their villain. It is actually very easy to write a character who is just plain bad. But the reality is that no person is completely evil.

Remember Johnny Ringo from the movie *Tombstone*? While we do not know much about this character, his plight was delightfully summed up in one line from Doc Holliday, who says of him, "Poor soul. You were just too high strung."

In summation, get to know your villain. Give them a backstory that lets the reader know why he does what he does. Give him both strengths and weaknesses and allow one or the other lead to their downfall. And lastly, create a character you can love...because if you love him, so will your reader!

Find out more about Elizabeth Ludwig at the back of the book!

Chapter 8
Dynamic Dialogue
By Ane Mulligan

I cut my authorial teeth writing stage plays—a lesson in humility, but one well learned. I was the Creative Arts Director for my church, and the pastor gave me his sermon titles and main points. It was my job to write a short script to illustrate those. Sometimes, the sketch introduced the sermon topic, and other times it fell in the middle of the sermon. When the script was ready and approved, I gathered the actors and had a rehearsal. That's when my lesson began. They had the audacity to change what I'd written. But in truth, once I heard their version, I realized my words were stilted and stiff—not at all the way real people spoke.

Now, I might not be the brightest spotlight in the theatre, but I was smart enough to hear the difference. I pulled out my trusty pen and changed the script. The next one I wrote was better, with more natural dialogue. There were only a few changes. Again, I listened and made corrections. Was I tickled pink when the actors stopped making changes to my dialogue? You bet!

When I turned to writing novels, I didn't know anything except how to write good, realistic dialogue. Dynamic dialogue. So, you might ask, what is dynamic dialogue? By definition, it's purposeful, active and changing. There are other definitions, but those suit what dialogue needs to be in a novel.

Let's take a look at those.

- **Purposeful**: Dialogue needs to make a point. You don't want to read about two people discussing the weather, unless weather is important to the story. If your story is about an island during a hurricane, then it's appropriate dialogue. In my current novel-in-progress, *On Goose*

Island, the main characters are shrimpers who go out on the open ocean. Weather is very important to them, lest they be caught in a storm their boats aren't fit to withstand.

- **Active**: Unless you're creating a mood of passivity for an introverted character or one struggling with health issues, make the dialogue active and energetic.
- **Changing**: As your character goes through their arc of change, their dialogue should reflect that. In *Chapel Springs Survival,* my protagonist's husband makes a 180-degree turn around. In the next book of the series, his dialogue and manner of speaking show his change. He's no longer gruff and demanding.

Another aspect of dynamic dialogue is by the character, themselves. Each character should have his or her own unique speech patterns and manner of articulation. One person may enunciate their words clearly, while another slides over consonants or drags out vowels. I write Southern fiction with characters from the South. In *Chapel Springs Revival,* to get the reader hearing the characters' Southern accents, I said of one: "The woman added extra syllables to every vowel and dropped so many word endings she could be fined for littering. North Georgia accents were a teeny bit more civilized." Now the reader will hear her, and I don't have to write her any differently. Once shown, the reader remembers, and only an occasional word will remind them.

What makes up their patterns and articulation? Several things contribute to our dialogue patterns:

- Gender
- Origin (where the character is from)
- Education
- Age
- Type or Personality
- Worldview
- Setting

As we go through each bullet point, I'll give you some examples and hopefully point you in the direction of writing dynamic dialogue. In each section, we'll take a look at some flat dialogue. You know, the kind I *used* to write.

I. Gender

Let's face it: men and women speak differently. They *think* differently, too. A woman's thoughts can be in two or more areas at one time, and she can still keep up with the conversation. Mark Gungor has a funny video on this I suggest you watch. It's on YouTube, and called <u>Women's Brains vs. Men's Brains</u>.

Gungor explains, "A man's brain is made up of boxes, and the rule is the boxes don't touch." And then, "Women's brains are made up of a big ball of wire and connected to everything. It's like the Internet superhighway. And it's all driven by energy we call emotion." It's hilarious but so true.

Here's an example of a conversation between two men and between two women, first showing a bad example of stilted dialogue between the men:

"Good morning, Bob. Where are you headed this fine morning?"

"Good morning, John. I'm going to the hardware store to get a new float for the toilet."

First of all, we don't really care about Bob's toilet, unless his four-year-old flushed the latest Wiki-leaks state secrets down it. A bit more realistic might sound like this:

"Morning, Bob. Where you off to?"
"Hardware store."
"Anything I can help with?"
"I got it."
"Okay, holler if you need me."

However, if it were women having a morning discussion, it might go something like this:

"Morning, Sally. Going shopping?"

"Macy's is having a huge sale, and you know that new slip cover I got for the den sofa? John ruined it with cranberry juice."

"I hear you. Bob got mustard on my bedspread. Why can't they be more careful?"

"I think it's in their genes."

"Yeah, he got mustard on those, too."

You can see how the women's conversation veered off the main track. That's realistic—dynamic. So listen to people. Eavesdrop—it's a writer's best research tool. Dialogue between two or more women will nearly always rabbit trail onto several subjects before ever coming back to the main topic—especially if they're good friends and share common ground.

This difference is a good guide to the way you make your characters speak and think. Yes, *think*. Dynamic dialogue includes interior monologue. A character that speaks in a certain way but doesn't think that same way won't be believed by the reader. They'll be confused and wonder what happened to him—where did he go?

Take Jack. He's a logical engineer. Everything he does and says follows logic. He plans out every step in his work and his leisure. Throughout the story, Jack is the same. Then in chapter fifteen, we come to a section of interior monologue, where Jack is suddenly a Sanguine, thinking with his heart instead of his logical brain. Readers will wonder if you head-hopped, had a name typo, or did they miss a scene in which Jack had brain surgery.

Have you ever read a book where the male hero thought like a woman? Unless a man is an investigative reporter, he won't notice anything about your living room sofa except if it's comfortable. He might notice the cat hair if he's allergic, but color or fabric? No way. So don't have your hero thinking about Julie's lovely mauve, velvet sofa.

And if you're in his POV, her dress will be a pretty thing. It's soft—silky maybe, but never name the material. Men generally know cotton and wool; it's itchy. Beyond that, they aren't interested. As far as the color of her outfit, it's black or red or blue. Never shades of those colors unless he's an artist. And even then it's suspect. My husband *is* an artist. He was a businessman for most of his career, then in retirement took up art. He's very talented, but every shade of red, whether dark pink, deep rose, or wine ... is red. Drives me nuts! He says red; I think cherry red or Christmas red. I turn to see where he's pointing, and it's absolutely a burgundy color. When I point out the difference, he looks at me like I'm the nutty one.

On the other hand, if you're hero is describing a car or truck, he'll go into eloquent detail, right down to the chrome wheels, or whatever they're made out of. He'll know the exact shade of blue that vehicle is painted, whether it's Chevy blue, GMC blue, or a custom metallic blue.

Men's conversation about the color of Jack's new truck won't evolve into discussing his new suit with a trace of blue in the thread. But a woman? Absolutely. That truck's color would match her new handbag perfectly.

Maybe because I raised boys, I can think in "manspeak." When I write a male POV, I make sure it's without a woman's sensibilities. Women are relational. Men are literal. Remember the non-emotional separate boxes that make up the male brain.

II. Origin: Where your character was raised.

Our country is vast and each area has certain traditions and indigenous peculiarities, along with unique colloquialisms deeply ingrained in those who are raised in that region. If you set your novel in a region you're not from, then you'd better get to know those things that make a Southerner Southern; a Midwesterner Midwestern, a Texan, well, a Texan.

I was raised Southern. I say "hey" instead of "hi" and "y'all" instead of "you," and "all y'all" is plural for everyone. Southerners refer to eating biscuits with sausage gravy for breakfast (except for *this* Southerner—love biscuits but not the sausage gravy). And never argue with a Southerner on the proper way to eat grits. The correct accouterments for grits are butter, salt and pepper, cheese, or shrimp. Don't have a character ask for sugar to put on his grits or everyone will know you aren't from the South.

That said, if the hero is transplanted to the South and ask for sugar for his grits, that might make a fun scene and add a bit of conflict. Likewise, if your Southern heroine finds herself in New York, she may try to order biscuits and gravy, but she'll be hard-pressed to find any. The waiter might look down his nose at her plebeian tastes.

Comparing regions is fun, and I gleaned a few from all over the U.S.A. Starting with Coke (Southern), Pop (Midwestern), and Soda (everywhere else). Characters from the South will say they want a "coke." Someone needs to ask them what kind, because it could be 7-Up or Dr. Pepper, not necessarily Coca Cola (also known as Co-cola, especially if your character is over fifty). The Midwest is "pop" country. Most other places will say soda, so you're always safe with that. But if your character was raised in the South, it's coke and you put peanuts in an RC Cola.

When grocery shopping, be sure to use the correct terminology. The conveyance in which you put your groceries and steer it around the store is generally called a shopping cart. That is, unless you're in the South; then it's a buggy. In New England, it's a carriage (unless you're from old England, then it's a trolley). The West Coasters say a cart, either grocery or shopping.

When researching a few tricks to make your character sound like they are from a region, look for pattern of speech. Midwesterners tend to drop helping verbs. Verbs like "to be" are often omitted to make awkward sentences shorter. They somehow make sense to locals. For instance, "the dishes need to be washed" becomes "the dishes need washed." Your character can say, "My car needs fixed" or "my lawn needs cut." Whatever is in your dialogue, using these will make a Midwesterner relate to your character as one of their own.

My first ever novel was a Biblical saga, which served as my college degree in novel writing. I did a lot of research while writing that book. And I learned that I love research. After I retired it under my bed and moved to a contemporary story, I thought I didn't need to do much research. *Au contraire, mon ami.* Nearly as much research goes into a contemporary novel as a historical one. You're just researching different things.

When you decide that even though you've never been to the breadbasket of America, and you're going to have your Southern belle transplanted by her job to Indiana or Kansas, either plan a research trip to visit a writer buddy who lives there, or plan to spend a lot of time on the Internet, the telephone, or in the library. You're looking for the cadence of the accent, the colloquialisms, and those indigenous peculiarities that set them apart from any other region.

A quick caveat here: do not try to write accents beyond a few words to give the reader an ear for them. When I write, I develop a *think* Southern drawl. Yes, I said think, not thick. I think in their accent. If a new character enters the scene, you can use a word or two in dialect to give the reader a feel of their voice, then write the dialogue normally.

If you're writing a character from Europe, study the way they speak, not the accent. For instance, the Irish have a lilt and rhythm to their sentence structure. A normal statement may rise at the end to sound like a question. They also use the to be verb more than we do. Instead of "Do you want a coat?" an Irishman would say, "You'll be wanting a coat." In my book, *When the Bough Breaks,* the main character's father is from Ireland. The first time he speaks, you'll see a tiny bit of dialect. After that, it's only the cadence: "What a delight, me darlin'. But your old dad's gettin' a mite long in the tooth for this kind of surprise. Next time you might be warning me." He kissed her cheek soundly then thrust one hand toward Reese while keeping the other around her shoulders. "Welcome, young man." He glanced down at Sienna. "Would you be introducing your friend, daughter?" That was it. Every other time, it's sentence structure that makes the "sound" of an Irish accent.

It used to be vogue, eons ago, to write the dialect. If the character was European and the author wrote in dialect, I spent a lot of time trying to pronounce those words. I'd usually give up and skim. Readers are much more savvy nowadays. They'll catch the cadence and sound of the accent and hear it all the way through the story.

III. Education

A character's education level plays into their dialogue and internal monologue. Someone with just a high school education doesn't often use words even your reader may have to look up to understand the meaning. While I'm on that, if you use an obscure word, make sure the reader can get the idea of its meaning by the context in which you use it. Robin Lee Hatcher is good at this. I've read a few words in her books that I didn't know but understood by the way she used them. I like that. I learn a new word and didn't have to stop to pull out my dictionary.

In my *Chapel Springs* series, I have 131 characters in the town, all of whom show up in almost every book. They have a variety of educational backgrounds. I had fun with the mayor's brother, Dale, who was a villain in one book. Dale didn't finish high school but went into the army. He spoke like it too. I gave him a trait for getting words wrong.

Dale and several other townsfolk were two-dimensional characters and lots of fun to create. In my workshop on Lies & Motivation, I teach about two-dimensional characters as well as three-dimensional. I added it in this section because the two-dimensional character's dialogue serves as the background for the main character's dialogue.

A master novelist paints his story with dynamic two-dimensional characters. The characters are woven into the story like little puzzle pieces. Each is important to the final picture, but standing alone they bring no significant revelation to the final image. However, they are still needed.

Two-dimensional characters are flat. They lack depth, are partially developed, and often are stereotypical.

But stories need two-dimensional characters. They bring the story to life, birthing a necessary reality for the main characters, and layering a believable background.

When my husband starts a painting, he paints the background. It's two-dimensional. When he adds a three-dimensional object, using a pallet knife to build up the paint, the two-dimension background allows the three-dimensional to pop. But without the 2-D? No pop.

Well-crafted two-dimensional characters:

- Resemble an archetype,
- Exist as a typical example or stereotype of a type of person,
- Fit neatly into the story and setting,
- Blend into the background to enhance mood, setting, plot, etc.,
- Are predictable and logical,
- Act in ways that are predictable for the main character so as to not draw attention away from main or sub plots,
- Have no past or future,
- Exist only in the moment, and are not fleshed out for the reader,
- Are perfect,
- Have flaws that are never revealed, and exist in perfection for a moment,
- Lack depth and personality,
- Have a personality, character, attitude, and behavior that is never explored.

Attempting to create a story without two-dimensional characters is like painting a Bob Ross style painting without the happy trees. The painting would look bland, lacking depth and vibrancy.

Which brings in another dimension.

IV. Age

If your age is over say fifty, and you're going to write a Young Adult novel, you'd better make sure you spend time around those young adults. Listen to them talk to one another, to their elders, and to children. The generations have been given names by when they were born:

1925-1942: the Silent generation.

1943-1964: Baby Boomers

1965-1980: Generation X

1981-2000: Millennials

2001-2013: iGen

If your main characters are Millennials, be aware they have a whole different philosophy on life than Baby Boomers. They don't want the same things. Millennials want to work less, travel now, and experience life instead of being tied down to a mortgage. They're buying tiny houses with cash.

And now, we have the iGen group. These kids are being raised in a world of technology. They know nothing different. Have you seen the commercial with a kid working on his tablet, and his mother asks what he's doing on his computer? The kid answers, "What's a computer?"

When writing dialogue, factor in what generation your character is in. It will affect their thinking and the way they speak.

V. Personality Type

There are several personality type tests out there. Probably the three most used are the DiSC test, the Myers Briggs (ENFJ), and Florence Littauer's Personality Plus (Sanguine, Choleric, Melancholy and Phlegmatic Types). Whichever you prefer, I highly suggest using one. These tests give you personality types. And personality type shows up in dialogue as well as action.

Look at these types from Florence Littauer:

- The **Sanguine** is the **popular person** who wants to have fun out of every situation and be the life of the party. Sanguines love to talk.
- The **Choleric** is the **powerful person** who wants to take control of every situation and make decisions for others. Cholerics love to work.
- The **Melancholy** is the **perfect person** who wants everything done in order and done properly and who appreciates art and music. Melancholies love to analyze.
- The **Phlegmatic** is the **peaceful person** who wants to stay out of trouble, keep life on an even keel, and get along with everybody. Phlegmatics like to rest.

Once you have your character's personality type, you format their dialogue accordingly. The most dynamic dialogue comes when you pair opposing personality types. They think and talk differently, which creates great dynamics in dialogue—and misunderstanding between the characters. Let's say you have a Sanguine, who loves to talk, and a Choleric, who just wants to work. The dialogue might go something like this:

"John, why do you think we need a bridge over the highway? What's wrong with waiting for the light to change?"

"It's a time waster. I can be across a bridge and on the train by the time the light changes."

"Or you could have a meaningful conversation with your co-workers, like Janice, while you wait."

You can see where their focus is by the dialogue. You can also guess their personality type by it too.

If your character is a Choleric and all about work, they don't turn into a Sanguine as the novel progresses. They might soften the edges of their Choleric personality, but they are still someone who likes to take charge. Their dialogue will show that, even as they are trying to control it.

The Phlegmatic is the poster child for the 1960s. But what if you suddenly dropped that same flower-child-Phlegmatic into a law office with a bunch of Cholerics? Come to think of it, unless they were the secretary or receptionist, they probably wouldn't be in a law firm except as a client.

Whatever your main characters' personality types are, be sure their dialogue reflects that. Their emphasis and word choice will be different for each.

VI. Worldview

First of all, what is a worldview? It's how people view the world and life from their perspective. Everyone has a worldview, and that worldview is a product of their ancestors. What they believed, they passed down to the next generation. That generation either accepts or rejects that worldview.

Your character's worldview should remain consistent in their thinking and their dialogue throughout the book. Let's say your character's worldview is filtered by distrust, learned at an early age through their parents' worldview and their own experience. Learning to trust someone is going to be difficult. Their dialogue and interior monologue will reflect that.

In one novel, set in 1929-30, I had to go back several generations to find out why the sisters have the worldview they do. Growing up, one sister accepted their ancestors' worldview, while the other sister rejected it. During the course of the story, the first sister wished she hadn't been taught that worldview. Even her sister's name indicated the parents' worldview. And it showed in their dialogue:

Duchess turns on her side and rises on one elbow. "I've never had a dream like yours. I don't know how to *do* anything but play the piano and serve tea. How am I going to earn my keep?"

I swanney, if Mama were still alive I'd wring her neck for not teaching Duchess anything but manners. "I'll teach you."

Let's say your character is raised in the slums of New York. Her worldview is one of survival at all costs—every man for himself. That will carry over, even if she gets out of the slums, and it will show in her dialogue. It will have an edge to it. For instance:

"Hey, Olivia, where'd you get the cool shoes?"

"I bought them." She thinks I stole them.

"Duh. I meant where?"

Oh. "Macy's."

That's an example of both the dialogue and interior monologue for that type character. She's hard because she had to be tough growing up. Her view of the world is it's against her.

And finally …

VII. Setting

Setting and origin both play into a character's dialogue. If a character is raised in Southern California and goes to college in Atlanta, she's going to come home with a strange accent. She's still young enough to pick up some Southern and mix it in with her surfer chick dialect. I know. I've heard it with my own ears. Some words were southern and some were valley girl. "Like he was totally grody to the max, y'all."

My husband is from northern England and immigrated to the U.S. in the … well a long time ago. When I first met him, his accent was very strong, swoon-worthy, really. But time spent in the U.S. Army and in business mellowed his accent. Now people aren't sure where he's from.

Those are both examples of origin and how the setting can change that. Does your Connecticut Yankee hero find himself in the Deep South, surrounded by y'alls and banana pudding? How is that going to affect his speech? How do other characters see him and react to him?

Remember during our gender discussion, we mentioned office relationships could be different? Co-workers don't share the same life outside the office, so Larry won't talk to his boss about his kid flushing whatever down the toilet. Your setting will add to that difference. There isn't always as tight a bond between co-workers.

Sally might share about a sale at lunch, but that depends on a whole lot of other factors: what's her job in that office? Is she in management? If so, she'll most likely retain a professional manner. Her dialogue in the office will reflect that, and not that her husband spilled cranberry juice on her sofa.

That said, if your setting is a small town, they most likely have that closeness in the workplace. After all, the librarian lives next door to the mayor. The mayor's secretary's bestie is the sheriff's sister. Dialogue will be totally different in a New York law firm and a Mayberry police station.

All these seven areas play into your characters' dialogue. If you incorporate them into their dialogue, it will be dynamic and believable.

Find out more about Ane Mulligan at the back of the book!

Chapter 9
Ramping up the Sigh Factor in our Heroes
By Julie Lessman

Question: What's one of the most—if not *the* most—important components in a romance?

Answer: The Hero. I mean, seriously, how many women do you know who went to see *Twilight* because of Kristen Stewart or *The Notebook* because of Rachel McAdams?

Question: When you finish a *reallllly* great romance novel that lingers in your mind long after the last page—key word being "romance," *not* women's fiction—what exactly are you thinking about ... the heroine, the hero, or the plot?

Okay, if you said the heroine or the plot ... you might want to move on to the next chapter, because I'm not sure this one is for you. Seriously, do you think Scarlett would have stood a chance with the female audience if Rhett wasn't laying lip-locks on her? And go ahead, name one women you know who'd shell out money to watch Rachel McAdams get caught in a rainstorm *without* Ryan Gosling.

So, why exactly is the hero a key element in a romance novel? I contend that the thoughts and actions of the hero generate more feelings/reactions from the readers than the heroine's because HIS desire translates into the desire every woman wishes she could elicit. The truth is women long to be pursued, loved, cherished for who they are and made to feel they are the most special woman in the world—if not to the man they love, then to the man they hope to love someday. And that's okay, because that's how God made us—to be "cherished" in a romantic relationship, per Ephesians 5:28-29. *"So, husbands ought also to love their own wives as their own bodies. He who loves his own wife loves himself; for no man ever yet hated his own flesh; but nourishes and cherishes it."*

So ... the bottom line is—when it comes to the romance novel, only a hero can satisfy that longing, not a heroine, which is why in order to hook your readers with a romance story, you *have* to hook them with the hero.

It's just plain common sense that when it comes to romantic fiction, the only one who can make a woman swoon is the hero. So, what exactly does it mean to "swoon"? Well, *Merriam-Webster Dictionary* defines it as follows:

To become very excited about someone or something; to become enraptured; to suddenly become unconscious.

Now, for the sake of this chapter, let's go with the first two definitions, although I have to admit that in my tenure as a die-hard romance reader, there have been one or two heroes who were so flat and swoonless that I wished I were unconscious. But I digress ...

When it comes to romantic heroes, all women swoon. Just not in the same way. For instance, the Novel Crossing blog ran a poll a while back among Christian romance readers as to the "Five Swoon-Worthiest Heroes in Christian Romance," and there were no less than 25+ contenders. Now, that's a lot of swooning if I must say so myself, proving that the parameters for "swoon-worthy" are as diverse as the number of heroes in Christian romance.

Why am I telling you this? Well, yes, I'm pretty darn proud that my bad-boy Collin McGuire from *A Passion Most Pure* made it to the top five because frankly, he needed the boost. Trust me, if you know anything about Collin regarding his lack of athletic ability and the heckling he takes from his brothers-in-law in the next five books, you would know why!

But ... the main reason I mention the poll above is because it validates my point that swoon- worthy heroes are as diverse as the women who read about them, so there's no cookie-cutter approach or template to create such a hero.

However, there *are* characteristics, flaws, quirks, etc. that can help ramp your hero from sweet to swoon-worthy in the blink of a word, and we'll explore those later in this chapter. But first, I thought it might be fun to take a look at the following six most common types of heroes you will encounter in Christian romance along with excerpts from my books depicting each one.

Ready? Here we go!

THE SIX MOST COMMON TYPES OF HEROES IN CHRISTIAN ROMANCE NOVELS

1. THE BAD-BOY HERO: What is it about the Bad Boy that makes him the most popular hero? In a survey on hero types polling approximately 350 women, the Bad-Boy Hero tied for first with 28% of the vote out of ten heroes listed. Why is that? I allege it's because *he* represents the unobtainable male whose head every woman wants to turn, but only one woman can—the heroine. You know the type—dangerously handsome, in control, and living life on their own terms—men like Rhett Butler from *Gone With the Wind*, James Dean from *Rebel Without a Cause*, or John Travolta from *Grease*.

In Christian romance, there is nothing stronger than a wayward guy gone good. It takes strength of conviction and a lot of humility for a man to bend his knee to God, but when he does, he rises as a tower of strength and manhood, not in his own power, but in God's. It's like epoxy—the strength of a man combined with the strength of his Savior, recreating man as he was meant to be—a warrior, a protector, and fiercely devoted to both God and the woman he loves.

To me a "bad boy" hero in a romance novel is a rogue who is cocky and sure, knows he's attractive to women, is very experienced with them, and has no compunction whatsoever about stealing a kiss. A good example is in this scene from *A*

Passion Most Pure, when bad-boy Collin McGuire makes advances to heroine Faith O'Connor out of sheer anger after she causes problems for him with her parents by exposing his clandestine meeting with her sister.

Faith shot off the blanket and glared down at him. "You leave my sister alone! She's not one of your common girls at Brannigan's. She's a good girl. Too good for the likes of you."

"Too good for the likes of you ..." The words of his mother assaulted Collin's memory, flaming the fuse. Springing to his feet, he towered over Faith and gripped her shoulders, fingers digging in. For an instant, it appeared as if she didn't dare breathe.

"Don't ever say that again," he whispered, his jaw hard as rock. Fury pulsed in his temple as he tightened his grip. "Too good for the likes of me, is she now? Well then, what about you, Faith O'Connor? Are you too good for the likes of me?"

She caught her breath just before his lips found hers, and he felt the fight within her as he locked her in his arms. The taste of her mouth was so heady to his senses, a soft moan escaped his lips at the shock of it. She shivered before she went weak in his arms, and instinctively, he softened his hold.

She lunged back and clipped the edge of his jaw with a tight-fisted punch, her breath coming in ragged gasps. "How dare you—" she sputtered, the green eyes full of heat.

He grinned and silenced her with his mouth. She made a weak attempt to push him away, but he only drew her back with a force that made her shudder. He felt her pulse racing as his lips wandered her throat. The scent of her drove him mad. He kissed her with renewed urgency, the taste of her making him dizzy. And then, before she could catch her breath, he shoved her away, his heart thundering and his mind paralyzed.

2. THE BROODING HERO: There's just something about a brooding hero, the still-waters-run-deep concept with just a hint of the rebel thrown in to make him mysterious, passionate, and almost dangerous. Heroes like Edward Cullen from *Twilight* or James Dean from *Rebel Without a Cause* or even Mr. Darcy from *Pride & Prejudice* come to mind, evoking a hero that not only races the heart, but sends a shiver of warning down the spine of any woman upon whom he sets his sights.

When it comes to a brooding hero, I personally like to contrast all that lovely male moodiness with a little heroine humor to soften the edges of the brooder, such as in this clip from my contemporary novel, *Isle of Hope*. I actually *love* writing cranky, crusty heroes, so I had blast with both Mitch Dennehy in *A Passion Redeemed* and Nick Baronē in *Dare to Love Again*, which is why I made the older subordinate hero in *Isle of Hope* a brooder as well.

Meet Dr. Ben Carmichael, otherwise known as Dr. Doom to the neighborhood kids ever since his wife ran off with his best friend and neighbor. It's been eight years, and his ex-best friend's ex-wife, Tess, has decided that's long enough to hold onto a grudge, so she sets out to reconnect with the brooding neighbor on the other side of the mile-high hedge.

"The UPS man delivered a package for you, so I thought I'd bring it over as well as bacon for Beau."

The man didn't move, didn't speak, didn't blink. Just stared like she'd dropped in from the next galaxy rather than merely next door.

Despite the smile on her face, her chin notched up along with the plate in her hands. "And I have monster cookies," she said in a sing-song tone usually reserved for her children.

Silence. Except, of course, for Beau's whimpering lament. Her smile compressed. *Okay, buster, have it your way.* Eyes never straying from Dr. Doom's, she sailed the bacon far into the yard, grit girding her smile as Beau bolted away with whines of euphoria. *Because when it comes to the evil eye, Doc, I can outlast a dirty eight-year-old Power Ranger who doesn't want to get a bath, so bring it on ...*

"Why." It sounded more like a grunt than a question ... and still nothing moved on the man's body.

Tess hiked a brow, a challenge in her smile. "Why, because they're your favorite, silly ... or at least they used to be."

"No," he bit out, the hard planes of his face calcifying even more. *"Why* are you *here—now?"*

Tess blinked, a wee bit worried for his patients if he couldn't figure this one out. Package snug under her arm, she tapped it with her fingers, head dipped as if talking to her eight-year-old son, Davey. "Uh, your package?" She paused, expectant. "You know—it needed a signature?" She battled a full-fledge grin at stormy eyes shadowed by beetled brows. *Come on, Ben, you can do this.*

The fog cleared from his gaze, but the snark remained. With a grunt of thanks, he extended a muscular arm over the fence, his large palm surprisingly calloused for one of the state's top heart surgeons.

She angled a brow, stealing a page from the Dr. Doom playbook when her body didn't budge.

The scowl on his stone face slashed even deeper, revealing a hint of temper that didn't faze Tess in the least. If she learned one thing from being best friends with the Carmichaels for almost a quarter of a century, it was that Ben Carmichael was all bluff. Serious, moody, yet a depth of passion and integrity she'd always admired. A bottomless well of emotion roiling beneath a mirror-lake he worked so hard to convey.

Still waters run deep.

Her smile tipped. *And, turbulently, it would seem.*

3. VIRTUOUS HERO: In Christian romance, one would certainly expect more virtuous heroes, those men who live for God and hold virtue in high esteem, which makes the wrestle with evil all the more attractive. Men like Lancelot in *Camelot* or Ashley Wilkes in *Gone With the Wind*, fiercely devoted to God but subject to the frailties of things like temptation, a secret vice, or past mistakes. To me—a die-hard romantic-tension queen—one of the most attractive things about the virtuous hero is the **untapped passion/attraction** he feels for the heroine, such as in this scene from *A Passion Denied.*

Virtuous hero, John Brady (a Billy Graham-type character), is caught off guard by the sweet heroine he views as the little sister he's spiritually mentored since she was fourteen. Now, at the age of eighteen, Lizzie (whom Brady still calls Beth) is in love with John and wants him to see her as a woman, which, of course, Brady refuses to do. *Until* ... Lizzie's seductive older sister teaches her how to turn his head ... by stealing a kiss!

"Beth, are we okay?" He ducked to search her eyes, then brushed her hair back from her face. A smile shadowed his lips. "Still friends?"

Friends. A deadly plague only a kiss could cure. Resolve stiffened her spine. "Sure, Brady ... friends."

He smiled and tucked a finger under her chin. "That's my girl. Now, what do you say we pray about some of these things?" He leaned close with another quick kiss to her brow, and in a desperate beat of her heart, she lunged, uniting her mouth with his. She felt the shock of her action in the jolt of his body, and she gripped him close to deepen the kiss. Waves of warmth shuddered through her at the taste of him, and the essence of peppermint was sweet in her mouth.

"No!" He wrenched back from her hold with disbelief in his eyes.

Too late. She had never felt like this before. Years of seeking romance from flat parchment pages had not prepared her for this. This rush, this desire ... her body suddenly alive, and every nerve pulsing with need. All shyness melted away in the heat of her longing, and she pounced again, merging her mouth with his. *John Brady, I love you!*

A fraction of a second became eons as she awaited his rejection. His body was stiff with shock, but no resistance came. Then in a sharp catch of her breath, he drew her to him with such force, she gasped, the sound silenced by the weight of his mouth against hers. He groaned and cupped the back of her head as if to delve into her very soul, a man possessed. His lips broke free to wander her throat, and shivers of heat coursed through her veins. In ragged harmony, their shallow breathing billowed into the night while his arms possessed her, molding her body to his.

4. ALPHA HERO: Okay, you know who these guys are—those gruff, no-nonsense types who are natural leaders and stubborn to the core—cool, confident, steady, strong, and like to be in control. Men like Jethro Gibbs from *NCIS* or the highlander type from a Scottish romance. Utterly male and utterly determined to be in control by staking his claim on the woman he loves.

In this scene from The Daughters of Boston series, alpha hero Mitch Dennehy has painfully adhered to intimacy boundaries set by the heroine with whom he's falling in love. *Until* he learns she still has feelings for another man, and then the alpha male in him becomes very territorial.

When Mitch took her home that night, he had given her his usual gentle kiss.

"I'll see you Monday," Faith whispered, pushing the door ajar.

Something inside had compelled him to pull her close. "No, you'll see me tonight, in your dreams, and that's an order. But just to make sure ..."

Never would he forget the look—eyes blinking wide as he dragged her to him, her soft lips parting in surprise when his mouth took hers with a hunger long suppressed. His hands wandered her back, urging her close while his lips roamed the curve of her neck, returning to reclaim her mouth with a fervor. For one brief, glorious moment, the terms were his, and by thunder, she would feel the heat of his kiss in her bones.

In a raspy gulp of air, she lunged back. "I can't believe you did that!" she gasped.

"Believe it," he quipped, tone nonchalant.

"But, why? After what I told you tonight, why would you do that?"

"Why? Let's just call it a bit of insurance."

"What?"

"Insurance. If the woman I love is going to have memories of passion, it's going to be with me, not him."

"I don't entertain memories of passion." Her voice was edged with anger.

"You will tonight," he said. And turning on his heel, he left her—hopefully with a warmth that defied the coolness of the night.

5. SWEET AND EASYGOING BETA-MALE HERO:
The Beta Male are those "nice guys" who are sweet, kind, decent, and loaded with best-friend potential. But, oh my, once you scratch the surface, you uncover a past or a wound he doesn't want anyone to see. Like my hero in *Surprised by Love*, Bram Hughes, who has always been the easy-going, big-brother mentor and best friend to the heroine, a once shy and frumpy little girl. But when Meg returns from a year in Paris, she's suddenly blossomed into a beauty who races his pulse, which disturbs him enough to avoid her. That is, until he manages to get their friendship—and *only* friendship—back on solid ground.

The softest of smiles played at the edge of her lips. "Really counselor—bribery?" Those remarkable green eyes twinkled. "I would have thought better of the noble Bram Hughes."

His smile faded as he shifted to face her, her words pricking his conscience. He strove for a casual air with one arm over the back of the seat while the other absently fiddled with the leather head of the tiller. "Yes, well, maybe you shouldn't,

Bug, because it wasn't very 'noble' of me to avoid you for over two weeks, which is why I wanted you to come with me to get ice cream—so I could apologize and explain why."

She picked at a seam in her skirt as she looked away, a hint of rose stealing into her cheeks. "I already know why," she said softly, "and the truth is, it's I who owes you an apology."

"No, Meg, you're wrong—"

"Am I?" A sweep of dark lashes lifted to reveal a gaze riddled with regret. "You're my best friend in the whole world, Bram, and I made you uncomfortable with my—" A nervous lick of her lips told him this was not easy for her. "Brazen overtures," she whispered.

He tipped his head, gaze softening while a crooked grin skimmed across his lips. "Come on, Bug—brazen?" He nudged her chin up, coaxing her eyes to meet his. "There's not a brazen bone in your body, Megan McClare, and an apology is hardly necessary."

Boosting his courage with a fortifying breath, he leaned back against the car door with a fold of arms, his smile sloping off-center. "Trust me—you had every reason to assume that mindset the way I gawked at you when you first walked into the room, like I was some starry-eyed adolescent."

Sobriety stole into his manner, dimming his smile. "You've grown into a beauty, Meg, and some lucky guy will be blessed beyond his wildest dreams with a woman who is bright, gentle, and beautiful—the perfect girl, really." His chest rose and fell with a heavy sigh. "It just can't be me, Bug," he said quietly.

6. PROTECTOR HERO: This is the hero whose major goal—protecting those he loves—becomes who he is, be it a cop, firefighter, soldier, spy, etc. Many times these heroes have become protective because as children, they suffered some great loss or hurt, which is something you always want to convey if this is the case in your story.

In this scene from my novel, *Dare to Love Again*, the hero is a grouchy police detective who's been coerced by the heroine's wealthy uncle—whom the hero hates—to protect his adventurous and scatterbrained niece without her knowledge.

Unease skittered his spine like rats skittered the alleys of the Barbary Coast, and hands cupped to the window, he peered through the crack in the curtains.

Words he hadn't uttered since the war ground from his lips, eyes gaping as Allison McClare wobbled on the top rung of a ladder. Nick would have sworn she was swaying as she attempted to paint scenery—the red roof of a house facade Mr. Bigley was supposed to finish—with a paintbrush taped to the end of that confounded stick.

*So help me, Allison . . .*He bit back another colorful word as he quietly made his way to the front door, silence essential so he wouldn't scare the brat half to death and risk her toppling from the ladder. Pulse hammering, he attempted to unlock the front door with the key Mrs. McClare had given him, incensed all the more to find it unlocked. "Blue blistering blazes," he muttered under his breath, easing the door open with nary a sound before silently stealing into the gym.

One glance at the stretch of her lithe and curvy form confirmed proximity to Allison McClare was not a good thing. At least, not anymore. Apparently too focused while she hummed quietly to herself, she never even heard his approach, and releasing a silent sigh, he slowly mounted the steps to the stage.

The humming and painting happily continued, confirming once again that this woman lived in a world all her own. Nick's lips went flat. A world in which he was becoming entirely too comfortable. "Alli," he said softly, taking great pains not to startle her.

"Oh!" Jerking straight up, she whirled around at the waist, body and ladder teetering so hard, the paint bucket went flying, hitting the paint-stained sheet beneath her with a clunk and a splat.

Pulse in a sprint, he sprang forward with instinct and speed honed to near perfection in jiu-jitsu, heart crashing into his stomach while Allison crashed into his arms. With a harsh catch of his breath, shock gave way to temper at the risks that she took. "What is it with you and climbing on things, anyway?" he snapped. "You trying to break your silly neck?" Rib cage heaving, he glared, waiting for the tongue-lashing that never came.

"Oh, Nick!" she whispered, hand quivering while she gently stroked his cheek. "I've missed you *so* much!"

_So_ ... how do _I_ like to ramp up the swoon factor in a hero to take him from ho-hum to hot?

Well, the ways are ENDLESS, but here are a few of my favorites that I employ over and over. We'll go through each one in detail, along with excerpts to show you what I mean.

1. Make the Hero Decidedly Male through Speech, Body Language, and Mindset.
2. Make the Heroine Affect Him Like No Other Woman.
3. Make the Hero's Attraction/Love for the Heroine Reform Him.
4. Make the Hero Be Able to Walk Away from Temptation.
5. Make the Hero Sacrificial.
6. Give the Hero a Sense of Humor.
7. Show the Hero's Love for Kids, Family, and Animals.
8. Make the Hero Dominant.
9. Give the Hero an Endearing Quirk.
10. Make the Hero Aware of the Heroine's Interest.
11. Make the Hero Aloof and Unavailable.
12. Show the Hero's Humility and Gentleness.
13. Show the Hero's Mental Desire for the Heroine.
14. Show the Hero's Spirituality.

15. Give the Hero a Noble Cause.
16. Give the Hero a Wounded Heart.
17. Show the Hero as Wise and Intelligent.

Shall we get started?

1. MAKE THE HERO DECIDEDLY MALE THROUGH SPEECH, BODY LANGUAGE, AND MINDSET: It's no shock to anyone that there are MAJOR differences between men and women, and as the old saying goes—vive la difference! So, it just stands to reason that when we see guys doing guy things or talking like guys talk, it's a natural pull for a woman even if we are shaking our heads and smiling at the time. Now, there are a zillion ways to make a guy "decidedly male," but here are a few of the more important ones that will help give your heroes a testosterone boost.

A.) Speech: Statistically speaking, women say 20,000 words compared to men's 7,000 per day, which means most men have a tendency to talk in short, to-the-point, and sometimes clipped conversation. They do NOT dwell on things like women do and their rationale for doing something is usually pretty basic, bottom-line, and right up there on the surface.

One of my favorite examples of this comes from an old *Home Improvement* TV episode where Tim "the Toolman" Taylor holds up a stop sign to the audience and says something like.

"This is a stop sign, and it was invented by a *man*. Do you know how I know that?"

"No, how do you know that?" the audience shouts back.

Tim taps the front of the sign and says, "Because it says 'stop'! If a woman had invented it, it would say ..." He then flips the sign over to reveal: If you really loved me, you would know what to do right now.

Now, honestly, is that not one of the truest stories you've ever heard? Because let's face it—women expound and men generally … *don't!* More often than not, in fact, men speak in monosyllables or mono-sentences, such as the example below from *Dare to Love Again.* Hero Nick Barone is a grouchy, no-nonsense Italian police detective who has implied the heroine is not very "bright" for strolling the Barbary Coast at night by herself.

Her eyes locked with his, completely void of any guile. "I'm learning, Mr. Barone—slowly, mind you, because I'm not all that bright," she said with a hint of jest before those green eyes deepened with true sincerity, "that you're just a very frank person who hates to see people so oblivious to harm."

He blinked, wishing they could just go back to insults. He was pretty sure anger was a lot safer than this dizzy heat whirling inside, leaving him tongue-tied.

"Nicholas?" Miss Penny lifted her chin. "What do you say?"

He mauled the back of his neck. "Uh … okay, I guess."

"Oh, for heaven's sake, Nicky," she said with a fold of her arms, tone stern despite a bare hint of a smile. "You say, thank you, Miss McClare and I'm sorry for being so brash."

He swallowed the foot in his mouth, eyes on Miss McClare as he inclined his head towards Miss Penny. "Yeah, what she said."

B.) Body Language: Facial and body expression in a male (or at least a hero) is usually **calmer and more relaxed,** with just a hint of something going on under the surface when he's upset. It could be a tic in his jaw, a muscle flickering in his cheek, or a twitch in his temple. A male's look is never wide-eyed like a female's, but generally more slatted or shuttered, pupils possibly dilated in surprise. Some men will run their fingers through their hair—slashing or gouging for anger, threading, fanning or tunneling in frustration or confusion, or just combing and spiking after exertion or exercise.

To me, most men (especially cowboy types) are more casual in motion, seldom standing ramrod straight, tending toward a more relaxed, leisurely stance with a slack of a hip and palms propped low on his thighs. Relaxation is also key for sitting positions where they straddle a chair, brace arms to the back of their neck with elbows flared, or clasp hands loosely over knees splayed wide.

To show fatigue or frustration, they'll do things like knead the bridge of their nose, gouge their foreheads with the ball of their hand, or massage their temple. When angry or frustrated, they may kick or throw things, punch a wall, slouch their shoulders, bury hands in their pockets, or grunt and swear. Whatever they do, *they're male, not female,* so always remember that their **language and thoughts are more abrupt, and their movement more casual**.

In this scene from *A Passion Redeemed*, the hero is a gruff, no-nonsense type with no patience. So, I utilized monosyllabic language as explained in Point A above, abrupt action, and almost rude manners to convey him as such, all of which I bolded for ease of identity. Per the request of the heroine's grandmother, the hero is assisting the heroine on a voyage from Dublin to Boston because she has a broken arm and leg and cannot walk.

"Do you think I could have a glass of wine?"

He turned around. "What?"

"You heard me."

He scowled. "No wine. How 'bout ginger ale?"

"But I don't want ginger ale. Can't I have wine instead? Please?"

His mouth snapped closed. He **snatched** the pitcher from the table and poured two glasses of water. "It's water or nothing at all." He set the glasses on the nightstand and sat back down.

She squared her shoulders and cradled the basket in her lap. "Fine. No wine, no food."

His jaw shifted back and forth the tiniest bit, a mulish habit she was quickly becoming familiar with. "No wine," **he ground out.**

She turned away and closed the basket. "Enjoy the dining hall, then." She felt the **heat of his stare** and released a deep breath when **he finally stormed out, door slamming behind him.**

Minutes later he returned, **mouth flat** and bottle in hand. He poured her wine, then **clunked the bottle on the table** and handed her the glass. "One per night. Take it or leave it."

"I'll take it, thank you."

Plopping into his chair with a grunt, he reached for his bread once again, **shoving a hunk in his mouth. He stared straight ahead, chomping hard.**

She smiled. "Now, isn't this nice?"

He gave her a **half-lidded glare** and continued to chew.

She took a sip of wine, then held her glass out. "Would you mind setting this on the table, please?"

He muttered under his breath and got up to lift the table—water pitcher, wine bottle and all— to the side of her bed. He nabbed several pieces of meat and sat back down.

"Perfect. Thank you."

He watched as she picked at the meat in the basket. She foraged through the pieces, fiercely intent on selecting just the right one.

He stopped chewing and swallowed hard. "Are you always this much trouble?"

C.) Mindset: Pride is a huge factor in the male persona, so generally you'll see more **stubbornness, control, and obsession with achievement**, be it sports, work, competition with other men, or just plain **dominance**. Such is the case in this scene from *A Passion Most Pure,* where the subordinate hero's pride has been trampled by his wife.

In several abrupt steps forward, Patrick loomed before her, eyes intense. He didn't touch her, but pressed uncomfortably close, hands fisted at his sides. "When it comes to the welfare of my children, Mrs. O'Connor, you will, in the future, consult me regarding your decisions. Am I making myself perfectly clear?"

For a moment her breath wedged in her throat before spilling forth in a rush of angry defiance. "And you, Mr. O'Connor, in the future, can find somewhere else to sleep! Am I making myself perfectly clear?" Her tone was shrill.

He flinched, as if she'd just spat in his face. For a brief moment, hurt flecked in his eyes before giving way to the coldest of steel. His jaw hardened to granite. She watched in disbelief as he reached for his coat and jerked the door open wide, allowing the wind to bang it against the wall.

2. MAKE THE HEROINE AFFECT HIM LIKE NO OTHER WOMAN: When I first read *Gone With the Wind* at age twelve, I was mesmerized by the emotional tug-of-war between Rhett and Scarlett. Here was a strong, dominant male in total control of his life and whom no woman could tie down and then, BOOM! The moment Scarlett sears him with a look on the winding staircase of Twelve Oaks, he's a goner, spellbound by this woman he just *has* to have, even if it means marriage—something he vowed he'd never do! So, it's key to show the impact of the heroine on the hero, which can be done in the following ways.

A.) It can be as simple and subtle as A LOOK, such as in this clip from *A Passion Most Pure* in which the hero Collin McGuire is engaged to one sister but in love with the other:

A hush settled on the room as her father read the Christmas story. Collin closed his eyes to listen, his face calm as he held Charity on the loveseat. Faith found herself watching him, amazed at the way he seemed to fit in so easily. Her heart melted into an ache.

All at once, his eyes opened and met hers. She dropped her gaze, heat fanning her cheeks. Out of the corner of her eye, she saw him draw Charity closer.

B.) Or by showing the HERO'S INTERNAL MONOLOGUE or thoughts, as in this clip from *A Passion Most Pure,* when the hero is adamant that he does *not* like the "control" the heroine has over his heart. **(Note: Male internal monologue needs to be short and infrequent since men do *not* dwell on their feelings like women do.)**

Collin had never felt like this, and it scared him. *She* scared him, and he didn't want anything to do with her. From that moment in the park when he kissed her, it was like he'd been possessed, cursed to dream of her, think of her, want her. He'd known woman far more beautiful, far more accommodating, far more easy to control. But this! Two encounters and she traveled his system like poison. The very same poison that had killed his father …

C.) Or by showing the HEROINE'S INTERNAL MONOLOGUE or thoughts like in this clip from *A Love Surrendered.* The heroine, who was disfigured by an abusive husband and feels anything but beautiful, is not only made to feel beautiful despite her scars, but knows to the depth of her being that her current husband loves her.

"Are you conspiring with those cats, Emma O'Connor?" Sean assessed her with a shuttered gaze, arms folded and hip cocked in the doorway. Sculpted chest bare, he ambled into the room in boxers and blond hair damp from his shower. A slow grin of warning stretched across wide lips as he eased onto the bed to lie beside her. Elbow cocked and head in hand, he massaged Guinevere's ribcage, warming Emma with a dangerous smile. Leaning close, he grazed her lips, then pulled away, the blue eyes tripping her pulse. "You're next," he whispered, and Emma was certain he could unleash a purr from her throat as easily as Guin's.

"I best get ready for bed," she said, attempting to get up.

A firm wrist gently tugged her near. "Not yet," he whispered, and with the grace of an athlete, he rolled on his back and pulled her along to lie on his chest. His tall frame dominated the bed, prompting Lance and Guin to find elsewhere to sleep while Emma's body relaxed against his.

His kiss was slow and sweet, and her eyelids fluttered closed while magical fingers kneaded the nape of her neck to coax her closer. His scent surrounded her, drugging her body as much as his kiss—the clean smell of soap and shaving cream and the taste of mint in his mouth.

Never had she felt so alive, so loved, so beautiful as she did in Sean's arms. "I love you, Emma," he said softly, "more than Snickers and baseball and beating Brady and Luke at sports." The tease in his words faded with another tender kiss, and when he pulled away, he caressed her with a look that nearly stole her breath. Never had she known a man more who could make love with his eyes. "I adore you," he whispered, "and sometimes I wonder how I survived without you."

D.) Or it can be a BOLD STATEMENT, such as Rhett Butler's declaration to Scarlett O'Hara in Margaret Mitchell's classic, *Gone with the Wind.*

"I want you more than I have ever wanted any woman— and I've waited longer for you than I've ever waited for any woman."

E.) Or an ACTION, either bold or reluctant, such as in this clip from *A Passion Redeemed,* where the hero does *not* want to be drawn to the heroine but can't fight it when he brings her home in his car after an innocent evening as friends.

His gaze settled on her mouth, and a rush of heat chased the smile from his face. His heart began to pound.

Friends. Only friends.

She pulled away, slowly scooting to her side of the seat, poised to open the handle of the door.

His hand clamped her arm. "No."

She turned. Shock flickered across her features. "No?"

His throat worked as his eyes settled on her mouth once again. "Stay. Please."

3. MAKE THE HERO'S LOVE/ATTRACTION TO HEROINE REFORM HIM: Nothing is more exciting to a woman—*especially* a Christian woman—than a man who is willing to change and become a better man, not only **for** her, but **because** of her. Again, this can be accomplished by the hero's thoughts, statements, or actions such as in these excerpts from *A Passion Most Pure*.

The first clip depicts the hero's thoughts right *after* he's turned his life over to God, knowing full well it was the heroine's prayers and actions that did it. The second clip, then, is his actual statement to the heroine that she's changed his life for the better.

The Hero's Internal Monologue/Thoughts/Action:

Slowly Collin rose from the dirt, astounded at the serenity he felt. He breathed in deeply to fill his lungs with the cool, night air. He couldn't have her, but she would always be a part of him. He knew to the depth of his soul that it had been her prayers that had saved him. It was a debt for which he would always be grateful. He wished her well.

No, he thought, there was no wishing to it. He would pray that God would bless her with the marriage she deserved. He owed her that. Quietly, he entered the billet and returned the Bible to Brady's side. Crawling into his own bunk, he closed his eyes and slept, finally, the slumber of a man with peace in his heart.

The Hero's Statement:
He gently stroked her cheek, blotting a tear with his finger. "Look, I didn't mean to make you cry. I just wanted you to know you've had a profound impact on my life, and I'm grateful. Because you see, Faith, just knowing you has made me a better man."

4. ONCE REFORMED, MAKE THE HERO ABLE TO WALK AWAY FROM TEMPTATION: Yes, we want the hero to have an almost irresistible attraction to our heroine, but ... we still expect him to resist! After all, this *is* Christian fiction, and to the Christian woman, a man who can control his passions demands a lot of respect from the reader, which is what we want for our heroes—a man we can respect!

Here's a scene from *A Passion Redeemed* in which the hero (who the family thinks is married to the heroine and actually will be within mere hours) resists the heroine's temptation via internal monologue, action, and finally a statement:

"Mitch, please . . . ," she whispered, and his gaze trailed from the deadly source of that plea to the soft curve of her nightgown as it clung to her body. Lust invaded his mind, bidden by thoughts of what lay beneath, and against his will, he found himself moving toward the bed.

All at once, he thought of her sister in a room down the hall, and his ragged breathing stilled. Faith had given him a glimpse of something holy and rare, a passion most pure. And despite the raging desire pumping through his veins at the moment, he meant to have it as well. With—or without—the woman before him.

He turned and ripped the cover off the other bed and retrieved his shoes. "I can't do this, Charity. I'm sleeping downstairs."

5. MAKE THE HERO SACRIFICIAL: Okay, almost nothing is more appealing in a hero than a man willing to sacrifice his own happiness for the sake of someone else. Not only does it reflect strength of character in making a selfless decision, but it reveals a core of strength and discipline that is so very attractive in a hero.

One of the reasons that Luke McGee from my novel, *A Hope Undaunted,* is one of my top two favorite heroes I've ever written is because he does just that—he sacrifices his own happiness in order to rescue his best friend, Betty, from an illegitimate pregnancy. That is noble in itself, but when Luke stays the course with Betty even *after* he discovers that the heroine he's loved since he was a boy—Katie O'Connor—is *finally* ready to love him back, it becomes even more powerful, not only deepening the respect and love of the heroine, but the reader as well.

Luke stared out his bedroom window, body numb and eyes glazed in a hard stare. The lamppost across the street blurred into a halo of light, foggy and out of focus—like his mind at the moment—and as dim and surreal as this nightmare that wouldn't end.

The scene in his office replayed, and the tragic turn of events twisted his gut once again.

"I . . . I think I'm in love with you, Luke . . ."

He slumped at his desk, hand to his eyes, never believing those words could have caused him such pain. Katie wanted him to stay, but he had promised to go. Two women who stirred the love in his heart . . . but only one who stirred his passion.

He closed his eyes, and thoughts of Betty were immediate, producing an ache so deep, more tears welled beneath his lids. Like him, she had lived in the gutter all of her life. Not just in the streets of New York, but in the littered ruts of destiny as well, where life denied her any chance at happiness. A father killed in the war and a destitute mother, a stepfather who thrived on abuse, and a lover who took it a step further. The result was a baby destined to be born a bastard, and a friend who had vowed it would never happen.

Betty and he were blood, not in the literal sense of heritage, but in the true sense of all they had shared . . . as friends . . . as family . . . *as lovers*. Grief pierced anew, and the emotion shifted in his throat. Brady and the O'Connors had taught him well. Luke had little or no experience with family, but one thing he knew to the core of his being—family didn't desert family . . . not in their time of need.

6. GIVE THE HERO A SENSE OF HUMOR: I love brooding heroes as much as the next gal, but a hero with a sense of humor can soften a reader's heart in the quirk of a smile, such as this scene from *A Heart Revealed* in which the hero's humor gives him a lovable, little-boy air.

He released a huff of frustration and looked up, his gaze pinned to hers. "I'm happy with my life, Emma. I don't need anything to complicate that, which is why I'm not looking to get involved with a woman. But there's a young lady at the store"—his lips slanted into a wry smile—"and I use the term loosely, given today's flapper mentality—who has, well, made it pretty clear she'd like to be on 'friendlier' terms."

Emma's eyes widened. "A customer?"

"No, not a customer... ," Sean began.

"Oh my goodness, not an employee, is it? You're the manager, Sean—I certainly would put this young woman in her place, gently but firmly."

Sean grimaced and scratched the back of his neck. "Well, she doesn't exactly work for me, either." He blinked at her, clearly perplexed. "You see, she's the owner's daughter."

Emma's lips circled into a soft "oh" before the words even left her mouth. "Oh, my."

"So, you see, it's a rather awkward position."

"Oh my, yes," Emma whispered. She listed against the counter and propped a palm to her mouth. She took a deep breath. "Well then, you'll just have to do your best to avoid her."

The corner of his lips swagged into an off-center smile as his eyelids lowered enough to indicate skepticism. "Yeah, well, that's hard to do when one is cornered in the supply room."

A soft gasp popped from Emma's lips as heat skimmed into her cheeks. "No!"

"Afraid so. Turned around with a clipboard in my hand, and the woman had me in a lip-lock so fast, I forgot which one of us was taking inventory."

7. SHOW THE HERO'S LOVE FOR KIDS, FAMILY, FRIENDS AND ANIMALS: Seriously, in romance ... is there anything sweeter than a big, hulking hero in love with a child? Anything more powerful than a friend who'll lay down his life for a friend? Anything more satisfying than a man who cherishes God and family above all else?

Well, not many things, that's for sure, because when you see how a hero treats his family, friends, or animals, you see clear into his heart, telling you he's a man—or a hero—worthy of your respect and love.

The following scene from *Dare to Love Again* shows the impact that a little six-year-old orphan has on one of my most hulking, grouchiest heroes—Nick Barone—and I can't tell you how many letters or reviews I've received where the readers loved Nick the most for the tenderness he showed Lottie.

Nick circled Lottie's waist, the scent of baby powder and Pear's soap calming his senses.

"Are you going to spank Mr. Nick with a stick, Miss Penny?" the little dickens asked his landlady, making him smile.

Miss Penny's lips squirmed while Mrs. Lemp chuckled. The steel in her eyes melted into affection. "I'm considering it, Lottie, if Mr. Nick doesn't behave."

Clambering up on Nick's lap, Lottie hugged him with a husky, little grunt before she braced his face with two tiny palms, depositing a sweet peck to his lips that dissolved any frustration he had. "Don't be bad, Mr. Nick," she whispered with a gloss of moisture in her eyes that nearly wrung tears from his own, "I don't want Miss Penny to hurt you."

He released a silent sigh and tucked a curl over her shoulder, the risk of disappointing her a far greater deterrent than any piece of wood. "I'll be good, Lottie," he said quietly, "I promise."

Okay, in our next example, I'm sorry, but I can't help it—when I see a hero with a fierce loyalty and affection for his best friend, I melt just a little bit more. Why? Because that demonstrates the loyalty every woman out there is looking for in a man ... *especially* a hero! Which is why friendship scenes like the one below from *A Passion Denied* affect me so greatly. The loyalty and love between my heroes Collin McGuire and John Brady—who are partners in a printing business—greatly enhance my own love for both men.

Brady continued to stare, his bleary gaze lost in a sea of bitter coffee. "I'm not hungry."

"Yeah, well you need a little something other than vodka to sustain that thick head of yours."

That woke him up! His head shot up, and the red in his eyes singed like fire. "Go to the devil, Collin. As if I didn't pull your head out of the latrine more times than I can count."

Collin eased back into his chair, all humor depleted. "That's right, John, you did. Which makes this all the more upsetting. What's going on?"

Brady closed his eyes and ran a shaky hand over his face. "I can't tell you."

"Why? From the very beginning, you've known everything about me—my past, my present, what I think, what I feel. The best of friends, closer than brothers. Don't you think I deserve the same?"

Brady lowered his head. "You do, but I can't tell you."

Collin's jaw tightened. "Why?"

"Because I'm not ready."

Collin slammed his fist on the table. "Not ready for what? To be a friend?"

Brady's head lunged up, his eyes swimming with pain. "No, Collin, not ready to lose one."

Collin blinked. He swallowed the emotion lumped in his throat and nodded. "If I leave, will you promise to talk to Father Mac?"

Brady nodded slowly, his eyes dull.

Collin stood. He glanced at Father Mac. "Can you try to get him to eat? I want him healthy at work tomorrow." Collin gave Brady's shoulder a quick squeeze. "I'm tired of carrying him." He started for the door.

"Collin?" Brady's voice suddenly had an edge.

"Yeah?"

"I'll have half of day's work done before you even shadow the door."

Collin turned, hand poised on the knob. His throat tightened. "I want you to know, John, whatever you did, no matter how bad you think it may be, I will stand by you. I'm proud to call you my friend, because I know who you are—a man of integrity, honor, and passion for God.

"And nothing—*nothing*—you can say will ever change that for me. I love you like a brother, John, and always will."

The door clicked softly behind him.

And finally, when I see a hero who is fiercely protective and loyal to his own family, it goes a long way in redeeming a rogue like Logan McClare in the clip below from *Dare to Love Again*, not only winning more of the heroine's heart, but hopefully the reader's as well.

He cocked a brow. "So, we take precautions. We hire a full-time handyman/guard to assist Mr. Bigley year-round, not just for a few months. Then we put our foot down with Allison as well, restricting her working at the school past five or taking the cable car on her own."

Cait's lips wobbled into a faint smile. "We?" she whispered, not wanting to burden Logan further but painfully aware he was becoming more and more a part of her life every day—her decisions, her problems, her responsibilities.

And my heart?

He paused to study her, the potency of love she saw in his eyes making her want to weep all over again. "Yes, 'we,'" he whispered, skimming several fingers along the line of her jaw. "We're a team, Cait, you and I. We may not be a 'couple' in the true sense of the word, but we are two people in love with the same family, nonetheless. Which means your family is my family, and I will support and protect you—and it—until I take my last breath."

8. MAKE THE HERO DOMINANT: Yes, women are notorious for trying to change a man or push him around, but the truth is that most women are drawn to a man they *can't* push around. A man who is his own man, in control, and won't allow a woman to take the upper hand.

From early cavemen and Viking warriors, to the more genteel gentlemen of the South like Rhett Butler or the likes of rough-and-tumble cowboys like John Wayne, it is *Taming of the Shrew* all over again because women *want* heroes who are strong. And when that strength and control is spiritual as well as physical, even better!

Here's a scene from *A Hope Undaunted* that demonstrates the iron-will dominance of hero Luke McGee, something that is desperately needed with a strong-willed heroine like Katie O'Connor.

"Wait!" She ran to grasp his arm in a death hold, fingers clenched as tight as her stomach. "Don't do this, please—don't just walk away. I care about you, Luke, and I need your friendship. And you need mine."

His gaze fixed on her hand where Jack's diamond glittered in the lamplight, then slowly rose to her face, his blue eyes almost black. "No, Katie," he whispered with a thread of pain in his voice, "I need your love."

Her heart crashed to a stop. She removed her hand and lowered her eyes, her gaze fused to the fringed tongue of his brown leather shoe. "I . . . care about you, Luke, I do." Her voice trailed off, fragile and reedy with regret. "But please . . . why can't we just be friends?"

Taut fingers gripped her chin and jerked it up, the dominance of his hold matched by the anger in his eyes. "Because it will be lovers or nothing, Katie Rose. The choice is yours."

Of course, when it comes to dominance in a hero, I would be remiss if I didn't include Rhett Butler in this famous kissing scene from Margaret Mitchell's *Gone With the Wind,* in which Rhett dominates Scarlett with a proposal few women could refuse. Following is a mix of the book and the movie:

"You've been married to a boy and an old man. Why not try a husband of the right age, with a way with women?"

"You're a fool, Rhett Butler, when you know I shall always love another man."

"Stop it. You hear me, Scarlett, stop it! No more of that talk."

(He jerks her to him and kisses her)

"Don't, I shall faint," she whispered, trying to turn her head weakly from him.

"I want you to faint. This is what you were meant for. None of the fools you've ever known have kissed you like this, have they? Your Charles or your Frank or your stupid Ashley."

"Please—"

"I said your stupid Ashley. Gentleman all—what do they know about women? What did they know about you? I know you."

His mouth was on hers again and she surrendered without a struggle, too weak even to turn her head ...

9. GIVE THE HERO AN ENDEARING QUIRK (especially if he's an alpha-male): Come on, I dare you to deny it—endearing quirks make us smile. And when they belong to a hero? Sigh ... they can soften the crustiest of men, making our hearts smile, too, with added affection.

In *Dare to Love Again*, my alpha-male hero Nick Barone is a fearless and armed rough-and-tumble Italian police detective who, like Leroy Jethro Gibbs of *NCIS*, is not afraid of anybody or anything. You know the type—rock jaw, perennial shadow of beard, and gruff manner?

Well, Nick is railroaded into escorting the heroine home every day on a cable car. The quirk I gave him? He's afraid of cable cars, of course, as depicted below, a flaw that provides levity, I hope, as well as humanizes our grouchy hero and endears him to the reader. And just to be ornery, I tossed in an addiction to animal crackers that not only help settle his stomach, but give him animal-cracker breath throughout the book.

Her head wheeled to face him, eyebrows tented in shock. "What? This is your first time on a cable car? Then how on earth did you know you'd be sick? Do you get sick on boats?"

"No." It was a croak as he smothered what could have been a belch.

She squinted. "Then I don't understand. If you don't get seasick, then why—" Her eyes went wide. "Wait—you're afraid, aren't you?"

Well, that certainly helped his color. Blood gorged his cheeks. "Don't be ridiculous," he snarled, singeing her with a glare.

Her lips took a twist. *Oh, good—familiar territory!* "Sweet mother of mercy, you *are*, aren't you?" She clamped a hand to her mouth to smother a laugh, the idea of this mammoth, gun-toting grouch afraid of anything delighting her more than it should.

She forced a serious demeanor, noting from his ruddy color that their sparring had apparently taken his mind off the ride. "For heaven's sake, it's nothing to be ashamed of, Nick," she said sweetly. She tilted her head, attempting to contain the chuckles that bubbled up in her chest. "Unless, of course," she whispered in a voice hoarse with restraint, "you're afraid of mice too . . ." Her laughter broke free in a glorious swell of giggles.

The gray-green eyes narrowed over the handkerchief he held to his mouth. "Don't tempt me, Miss McClare—I had kippers for lunch."

10. MAKE THE HERO AWARE OF HEROINE'S INTEREST: Call me crazy, but to me, there's just something attractive about a man who's confident in the fact that the heroine is attracted to him. Call it a hint of cockiness if you will, but I think it gives the hero the upper hand, which plays right into the "dominance" mode that is so appealing to many romance readers.

In these two clips from *A Hope Undaunted*, we see the hero's awareness of the heroine's attraction, first in THOUGHTS where he's remembering her ready response to his forced kiss in a prior scene, then in ACTION when he reminds her of it in the second example.

His jaw hardened. But dirt beneath her feet or no, that hadn't stopped her body from responding to his, not that she would ever admit it. She may not be attracted to him as a person, but as a man, the passion in her kiss told him all he needed to know.

The memory suddenly surged through him like the sticky June heat outside his window, stifling his air. A silent curse hissed from his lips as he hurled his suit jacket across the room. Either way, she had made a fool of him.

Again.

Then later on in the story, when the hero and heroine are on speaking terms, he reminds her with one look and one word that he knows she's attracted to him.

Luke lifted the mammoth burger to his lips, pausing to give Katie a weighted gaze. "And unlike you, *Katydid*, some women actually enjoy doing what I ask."

"Ask maybe, but force? Do they enjoy that?"

He bit into his sandwich and chewed slowly, a smile surfacing at the edges of his mouth. "Sometimes," he said, heating her with a look while he took a slow swig of his drink.

Katie's cheeks flamed hot, and she itched to slap that smug smile off his handsome face. Instead, she turned to Betty while nibbling a scrawny piece of bacon. "So, how are the ribs?"

11. MAKE THE HERO ALOOF AND UNAVAILABLE: Mr. Darcy of Jane Austen's *Pride and Prejudice* is probably the epitome of the aloof and unavailable hero, immediately setting up a romantic conflict that the reader begs to be resolved. Not only does this conflict make the heroine acutely aware of the hero, putting her on edge whenever he's around, but it puts the reader on edge, too, heightening romantic tension, which is what a romance author wants to do.

I utilize this tactic in *A Hope Undaunted,* when the hero distances himself from the heroine following an altercation involving a kiss. His aloof manner only serves to draw the heroine in, however, increasing her ardor—and the reader's, I hope—especially when they discover his true reasons why.

A click of the phone in the cradle signaled he was through, and she looked up. "Do you mind if I sit down?"

He straightened and nodded, rolling his chair away, as if to distance himself.

Sucking in a deep breath, she slipped into a chair and tucked her arms to her waist. "Thank you," she whispered.

"What's this all about, Katie?"

She looked up then, and the guarded look in his eyes bolstered her intent. "Luke, last week I said some things that were really unkind and ... provoked you, I know." Her gaze diverted to the window, unable to bear the coolness of his manner. "But you took me by surprise, you see, and I reacted badly. Both in my words and in my ... well, my response to your—"

He shot to his feet. "Katie, it's over and done with. We've both apologized, so let it go. It's time to go home."

She rose to her feet and leaned forward, palms pressed to the front of his desk. "No, it's not over and done with, Luke. You treat me like a leper around here."

He cuffed the back of his neck and exhaled. "What do you want from me, Katie?"

"I want you to talk to me and not through me, I want you to joke with me like you joke with the others, and I want you to treat me like you treat Parker and Betty—as a friend."

He slacked a hip and crossed his arms. "No."

"No?" She straightened, disbelief raising her brows. "I can't be a friend?"

"That's right." He shifted, and a muscle twittered along the hard line of his jaw.

"But, why?"

He leaned palms on the desk like she had, rolled sleeves revealing two muscled arms corded with strain. "Because it's no good, Katie. Too much butting heads, too much bad history." He rose to his full height and sucked in a deep breath, releasing it slowly. His eyes burned into hers as his voice lowered to a whisper. "Too much chemistry."

12. SHOW THE HERO'S HUMILITY AND GENTLENESS: The gentlest, most humble hero I've ever written was a secondary hero in *A Hope Undaunted* who won the heroine's heart, but not her hand.

Parker Riley was so humble and kind that he almost upstaged my hero, prompting a ton of reader letters begging me to give Parker his own story. I have to admit, although I personally tend toward cockier heroes, Parker stole a piece of my heart, too, and the main reason is his incredible humility and gentleness and his utter loyalty to his best friend. In this scene from *A Hope Undaunted,* the heroine gives him a Christmas kiss he isn't expecting after telling him earlier she only wanted to be friends.

She stirred from her thoughts and returned to the present, a smile tilting her lips at the snow in his hair and the concern in his eyes. "Merry Christmas, Parker," she whispered, then lifted on tiptoe to brush her lips against his.

His manner stiffened for several seconds, as if the cold had iced him to the spot, and then in the time it took for a snowflake to dissolve against her cheek, he pulled her close with a low moan and deepened the kiss.

Suddenly he wrenched away, his labored breathing billowing into the night. "Katie, I'm sorry . . ."

She touched a hand to his cheek. "Don't be, Parker. I kissed you, remember?"

A smile tugged at the corners of his mouth as those serious eyes studied her, cautious and nervous and so full of love. "Why did you?"

She rested her cheek against his chest, drawing comfort from the steady beat of his heart. "I don't know. I had no intentions, as you know, but then . . . something happened tonight. Call it the holidays or family or the magic of Christmas, but I watched you playing chess with my father and mingling with my family as if you belonged, and suddenly . . . I . . . wanted to know you better."

He held her away as his eyes searched hers. "What do you want from me, Katie?" he asked quietly. "Friendship or more?"

She licked her dry lips before her eyes met his. "I think I want more. Slowly . . . but more."

A smile curved at the edges of his mouth. "You're in luck, Katie Rose," he whispered, "'slow' is my middle name." He gloved a hand to her cheek, his eyes suddenly serious. "But I think it's only fair to warn you—I'm falling in love with you, my friend."

The muscles in her throat worked hard. "I have to admit, that does scare me a little."

He suddenly grinned. "Me too." The grin gave way as he looked into her eyes, and the dreamy quality returned once again. As slowly as if time were standing still, he bent to caress her mouth with his own, and her body relaxed, gentled by his touch. He pulled away and she remained there, face lifted and eyes closed, thinking Parker's kiss was unlike any she'd ever had. Not hungry and tempestuous like Luke or Jack's, but quiet and steady . . . like the man himself.

13. SHOW THE HERO'S MENTAL DESIRE FOR THE HEROINE: For me, nothing enhances a hero more than knowing he desires the heroine but can't have her, something I utilized a lot in *A Passion Most Pure*. In this scene from that book, the hero's mental desire—and his restraint in not revealing that desire—stokes the flames of romantic tension for me, and I hope the reader as well.

"You wouldn't be interested in a quick game of rummy, would you?" Her green eyes issued a challenge.

A smile slid across Collin's lips, pulse quickening as the color deepened on her cheeks. Her gaze quickly dropped to assess the cards in her hand, and all at once, he was as high-strung as a cat. He hated the way his blood was coursing through his veins without warning. Was he interested in a game of rummy? A swear word bubbled into his thoughts. No, he wasn't interested in rummy! And the cold realization did nothing to temper the heat he was feeling.

After a month of devoting himself to Charity, a month of hoping these feelings were behind him, even now, one-on-one, she still affected him more than any woman alive.

"Sure, why not?" He palmed the cards she dealt and breathed in deeply—quietly—arranging his hand. He willed himself to be calm and relaxed. Like her, he thought, stealing a glance. She was oblivious to the flood of feelings she'd just unleashed in him. Completely into the game, she gauged her cards with a cool look, face unreadable except for the slightest tilt of her lips.

14. SHOW THE HERO'S SPIRITUALITY: In Christian romance, when you show the deep spiritual side of a hero, it's an automatic chick magnet for Christian women.

However, it's best done through the eyes of another character rather than the hero's thoughts in order to amplify the hero's humility and godliness. One of my most spiritual heroes is John Brady from *A Passion Denied*, whom we see through the eyes of his best friend in the following clip, giving you a true glimpse into the man's soul.

They had prayed tonight. For the last time. And after a day of moving and an evening of reminiscing, John Morrison Brady had once again proven himself to be the man of honor Collin knew him to be. John had wanted to pray for Lizzie and Michael, but Collin had balked. "I can't," he had said.

But he did, because John had taught him how. How to forgive and how to let go, lessons John had learned well, in far harder ways than Collin had ever known. He was a man of principle with an unprincipled past, bent on a path in which God would use both for his glory.

15. GIVE THE HERO A NOBLE CAUSE: In *A Hope Undaunted*, the hero Luke McGee is a street orphan whose only family are his two best friends, Parker Riley and Betty Galetti, for whom he sacrifices his own happiness throughout the course of the book. This noble cause not only drives the plot, but drives the reader to both love and forgive Luke no matter his stubborn actions.

"I don't need you two hovering over me all the time. I'll be fine, I promise."

Betty started to leave, but not before Luke blocked her way. "We'll do this our way, Bets, or not at all, is that clear?"

"You mean your way, don't you, Luke? It's not Parker obsessing over my safety."

Luke sucked in a deep breath and exhaled slowly. Painful memories tightened his gut— the guilt of their close friendship veering into something more before he'd finally broken it off.

Pain he'd never meant to inflict, forcing her into the arms of a monster. Cold fury shivered him at the thought of how he'd found her that night, battered, bruised, a woman with whom he shared a bond closer than blood. And a friend he loved better than any sister. He released a weary breath. "I just care about you, Bets—is that a crime?"

Her defenses softened, and he saw a glimmer of the feelings she still harbored for him. "No, Luke, but you're going to have to let it go. It's not your fault. And it's in the past, where it belongs—leave it there."

He looked away, moisture threatening his eyes. "I know, but we're family, Bets—Parker, you, and me. And neither of us are going to let anything happen to you ever again."

16. GIVE THE HERO A WOUNDED HEART: In *A Light in the Window*, the hero Patrick O'Connor is a rogue that no woman can trust, but when the readers get a glimpse at the wounds of rejection he bears, understanding dawns as to why he is the way he is, eliciting a sympathy from the reader that only a wounded heart can achieve.

His father hurled the paper aside with that lethal glint in his eye that told Patrick he was looking for a fight. He lumbered to his feet, face pinched above a perfectly tied Windsor knot and buttoned vest. "You think you're fooling anybody working at that soup kitchen, boy?" He strolled forward to thump several taut fingers on Patrick's chest. "You got your eye on a girl there, is that it? Because I can tell you right now that no decent girl would look twice at a scoundrel like you." His lips twisted into a sneer, a look Patrick had long become familiar with, at least since high school when he'd finally given up trying to win his father's approval.

No amount of good grades or obedience seemed to satisfy him, not since that fateful day. The day Patrick had stumbled in on the upstanding Joseph O'Connor in bed with the next-door neighbor's flirtatious daughter while Mom was visiting Aunt Rose in New York. From that moment on, it seemed his father had taken his anger and guilt out on his eldest son until Patrick finally rebelled in high school, their relationship little more than a bomb ticking away. Pop had long since cleaned his life up, but Patrick's reckless ways apparently rubbed salt in the man's wounds, which suited Patrick just fine. Until lately. Now all Patrick wanted was to save money for college, get his degree, then kiss the devil goodbye.

"Don't bother coming home if you knock some hussy up, you hear?" Pop shoved him with the ball of his hand, and his mother's gasp echoed in the room, a frail indication of shock that never seemed to make its way into protest or support on Patrick's behalf.

Patrick staggered back, tendons tight with restraint as his arm wrenched up in a knee-jerk reaction, grinding to a stop before he could ram a fist in his father's gut. *No, I won't give you the satisfaction, old man.*

"You gonna hit me, boy?" he whispered, a cold glaze of triumph in gray eyes that matched the color of sallow skin. "Go ahead, you worthless punk, because there's nothing I'd like better than to toss your sorry carcass out into the street. Let's see how many skirts you can lift when you're taking all your meals in a soup kitchen."

17. SHOW THE HERO AS WISE AND INTELLIGENT: Sometimes there are those people who just seem to have an authority about them, you know? A strength that draws people to respect them and seek out their advice. Such is the case with two of my heroes—John Brady from *A Passion Denied* and Bram Hughes from *Surprised by Love*.

In the clip below from *Surprised by Love*, the subordinate older hero seeks Bram's advice about his relationship with the subordinate heroine, Bram's aunt.

Logan kneaded his temple and released a heavy sigh before his gaze met Bram's, a rare sense of defeat in his eyes. "The blasted woman has ruined me for any other, Bram, and for the first time in my life, I really don't know what to do."

Bram sat forward, hoping to help alleviate Logan's grief. "Logan, you wanted to know how I do it—spend time with Meg when I know friendship is all we'll ever have. It's not easy, but the only option I can employ—and the only one that will really work—is a directive from the Bible I call the Abraham Factor."

Logan squinted, the tug of a smile on his lips. "You're telling me you have a Biblical directive named after you?"

Bram laughed. "Hardly, but he is my namesake." He sat back with hands on the arms of the chair, fingers limp over the edge. "I'm speaking of Abraham in the Old Testament, of course, the Father of the Hebrew nation and proclaimed 'friend of God.' The man of whom God required the sacrifice of his only son on an altar in the region of Moriah. It's not a comfortable story by a long shot, but an important one for two men faced with heartache such as you and I."

He propped elbows on the arm of the chair and steepled his hands, staring out the window over Logan's shoulder, the gloom of night the perfect backdrop for the subject he broached. "You see, I've learned the hard way that when it comes to the most precious things in my life, the safest place to keep them is in God's hands. To trust Him to do for them and me the very best thing." His eyes met Logan's. "No matter *what* that is." He expelled a weary sigh. "Because if I love someone—really and truly love them—I'll always want to give them God's best, not my own."

Rising from his chair, he nudged Logan's cup of coffee toward him before he picked up his own. "Abraham loved his son fiercely, waited decades for God to honor His promise to give him a son in the first place.

"And then one day, God—Abraham's 'friend,' mind you—asks him to lay that precious son on the altar and give

him up. Sacrifice him—just like that. And you know what?"
Against his will, tears glazed Bram's eyes as his gaze locked
with Logan's. "That man didn't balk or miss a beat. Nope.
Because Abraham's trust in God was so strong, he actually told
his traveling companions to 'abide ye here and I and the lad
will go yonder; and we will worship and come again to you.'"

Bram shook his head, overwhelmed as always at the
strength of Abraham's faith, the certainty that somehow,
someway, God's best would prevail. "And you and I both
know what happened, Logan. God stayed the knife in
Abraham's hand, giving him his son back because of his
remarkable trust."

"Trust," Logan whispered in a low drone, "the very reason
I've lost Cait."

Bram nodded, his tone quiet but sure. "And the very thing
that will help you find God in a way you've never experienced
Him before. He wants you to trust Him, Logan, to put your
love for Mrs. McClare on the altar where God can do with it
what He wills for your good and hers. And whether He stays
your hand or not, your sacrifice of obedience will be rewarded
with more peace and joy and hope than you ever believed
possible."

And that's it for this chapter! Keep in mind that these are
just a *few* of the ways to ramp up the sigh factor in your heroes,
and I'll just bet you'll be able to add some of your own.

So, get on your mark, get set … *ramp!*

Find out more about Julie Lessman at the back of the
book!

Chapter 10
The Right Woman for the Romance Job
By Connie Almony

That Girl

Now that we've gotten a gander at Julie Lessman's utterly delicious ... er ... I mean, strong and capable romantic heroes, I thought I'd take a moment to expound on the characteristics of the ladies with whom they fall madly in love. And though, like Julie, I write novels with romance in them, my books do include elements of women's fiction and suspense so might have a few differences.

However, it is important to keep in mind that when Julie and I talk about developing these male and female counterparts who will lead our stories, given our novels are both considered romance, we are writing for a mostly female audience. Conservative estimates have it at about 95%. And though readers come in all shapes and sizes with varying likes and dislikes, we can look at trends over time to see what most of them really want.

The Perfect Complement

If you've read my chapter on colorful characters, you'll know I love stories with a contrasting breadth of personalities who round out a full spectrum of light and intrigue a variety of reader. Have you ever heard the term "opposites attract?" Of course, you have. However, I'm going to adjust that phrase a bit. To be more precise, it should read, "Complements Attract." That's *complements* with an 'e' in the middle, not *compliments*, the word for praising people. In other words, things that are differently useful (or gifted) move toward each other, because the combination of the two creates a more productive whole--

each playing a role the other cannot. Such is the case with people.

In a novel, this phenomenon creates more intrigue, because attracting opposites don't always understand each other when they first meet. It's the challenge of coming to understand that makes the story fun--like riding a roller coaster to get from point A to point B.

The Perfectly Imperfect

In the previous chapter, Julie outlines a variety of romantic male archetypes for women to love. Female readers of romance absorb these characters with the hope of meeting someone like the hero of the story. However, the role of the heroine is to have a character with whom the reader will identify. But not just a character like her. Along the journey, this heroine will become the fullness of who she was created to be, thus inspiring the reader to do the same. It is important to note, however, that the concept of a relatable inspirational cast member is not limited to female characters. Nor is it exclusive to romance.

Have you ever wondered what made the Harry Potter books such a rousing success? I remember when my sister-in-law (an adult reader) described the first one to me. She practically trembled with excitement outlining the story of a young, ordinary kid, whose adoptive family treated him like a useless nuisance, making him sleep below the stairs and giving him the scraps of what the other children received. Then one day, a letter falls from the sky that begins the young man's journey of self-discovery. He is not just an unlovable orphan anymore. He is gifted, and his gift is of critical importance. This little nobody is really a somebody. We read books such as this one with the hope we may one day find out the same in ourselves.

The desire for meaningful purpose is wired within us. Why else would a non-fiction book titled *The Purpose Driven Life* become one of the biggest selling books of all time?

So how do we authors tap into these characteristics of both relatability and desire for purpose? Let's take a look.

Having worked in the mental health field and specialized in counseling successful, driven, perfectionistic women who never felt good enough, I've come to realize, that feeling inadequate is a common theme in life. Not just for women. Not just for driven individuals with anxiety disorders, but people plodding through each day trying to make tomorrow better than yesterday.

So what does this mean for the reader? It means many (if not all) of them feel they have some secret flaw, weakness, or sin that keeps them from being the person they aspire to be. For this reason, if they read a character who is too perfect, beautiful, or successful, they may withhold some element of emotional investment from that character. In other words, they will not relate. On the other hand, revealing the character's flaws will endear her to the reader. Why? Because a flawed human being is the type of person with whom she'd most likely bare her soul without fear of judgment. This is the girl we root for. The one we hope gets the *hot* (caring, thoughtful, rich, successful, powerful--pick your adjective) guy in the end. Oh yeah, we also hope she finds purpose in spite of her seeming inadequacy as well.

Beauty is in the Eye of the Beloved

Should she be beautiful? You've seen the covers of the novels and the actresses who play the heroines in movies. They are generally not hard to look at. However, when writing this everyman, uh, I mean ... woman, you may reconsider the idea of making her the pinnacle of gorgeousness, unless you plan to *curse* her with it--yes, there is such a thing.

I don't know about you, but every time I see descriptions in novels of petite women with twenty-four-inch waists, I cringe. In my head, I want to ask, "What about me? Can't I be loved, too?" My waist measures ... well, ... never mind that. The point is, I want to live vicariously through this heroine for at least the time it takes to consume her story. Reading that she is perfect pulls me from that experience. So please, dear authors, don't be afraid to shape your heroine as someone a little overweight, and allow the reader to believe that even a plain girl can win the heart of the most eligible bachelor in the world. It's the adult female version of Harry Potter among the Dursleys.

You don't have to repel the reader with graphic details of how she does not measure up. Just don't go overboard in making her the ultimate icon of feminine loveliness. The male counterpart will come to love her anyway. For, after all, he is inherently deeper than your average Joe, and because of this, is much more worth the earning. He does not think of her in terms of how she has been physically gifted (or not) by her Creator. Instead, he is intrigued by the spark in her eyes when she's conjuring a mischievous plan, warmed by the way she bites her lip when she's afraid, and obsessed with the idea of running his fingers through her unruly curls. She may or may not be attractive to the guy walking down the street, but one thing is for sure, she *will be* the only possible woman for this particular hero. And that makes him all the more desirable.

In my modern-day retelling of *Beauty and the Beast*, titled *At the Edge of a Dark Forest*, the character who parallels Belle of the fairytale is rather plain. She shows up at Cole Harrison's mansion for their first meeting sopping wet and grease striped from changing a tire in the rain. Cole, in all his sardonic bitterness, labels her "Beauty," partly because he has a difficult time remembering names due to brain trauma, but mostly to get under her skin. He becomes more and more enamored with the woman who speaks her mind even at risk of losing his investment, appreciating her zeal for her work and her heart for wounded veterans. As time goes on, the term *Beauty*, once meant to mock her lack of the quality, transforms to describe something more powerful, more permanent--her soul. It even colors how he sees her physically by the end.

So, what if you have cursed your heroine with incredible looks? I'd suggest two possible scenarios--that is, if you want your female audience (remember, 95%) to really like her. 1) She should have no clue she is attractive, or 2) Her beauty should immerse her in an empty life. Do the men around her truly love her, or do they desire her for all the wrong reasons? This is the reverse scenario from Mr. Darcy's predicament in *Pride and Prejudice*. His curse of wealth leaves him stranded in a phony social world where it is difficult to tell women of substance from those seeking an alliance with him for his money and position.

Tiffany Lundgren in *An Insignificant Life* is another example of this. Due to her mixed heritage, she has an exotic appeal which causes men to look twice, and she has learned to use it to what she thought had been her advantage. Only it left her in the position of being used by men, envied by women, and not taken seriously by either. Eventually, she meets the one man who will risk his safety to protect her from being used and who looks deep enough to find out she loves dogs, snorts when she laughs, and cares about the people who work for her. Even though she could have any man she wants, she chooses the one who will love her after she's grown old and wrinkled and shuffles behind a walker … that is, as long as she still snort-laughs at his jokes.

You Complete Me

Ah! Wasn't that an awesome line from the movie *Jerry Maguire*? It says, together we have purpose. Together we can do more than the sum of our parts. The perfect ending to a meaningful romance. So how do we create these extraordinary duos with a sustaining future?

Let's look at Julie's archetypes from the previous chapter and brainstorm some thoughts on the women who might love them best.

Success-proven tips from 10 award-wining authors

1. THE BAD BOY HERO: The point of this dude is to make the reader long for his redemption. If he does not reform in some way, we have just wasted time reading his tale. Of course, in a romance, the woman will play a role in the reformation. She may reluctantly find the need to enlighten (chastise) him because they've been thrown together for some reason, and now she needs him to *play nice* in order to reach her goal. She may ignore him until he wises up, having no interest in his recalcitrant ways--which of course, attracts him to her all the more. Or she could be someone he watches from a distance as she quietly displays how her integrity works for the good. You can choose an archetype that fits these models: Nurturer, Spunky Kid, or maybe The Father's Daughter. Either way, it's even better if she gains a little something from him as well.

In *One Among Men*, the newly reformed Samantha Hart inspires the somewhat bad boy, Chris Johnson, to rethink his bitterness toward her faith. He watches how she lives it in the male dorm she runs, not preaching or judging, but helping and guiding, and wants what she has in doing so. Though he has been antagonistic to Christianity in the past, it is Samantha's human, and somewhat flawed, attempts that make living this faith seem more possible to him. In return, his protective instincts prompt him to keep her safe from the threats (both personal and professional) that lurk in her building.

2. THE BROODING HERO: I love Julie's example of a heroine with humor lifting this guy from his profound sullenness. Some guys are just so buried in their "deepness," they need a powerful geyser to spew them from it. A bubbly personality just might do the trick.

On the other hand, it's this man's depth that makes him rich. He's mysterious, which entices us with questions we must answer. He's passionate, which excites our own longings. But his dangerousness can be destructive if not checked. He needs a partner who will check him as much as the staid heroine needs a fire lit for her. Complementary characters work best when they eventually learn to respect and balance the strengths of the other.

Maybe he's the cynical type who questions the motives of all people he meets, inaccurately judging those around him. He needs someone who will challenge his assumptions, both through her actions and an informative debate. Liza Bennett does this for Mr. Darcy in *Pride and Prejudice,* countering his verbal assaults with humor and spirit. Later, she proves her point that not all women are after a man for money by refusing his original (though gloriously hideous) proposal of marriage. In the end, both discover, though there may be some truth in each person's beliefs, neither is as bad as initially thought. Each character's personality stimulates the other to think and grow.

3. VIRTUOUS HERO: In the previous chapter, Julie mentions that the most attractive quality of the Virtuous Hero is his untapped passion toward the heroine.

Oh, yes!

In my novel *An Insignificant Life*, the hero, Adam Grant, is a perfect example of this. He is picked on by his Campus police colleagues because he rarely dates and spends most of his day training his K-9 partner, Daisy. Suddenly, his job requires he associate more with the resident director of the all-female dorm who is best known for her beauty and her flirtatious way with men. Though he is not experienced in her world of dating, he is the one who shows her a greater love. One that is not about constructing an image to attract a man or about meeting physical desire only. His passion is in his newly unleashed longing to cherish a woman with his whole heart and soul. This is a completely new phenomenon to the frequently manipulated Tiffany. Her gift to Adam is not one of opening her physical self to him, but of unveiling the parts never revealed to anyone else in her life now that she has finally met the one person who will love her for them.

4. ALPHA HERO: This is the gruff, in control guy we see in Captain von Trapp from *The Sound of Music*. He creates an exhaustively detailed regimen for his children while he is traveling and chooses his fiancee based on the social mores of the time period. Then … in walks Maria, who is described in the song about her as "a problem," a wave that can't be pinned down, and a few other words I have no idea how to spell. She upsets a few apple carts (even juggling the fruit) and sends the children climbing trees wearing curtains. Oh my! Ya gotta love this pair, and yet the movie couple was inspired from real life.

Maria is exactly the kind of woman this man needs. She is someone who will help the Captain feel the emotion he locked away when his first wife died. He, in return, lends a degree of order necessary both in the care for the numerous children and in the possession of the hardened man's tender heart. She will need this quality as she and her new husband later escape the brutal control of the Nazis.

5. SWEET AND EASYGOING BETA MALE HERO: Again, I love Julie's example of how to shake a guy from settling into the predictable easy-going life of the Beta Male Hero. In the previous chapter, she demonstrates the use of what I like to call The Swan. The little girl, "all growed up" with new shape, sass, or even sophistication not before seen in the annoying brat she had been before.

Other good female archetypes that can zap this guy into an interesting storyline include The Dauntless, who pushes him to take risks in order to grow, or even The Truth Teller, who might challenge the comfortable misconceptions he holds dear. One thing is for sure, however, though The Nurturer might fit comfortably with this guy in real life, the pairing of the two as leads in a story would likely leave the reader snoring.

6. PROTECTOR HERO: I usually include a little Protector in all my heroes. However, there are those whose life choices begin with this quality in mind. My Protector Heroes tend to be in law enforcement positions. These guys often seem naturally attracted to The Nurturer and Father's Daughter archetypes. For the Father's Daughter, he seems to fill a void left for the girl who is now an adult. For the Nurturer, she is an extension of what is needed after the danger dissipates. Someone who will tend the injuries, both mental and physical.

In *The Long View*, J.T. MacGregor resists dating his mentor's daughter. First because he'd seen her for so long as an annoying little girl and later out of respect for her father. Even as children, he protected her both physically and emotionally, at one time carrying her a long distance to safety when she broke her leg. After coming back from college and discovering she had become an intriguing woman, he felt the need to protect his mentor's daughter from himself. However, his protective instinct, just like in the father-figure he idolized, can go too far. Destiny, having been the recipient of her father's over-diligent care, knew how to challenge J.T. and encourage him to open his mind to other possibilities.

An interesting pairing of the Protector-Nurturer is apparent in the book *The Hunger Games*, only in reverse. Katniss, the female protagonist, is the protector. She is a young woman who willingly agrees to participate in the Hunger Games in an attempt to save her sister. She knows her chance of survival, due to her ability to hunt with bow and arrow, is much higher than her sister's, so agrees to take the young girl's place. Her closest male friend is a hunter too. And though he teams with her to fight evil in later books, he is not the one she will need in the end. She chooses a man who will nurture her through the agony of PTSD as she recovers from the horrors of war.

I am Woman, Hear Me Roar

Anyone remember that song? Don't answer that. I'm showing some age by quoting it. At one time, this song was the battle cry of the Feminist movement. But before you assume I'm going to outline an Amazon, Wonder Woman character who likes to, well ... roar ... um, I think I'll have to disappoint you on that one. Roaring does not a relatable character make.

One of the new trends we see in fiction today is the apparent necessity of the Strong Woman character who can vanquish evil while cooking dinner and bandaging boo-boos all at the same time. These characters are meant to inspire women to be all they can be. However, sometimes in doing this, they leave the guy in the dust, often making him useless and, dare I say it, emasculating him. It's important to note that strength can come in many forms (both for the female character and the male), and the most satisfying romance is one where each member of the pair brings something to the table.

The Hunger Games, as mentioned above, though challenging traditional roles, gives us two individuals who truly complete each other. A movie that fails to do this is the Cinderella retelling, *Ever After*. In this movie, though the Prince figure is literally "charming," quite nice to look at, and speaks with a sexy accent, he serves no other purpose but to make her royal through marriage and satisfy a craving of the eye. The Cinderella character, Danielle, is smart, well-read, kind, shrewd, and can handle a sword. In the last scene, Danielle is faced with the prospect of being raped by her new master while the prince gallops off to save her. However, she outsmarts her captor before the prince gets there, leaving her counterpart with nothing to do but replace her old shoe with a bejeweled one. This is not the first time she saves herself in the presence of the prince while he watches and (hopefully) learns. How utterly unsatisfying! The audience may wonder why she wants him at all--except as eye candy. But even that will leave the individual consuming this tale hungry within the hour.

A Sustaining Feast

Have you ever heard the saying, "The whole is greater than the sum of its parts?" This means that when people with differing attributes work in communion with one another, they can do more than the added efforts of each person laboring alone. Such is the case in a story about a town organizing to save a historical landmark or a team coming together in order to defeat a foe. It is also the case when a couple's joining has reciprocal purpose. It may not be to rescue a child or build a skyscraper. However, if the one is rescuing the other while the other is building her up, the goals are not only satisfied, they come full circle. There is an *ah* feeling when we see how they fit and work together, a fulfillment that much will come from this relationship in the future.

That is a satisfying end!

Find out more about Connie Almony at the back of the book!

SECTION 4

Diving Deeper

Chapter 11
Hook Your Reader in the First Chapter
By MaryLu Tyndall

The first chapter of a book is by far the most important one. While every chapter needs to be superb and keep the plot, action, tension, and character change moving toward a magnificent conclusion, the first chapter is a do-or-die situation. If you don't have a fabulous first chapter, many impatient, stimulus-craved readers will not continue. Take it from someone who has put down many a book after the first chapter, never to pick it up again. That first chapter must stick so firmly in your reader's mind that they can't wait to pick your book up again and find out what happens.

It takes seven seconds for a reader to read the back cover of your book, another minute or so to read the first three pages, both of which you can do in a book store or online at Amazon. If you don't hook them right away, they move on. There are far too many other books to choose from, along with TV shows, movies, and videos. So it's your job to grab your reader in a choke hold and never let them go. Sorry for the violent visual. But it's true!

Having said that, I'll add that the first chapter is also often the hardest chapter in the book to write. There's so much that must be accomplished in those first pages in order to grab your reader. Here's my list of indispensable elements.

- Introduce protagonist
- Introduce other secondary characters, if necessary
- Ground reader in a setting: place, time period, etc.
- Introduce main plot or situation
- Introduce conflict and/or plot problem.

■ End with a bang that will force reader to turn the page.

You must incorporate all of the above in some measure if you want to:

■ Make the reader curious,
■ Connect the reader to the protagonist through empathy,
■ Invoke emotions in the reader, and
■ Introduce sufficient conflict to make the reader turn the page to Chapter 2!

Let's go through these one by one, and then I'll give you some examples.

1. Introduce protagonist

This is your main character. This is the character you want everyone to connect with and love, or even love to hate. The key is to give just enough information about them for the reader to make a connection, but not too much so as to either bore the reader or have nothing left to reveal in the rest of the book. Think of this introduction as just that—an introduction. When you first meet someone new, you don't know everything about them. You don't know their background, past, motivations, etc. Of course, this is a book, and we get to delve a little deeper into the protagonist's mind, but we still want the reader to get to know the character bit by bit through the story, just as they would with a new friend in real life.

Some general things I always try to convey about the protagonist in the first chapter are age, gender, general physical description or condition, profession, and a hint at personality type. This will generate a good visual of your character in the mind of your reader. Not all authors do this, of course. I've read books in which I had no idea what the age or appearance of the character was until halfway through the book. What happens in that case is the reader will create that character in their mind's eye, and when they actually discover the age or description later on, it's quite jarring. You might not be able to add all of those in the first chapter, and that's okay. We don't want to bore the reader with details, but it's important to give them a general idea of your character.

However, the most important thing you need to do is create empathy for your character. We want our readers to connect with our main character, to relate to them on some level, to understand them, to feel for them and their situation. How do we do this?

- Give your character a relatable dream or goal.
- Put your character in a situation that creates fear or empathy in the reader.

Here are some examples from published books. All this information was put in the first chapter.

Heroine has run away from an abusive uncle, endures a storm at sea, and is now shipwrecked on a deserted island. Her main desire is to find her real father and be loved and accepted. *The Redemption*, MaryLu Tyndall

My heroine is an impoverished mother of a four-year-old boy, struggling to care for her grandpa who suffers from malaria, and she is raising her sixteen-year-old sister, who tends toward rebellion. She doesn't know it yet, but she's just become a widow. *Gabriel's Atonement,* Book 1 in the Land Rush Dreams series. Vickie McDonough

Bookworm heroine's imagined life on a pirate ship becomes real when her Spanish nobleman's father's ship is overtaken by French privateers and she joins their crew. *The Pirate Bride*, Kathleen Y'Barbo

Journalist heroine is on a quest to discover what happened to the pirate Jean Lafitte after he supposedly died at sea. *My Heart Belongs in Galveston, Texas*, Kathleen Y'Barbo

Heroine has just lost her abusive father, and she desires to rule over his demesne herself but is encouraged to marry. *Sword of Forgiveness*, Debbie Lynne Costello

Maggie is a widow, raising her little boy alone in rural South Georgia at the onset of the Great Depression. *In High Cotton,* Ane Mulligan, the opening of the first chapter describes her:
Sadie always says, "Southern women may seem as delicate as flowers, but we've got iron in our veins." I believe her. After all, she's living proof—a lone Cherokee rose, whose thorns protect her better than any man could. Though older than my mama, she stepped into the role of friend the day I arrived in Rivers End as a new bride, and then later as mentor on the day my husband died. In my own defense, I've done a respectable job raising Barry, my just-turned-seven-year-old son, by myself while keeping Parker's Grocery afloat. Don't ask Big Jim for his opinion, though. My late husband's daddy is pigheaded when it comes to women working. He's pushing me to get married, but I like things the way they are, like being in charge of my life.

Heroine Travay flees a forced marriage in Jamaica and falls into the hands of a pirate. *In a Pirate's Debt*, Elva Cobb Martin

Heroine Rachel accepts a summer nanny job on a Charleston, South Carolina, tea plantation to discover if her brother really died in a plane crash over the Atlantic as reported by the Drug Enforcement Administration (DEA). No one at the plantation, including the new owner, knows of her job offer. *Summer of Deception* by Elva Cobb Martin

The hero is a very wealthy disabled war vet, with vestiges of arrogance from his old, unblemished youth, who thinks his life is now purposeless and seeks to end it on a cold snowy mountain in a blizzard. *At the Edge of a Dark Forest*, Connie Almony

A note on secondary characters. If there are other characters in the first chapter, but they are secondary characters, you don't need to reveal as much about them as the main character, but they should definitely stand out as unique.

2. Setting

This is a very important part of the first chapter. Without properly conveying the setting, the reader will feel lost in space and time, definitely not something you want, because even if you have a great protagonist, the reader may very well put the book down if they have no idea where or when the character exists. In the first chapter, you should answer the following questions:

- What year is it generally? You don't have to give the specific year, though sometimes this is listed at the top of the first chapter
- Where are we? What country, city?
- Are we outside or inside? In a church, ship, rowboat, island, city street, tunnel, outer space?
- What does it look like through the protagonist's eyes? (I encourage you to read my chapter titled "How to Write Like a Movie.")

Examples of Settings in First Chapters

The days right before the 1889 Oklahoma land run. -*Gabriel's Atonement,* Book 1 in the Land Rush Dreams series. Vickie McDonough

1724. Caribbean Sea. Heroine spies sails on the horizon and excitedly hopes for an adventure like one she's read about in her favorite books. *The Pirate Bride*, Kathleen Y'Barbo

Cumberland, England, 1398, castle heroine, now responsible for all the people in her demesne, struggles with what is best for her people as she works in her garden. *Sword of Forgiveness,* Debbie Lynne Costello

1720 Jamaica, Heroine is fleeing a forced marriage on horseback pursued by the jilted suitor. *In a Pirate's Debt* by Elva Cobb Martin

Contemporary heroine arrives late, *and unexpected*, at Barrett Hall Tea Plantation in Charleston, South Carolina, for a summer nanny position. *Summer of Deception* by Elva Cobb Martin

Current day, sometime after the Iraq War. In the woods, on the side of a mountain, in a substantial snow storm, on the extensive property of the wealthy protagonist. *At the Edge of a Dark Forest*, Connie Almony

Beautiful Mackinac Island, Michigan, in the Straits of Mackinac surrounded by Lake Huron.
My Heart Belongs on Mackinac Island by Carrie Fancett Pagels

Chapel Springs is a small mountain village on the shore of Chapel Lake. It's a tightknit community. From Chapter 1:
A spring breeze played with the edge of her shirttails as she stepped up onto the boardwalk along Sandy Shores Drive. She paused and lifted her hand, shading her eyes against the rising sun and welcomed the tremolos and wails of the loons floating up with the mist off Chapel Lake. She searched the reeds along

the shoreline for their distinctive black and white neckbands. Like Yankees, they'd soon migrate back to the north. She'd miss their plaintive cries. *Chapel Springs Revival,* Ane Mulligan

3. Situation

The situation is merely what is happening to the character. It's the situation at hand. It is what is happening in the setting and *to* the character. Essentially it is the very beginning of the plot and could contain elements of the major conflict.

Examples of Situations in first chapters

The following are from my books:

The Redemption: Heroine is in a storm at sea
Veil of Pearls: Heroine is escaping from slavery on Barbados
The Red Siren: Heroine is a pirate capturing a British ship
Falcon and the Sparrow: Heroine is traveling from France to London to become a spy for Napoleon.
Protector of the Spear: Heroine is shooting arrows at intruders who are seeking the Spear of Destiny

The hero is returning to his home town to become the sheriff after being gone eleven years. He left town after the gal he planned on marrying wed another man. When some youngsters throw rocks at him and his horse, he chases them into town. He catches one of the boys and is holding the wriggling boy when a woman steps out from a store and demands to know what he is doing to her daughter. The man instantly realizes the woman is his old love—and the kid is her child. - *The Anonymous Bride*, Book 1 in the *Texas Boardinghouse Bride* series. Vickie McDonough

1886. New Orleans. Heroine has gone undercover take a job as an assistant to a woman she believes can help her with the article she's writing for the New Orleans *Picayune* newspaper. Once employed, she learns her job also comes with the task of providing assistance in finding a lost relative. Unfortunately, her employer has also hired a Pinkerton agent to work on the search with the heroine, the same Pinkerton agent whose heart the heroine broke just a year ago. *My Heart Belongs in Galveston*, Texas, Kathleen Y'Barbo

Pressure to marry comes from every side as the heroine struggles to rule after her father's death. She has no desire ever to marry due to her father's abusiveness. But when the man who protected her nearly her whole life contacts the king about a marriage for her, heroine must make some tough decisions. *Sword of Forgiveness* by Debbie Lynne Costello

Maude has been waiting for her sweetheart to return home but hasn't heard from him. He unexpectedly arrives while she's at her uncle's soda shoppe. *My Heart Belongs on Mackinac Island* by Carrie Fancett Pagels

When confronted with a forced marriage, Travay Allston flees her stepfather's Jamaican plantation on horseback and dives into the sea. A pirate rescues her. *In a Pirate's Debt* by Elva Cobb Martin

When Rachel York arrives at Barrett Hall tea plantation for a summer nanny job, she finds the uncle who offered her the job had died and told no one about her job offer. *Summer of Deception* by Elva Cobb Martin

Cole Harrison agrees to try, and potentially invest in, the older man's prosthetics in order to save the man's (and his daughter's) business, and possibly the man's life. *At the Edge of a Dark Forest*, Connie Almony

Tourism, the mainstay of the village, is dying, and the town has grown shabby. To bring the tourist trade back, they need to revive the town. *Chapel Springs Revival,* Ane Mulligan

Chapel Springs achieved their plan to revive the village, but now landgrabbers move in to buy-up all the land and build a Miami style high-rise hotel. *Chapel Springs Survival,* Ane Mulligan

4. Character goal

This is really part of the protagonist's introduction, but it's so important, I wanted to list it separately. Many books fail at this point, but it's vital that the protagonist has a clearly defined goal in the first chapter. The reader wants to know what the character is after, what he or she wants most of all. This helps the reader connect to the protagonist, especially if that goal is something they can relate to. I've read countless books in which the protagonist wanders through the first chapter with absolutely no goal and no problem whatsoever. Yes, many writing books will tell you that you must introduce the protagonist's normal world before disaster strikes, and I agree with that, to a degree. Yet the last thing you want to do is bore the reader to the point where they close the book.

While I don't think this is essential and is a matter of style, most of my novels start with the main character smack dab in the middle of some huge disaster. Then in subsequent chapters, I reveal what the character's normal like had been like.

Examples of goals from published novels

Travay Allston determines to make it to Charles Towne to an aunt and escape the pursuit of the jilted suitor and her attraction to a certain pirate, Captain Lucas Bloodstone Barrett. *In a Pirate's Debt* by Elva Cobb Martin

While working as a nanny at a Charleston plantation, Rachel York determines to get in touch with her brother's last Charleston DEA partner. *Summer of Deception* by Elva Cobb Martin

Sienna would be the best lobbyist and then use that power to obtain her birth records. *When the Bough Breaks,* Ane Mulligan

Hero has to balance patient care with financial responsibility in a hospital where the board is demanding a new wing. *Love is Sweeter in Sugar Hill,* Ane Mulligan

Main character has to stop an unscrupulous man from winning the race for mayor. *Home to Chapel Springs*, Ane Mulligan

Heroine is a runaway who is searching for a father she never knew. *The Redemption*, MaryLu Tyndall

Wanted by the law for murdering her husband, Charity must find passage on a ship to Charleston where her family lives. *Charity's Cross*, MaryLu Tyndall

5. Conflict.

This is the person or thing that is trying to stop your main character from getting his or her goal. It doesn't have to be the main plot problem, but it's a good idea to have it somewhat related to the main plot problem. It can be a person, situation, event, or thing—anything that puts a roadblock in the protagonist's goal.

Examples from published novels

Two of the sheriff's cousins decide he needs a bride, and they each order one for him without telling him. *The Anonymous Bride*, Book 1 in the *Texas Boardinghouse Bride* series. Vickie McDonough

To protect her people, heroine is all but forced to marry a man who believes she was responsible for murdering his family. *Sword of Forgiveness* by Debbie Lynne Costello

Travay on horseback takes the wrong turn toward the Caribbean instead of toward Kingston and her jilted suitor in hot pursuit corners her on a cliff at the ocean's edge. *In a Pirate's Debt* by Elva Cobb Martin

Rachel York arrives at Barrett Hall for a summer nanny position, but no one seems to know about her job offer and the former owner, who made the offer, has died. *Summer of Deception* by Elva Cobb Martin

In order to run her family's inn, Maude's father is expecting her to marry Greyson. But Greyson has just returned to the island with another woman. *My Heart Belongs on Mackinac Island* by Carrie Fancett Pagels

Cole has agreed to try to invest in a product he'd hated in the past, and refused to use, in order to help the man's business. The arrangement requires him to work and live with the man's daughter, who despises him due to his obvious arrogance and thick sarcasm. She agrees to such distasteful conditions only because she is desperate to help her father. *At the Edge of a Dark Forest*, Connie Almony

Heroine is succeeding in running her late husband's grocery store, a fact her father-in-law hates. He believes women shouldn't work but should stay at home. He's been threatening to take the store from her. *In High Cotton,* Ane Mulligan

Heroine is determined to rescue the man she loves from the British Navy and marry him. The only problem? He doesn't want to ever see her again. *The Reckless*, MaryLu Tyndall

Heroine is on a mission by God to protect the Spear of Destiny when the Hero shows up, determined to steal it for the King. *She Walks in Power*, MaryLu Tyndall

6. End with a bang!

This is vital. You've created an empathetic character your reader can relate to. You've given them a goal or dreams that we all can understand and root for. You've created some sort of problem, person, or conflict that promises to keep them from their goal. So far, so good! But now you must end the chapter with an event or situation that will force the reader to turn the page. I have put down countless books after the first chapter and never picked them up again. This is something you never want to happen to your book.

So, what do I mean by a bang?

- Something completely unexpected, a surprise, or a shock
- A major disaster
- A hopeless situation
- An event that changes the course of the character's life

Examples from published novels

My hero has just gotten home from fighting in the Civil War after months walking to Texas. He's excited to be home and to see his parents again. As he walks through town, he sees a few familiar faces and notes how the town has changed in the years he's been gone. When he finally reaches his family's property, his excitement mounts. One more hill—and the house comes into view. But something's wrong. He hurries closer to discover the house is mostly destroyed. As he looks around, he discovers two graves—his parents' graves. *Long Trail Home, Texas Trails series,* Vickie McDonough

The first scene ends with us learning that Maude's fiancé has arrived home all right – married! *My Heart Belongs on Mackinac Island* by Carrie Fancett Pagels

Hero vows to find out the truth about his family's deaths, and if his bride-to-be is responsible, she will pay in blood. *Sword of Forgiveness* by Debbie Lynne Costello

After forcing her horse over a cliff into the Caribbean to escape a forced marriage, Travay is rescued but discovers her savior is a pirate—a murdering, thieving pirate. *In a Pirate's Deb*t by Elva Cobb Martin

Rachel York meets the distrustful, handsome new owner of Barrett Hall and is told the uncle she says offered her the nanny position died two weeks earlier. *Summer of Deception* by Elva Cobb Martin

Cole regularly insults Carly with his instinctual arrogance and sarcastic barbs, which he internally regrets, though these have become a self-protective habit. Carly fears she is living with a dangerous man, though she is willing to do almost anything to save her father and his business. *At the Edge of a Dark Forest*, Connie Almony

After numerous threats from her late husband's father to take her son and sell the store, the heroine receives a note from him. He's finally contacted a lawyer, and the word "loophole" leaps from (or off) the page. *In High Cotton,* Ane Mulligan

Heroine's rescue attempt causes the hero to jump overboard and the British Navy to shoot at him for desertion. *The Reckless*, MaryLu Tyndall

So, you see how important this first chapter is. I encourage you to spend a little more time when you begin your novel to make sure this chapter is the best it can be. I guarantee if you incorporate all these items in your first chapter, you will definitely hook your reader and keep them coming back for more!

Find out more about MaryLu Tyndall at the back of the book!

Chapter 12
The Tease: Scene/Chapter Endings to Lead your Reader On
By Julie Lessman

"Why don't you come up and see me sometime?"

—Mae West misquote

Yep, Mae West did it. So did Julia Roberts in *Pretty Woman*. Heck, even Scarlett did it dressed in her mama's velvet curtains when she visited Rhett in *Gone With the Wind*.

Let's face it—as human beings, we all "tease" at times. To persuade, to influence, to coax. Women do it when they doll up in their best dress, wear perfume, and put on makeup and flutter eyelashes at their boyfriends, hubbies or dates. Perfume companies do it when they offer handbags or umbrellas with the purchase of one of their scents, and Hollywood certainly does it when they entice us with movie trailers and previews of upcoming movies.

And guess what? Writers *should* do it too! Just like you need the perfect "pickup line" or hook (as MaryLu discussed in Chapter Eleven) to entice an editor or reader to pick up your manuscript or book, you *also* need great scene and chapter endings to keep them reading. To keep them turning pages far into the night, giving them insomnia. And to be honest, if there is one thing that bothers me as a writer more than a mediocre first line, it's an ending line to a scene or chapter that tells me ... *yawn* ... it's time to go to bed.

Case in Point—a few years ago I went to a writer's retreat in Chama, New Mexico, where, incidentally, Mary Connealy was my roomie, an insomniac who not only writes far into the night, but also reads into the wee hours as well. So, there we were, the two of us in all of our nighttime glory, reading our books. I was just finishing up *Twilight* by Stephenie Meyer because I wanted to see what all the fuss was about, and I liked it well enough, but had NO earthly intention of reading book two in the series.

None, zilch, nada.

So I heave a sigh and turn the last page and there, staring me in the face is chapter one of Book Two in the Twilight Saga, *New Moon*. Now, I wasn't tired and I didn't want to begin a new book that late at night, so I started reading it. And it was okay, but I still had NO intention of buying/reading it ... *until* I got to the last paragraph of the first chapter. Sweet mother of Job, Stephenie Meyer pulled a tease like I've never read in a book before. I'm telling you, when I finished those last few lines of *New Moon*'s first chapter, I was SO crazed to read on, that if there had been a store open at one o'clock in the morning in little Chama, New Mexico, I would have been there in my PJs, buying *New Moon*.

So ... ready to see that tease of a scene ending? Well, here it is—Bella is celebrating her birthday with both her vampire boyfriend, Edward, and his vampire family, when the party goes awry with Bella's accidental fall into a glass table. The table shatters, and Bella plunges into a sea of jagged shards of glass, causing blood to pulse from her arm. Here, then, is the final line of the teaser:

New Moon, by Stephenie Meyer

Dazed and disoriented, I looked up from the bright, red blood pulsing out of my arm—into the fevered eyes of the six suddenly ravenous vampires.

OH. MY. GOODNESS!! Stephanie Meyer cast her line, jerked hard, and reeled me in, hook, line and chapter ending. And, ladies and gentlemen—YOU can do the very same with a few tips I've learned over the years to "lead readers on."

Whenever I have done critiques in the past, the number one things I notice most are scene or chapter endings that could be ramped up. Now, maybe I feel that way because I am a CDQ (caffeinated drama queen), so I always want to end everything with a bang. Whatever the reason, **scene or chapter endings are unique opportunities to win your reader's heart and invest them more deeply into your book**. A pretty bow that wraps everything up while teasing the reader with what's inside the rest of the package.

So, when it comes to scene or chapter endings, think drama, drama, ***DRAMA!!!*** It's actually not much different than hook openings because you need to reel them in much the same way, but *this* time you're propelling them into the next scene or chapter *while* neatly wrapping the scene/chapter up at the same time.

Keep in mind that ho-hum actions (i.e. Mary turned, waved and headed down the street.), flat dialogue, (i.e. "Thank you for the lift home, Mitch, good-night.") or comatose thoughts (i.e. This was a great day.) are NOT going to entice your reader to shorten their beauty sleep. So, anything you can do to infuse DRAMA into your endings is imperative.

BUT—and here's the catch—it MUST make sense with the flow of the prior paragraphs, it MUST wrap the scene up like a period at the end of the sentence, and it MUST promise the reader something—a foreshadow of what's to come to keep them reading.

I'm pretty sure there are tons of ways to do that, but here are some that I came up with while browsing a lot of my own scene/chapter endings. PLEASE understand that these are not hard and fast rules, mind you, just suggestions of ways I've discovered to add DRAMA to my scene and chapter endings. Many of them overlap, but that's okay, because the more you can utilize in an ending, the richer it will be. The main purpose of the list below is to get you thinking about and exploring new ways to incorporate powerful scene/chapter endings that will lead your readers on. So ... here's what we'll cover:

1. Action
2. Analogy
3. Anaphora
4. Cliffhangers
5. Foreshadowing
6. Humor
7. Idioms
8. Internal Monologue
9. One Word
10. Play on Words
11. Question
12. Regret
13. Response
14. Reveal a Decision Made
15. Reveal a Truth
16. Reveal Something About a Character
17. Romantic Tease
18. Sarcasm
19. Scene Props
20. Scripture
21. Shock
22. Short, Punchy Sentence
23. Suspense
24. Suspicion
25. Threats
26. Triggered Memory
27. Witticism
28. Word Repetition

Ready? Let's get started!

1. ACTION: Dramatic action that is unpredictable, ups the ante, or is even jaw-dropping (cliffhangers) is one of the easiest and most powerful ways to propel a story forward, luring the reader along with it. I've listed jaw-dropper examples separately in the "Cliffhangers" section since they deserve a category all their own due to the impact they leave and the surprise twist factor.

The type of dramatic action I'm talking about here is unpredictable and moderately surprising, and generally offers insight into the characters via humor or drama. Following are some examples from my books—*A Passion Most Pure, Isle of Hope, His Steadfast Love, and Love's Silver Lining*—that although they don't rise to the level of cliffhanger, they definitely offer a deeper glimpse into the characters as well as redirect the course of the story.

Her mother's voice was distant as Faith turned, staring as if she were a stranger. Somewhere in the room, she sensed commotion and the faint sound of voices, farther and farther away until they disappeared altogether. And in a final swirl of darkness, with all energy depleted, she gave way to the spinning of the room, her eyes flickering closed as she fell limp to the floor.

***

"See you tomorrow," Jack called, turning halfway with a sudden notch between his brows. "Oh, almost forgot." He strolled around to Sam's side of the desk with his Red Bull to apparently throw it away, but dribbled the dregs over Sam's head instead.

"Are you crazy?" Sam vaulted to his feet with a growl, snatching the can from Jack's hand while he grilled him with a glare. "What the devil was that for?" he shouted, amber liquid dribbling off his nose onto one of his favorite ties.

Hands in his pockets, Jack strolled to the door with a satisfied chuckle, glancing back while he fisted the knob. "*That*, old buddy," he said with a smile a whole lot dryer than Sam's tie, "is for kissing my sister."

***

Face like granite, he slowly released her, clear grey eyes as cool as his manner. "Shannon asked me to find you."

177

"Of course she did," Cat muttered, ticked off that Chase Griffin would never seek her out on his own and then ticked off that it bothered her so much. He was the last guy she would ever be interested in, so why did it matter? She shoved the twenty-dollar bill toward the bartender. "Thanks, Alex—I had fun."

Alex's gaze flicked to Chase and back before he took a card out of his back pocket and slid it her way. "Call me sometime, or come see me again, okay?"

"Oh, you bet," she said in her huskiest voice just to get on Chase's nerves. Feeling smug, she tucked the card in her purse and eased off the barstool with a sultry look.

Right before she landed on the floor in a heap.

***

"How dare you manhandle me, you brow-beating barbarian! You're not a man; you're a bald-faced bully!" Raising her tiny fist, Libby whacked him but good, leaving Finn only one option to save his sorry campaign.

He scooped her up and tossed her over his shoulder like a sack of feed.

"No, ma'am, I'm a man," he said with a salute to the cheering crowd, then promptly carried her kicking and screaming right out of the deafening hall.

2. ANALOGY: Another way to infuse drama in a scene ending is the use of analogy, which gives the reader a double word picture that adds both punch and insight. The definition of analogy is "a comparison of two otherwise unlike things based on resemblance of a particular aspect."

In the first example below from *Surprised by Love*, the hero compares the need for milk of magnesia to both the acid eating at his gut *and* the guilt eating at his conscience. In the second example from *A Passion Redeemed*, the character's exhaustion is compared to the limp rag she just wrung out, two examples that hopefully create a stronger picture of how the characters feel.

Having had his say, Bram walked out, leaving Jamie to stew in his guilt. He reached in his drawer for milk of magnesia and threw back several hard swallows.

"A man putting his pride before the people he loves."

Issuing a silent groan, Jamie dropped his head in his hands. Bram's words gnawed inside like the acid that ate at his stomach, and he wished more than anything he had a remedy to alleviate his pain. Because at the end of the day, he could coat his nerves with milk of magnesia. But there wasn't a whole lot he could do about shame.

***

Faith closed her eyes and leaned hard against the sink, the rag limp in her hands. "Oh, God, help her to do the right thing. Please." She sighed and wrung out the cloth one last time. Her lips tilted in a tired smile. Limp and wrung out. Funny. She felt the same way.

3. ANAPHORA: An anaphora—repetition of the same word or group of words at the beginning of successive clauses, sentences, or lines—is a powerful way in which to tie up a scene with heightened rhythm and impact. In the clip below from *Isle of Hope,* the repeated words not only create more drama, but emphasize the risk ahead for the heroine, hopefully ramping up the conflict—*along* with the reader's interest.

No question about it—it was time, indeed.

Time to deal with the past.

Time to face her demons.

And God help her, she thought with a queasy roll of her stomach.

Time to face her father again …

4. CLIFF HANGERS: Ah, cliffhangers! There's no better way to keep a reader turning the pages than those wonderful and wild twists of fate that generally appear at the end of a book. Since I write straight romance rather than suspense, I generally only add one per book because, frankly, it's not all that easy to come up with a powerful twist that will drop your reader's jaw. But, oh my, when you *do* utilize the all-amazing cliffhanger, there is *no way* the reader can stop reading, just like Stephenie Meyers did to me with *New Moon*.

I like to think that I do have some whopper cliffhangers in my books, but unfortunately, the really good ones are spoilers that I don't want to reveal. But I have listed a few minor examples from my books, along with one each from two of my favorite "cliffhanger" author friends, Mary Connealy and MaryLu Tyndall, who *realllllly* know what a cliffhanger is all about.

The first two clips are from my books, *Surprised by Love* and *Love at Any Cost*, the first of which the reader doesn't know whether the man on the couch is the heroine's fiancé or her boss, Andrew, (who is also her mother's fiancé). In the second, the hero is a handsome fortune-hunter who falls in love with an oil heiress whom he discovers has no fortune. In both cases, the dramatic revelation completely alters the course of the story.

She had visions of Andrew sick or even bleeding on the floor from an accidental fall. Her pulse throbbed in her ears as she banged on the door, hysteria all but strangling the words in her throat. "Andrew? Are you all right?"

Ice slithered down her spine at the hiss of a curse, and heart in her throat, she heaved the door wide, eyes squinting to adjust to the shadowy light. "Andrew? Where are—"

She froze with a violent heave as if she'd been shot.

No air.

No pulse.

No sound save the ragged breathing of two people on a couch. Shirts untucked and clothes disheveled.

"Meg …" Her name issued forth on a broken groan. "What are you doing here?"

She couldn't speak or move, her mind in a stupor while Linda Marie fumbled to straighten her blouse. Tears of horror swelled in Meg's eyes and her muscles began to jerk, limbs like boulders as she slowly backed away.

"Meg, wait!" The male voice was gruff, rattled.

But she didn't.

She couldn't.

Nor would she ever again.

***

Foul words he didn't even think he knew spewed from his lips, defiling the summer day just like God had defiled his life, and with a rage he wasn't sure he could contain, he shot up and dove into the water, ragged air pumping in his chest like fury pumped through his veins.

"Jamie, I'm sorry... ," Patricia called.

But not as sorry as he.

Sorry he was too poor to help his sick sister.

Sorry his plans had been foiled.

Sorry he loved a woman who might be poorer than him.

Thoughts of Cassie assailed his mind, and his lungs burned in his chest till he thought he would die. Because therein burned the sorriest sorry of all.

Having to say goodbye.

***

A firm hand grabbed her arm and spun her around. Out of the darkness emerged an unusually large man, wearing a satin waistcoat and breeches. . . and a grin on his face as if he had just won a chest of gold. *Veil of Pearls by MaryLu Tyndall*

***

The dying horse staggered up, then fell toward her. Sally rolled aside but not far enough. The horse slammed her backward. Clawing at the rock-strewn trail, she felt the ground go out from under her.

She pitched over the edge of the cliff and screamed as she plunged into nothingness.

Wrangler in Petticoats by Mary Connealy

5. FORESHADOWING: Foreshadowing is a technique through which a writer gives a hint of what is to come later in the story by implying something with a loaded statement such as those in the two clips below. In the first, from *A Passion Denied,* the hero's neighbor just called him an angel, and in the second, *A Passion Redeemed,* the heroine's father sympathizes with the man his daughter sets her cap for.

Brady strode into Eileen and Pete's apartment and drew in a deep breath for the task ahead. An angel instead of a man. His lips quirked into a sour smile. That would certainly be nice. Especially at a moment like this. His jaw tightened. As if he could qualify.

Angels didn't have his past.

***

His thoughts suddenly returned to Charity, and his pace slowed considerably. She was the daughter who puzzled him the most. Beautiful, stubborn, wild—and so hard to reach. He fought a smile and made his way down the dark hall, shaking his head as he entered his room. *God help Mitch Dennehy!*

6. HUMOR: Humor is such a fun way to wrap up a scene because it can leave a smile on your readers' faces, hopefully enticing them to keep reading. Apparently, I use humor a lot in my scene/chapter endings because I have a wealth of examples that I hope will convey how nicely humor can tie a bow around your scene/chapter ending.

In the first example below from *Love at Any Cost,* the heroine and her cousin are discussing womanizers, particularly the ex-fiancé who just broke the heroine's heart. The second example is from *Love Everlasting,* in which the heroine is coerced by her brother to drive his drunk friend home. And the third is from *Isle of Hope,* where the subordinate heroine realizes she's falling for her grouch of a neighbor after she encounters a bikini-clad woman in his house.

"Well, serves you right, you little brat." Cassie pinched her waist. "But so help me, Al, if either of these two clowns corner me in the billiard room tonight, I'll wring your neck."

Allison lunged away, giggles bouncing off the walls as she sashayed to the door. She turned in a dramatic pose, hand on the knob. "Or thank me," she said with a dance of her brows. "Because trust me—these two make Mark Chancellor look like the rump of your prize filly."

A deep-down chuckle rolled from Cassie's lips, the first real laugh she'd had in way too long. Alli winked and closed the door, leaving Cassie with an image of Mark she could live with.

A horse's behind.

***

"Yeah, well that's when he's at his most dangerous, I'm afraid, catching women off-guard with his little-boy charm. So unconscious or not, keep your distance, okay?"

Shannon started the car with its customary sputter and growl, shifting into gear as she slid Jack a wry smile. "Distance would be a cab, Jack, but I'll keep that in mind."

"Good girl." With two firm taps of her roof, Jack closed the door, hands in his pockets as he watched her drive away.

A snort sounded from the back seat, and Shannon had no choice but to smile. A cab, definitely.

In another state.

***

The realization that Tess might suddenly be attracted to Ben—possessive of him—throbbed more than the gashes in her arm from the stupid hedge. Sucking in a sharp rush of air, Tess made an ironclad decision that tightened her jaw along with her resolve. He wanted privacy? Fine. She'd give him all the privacy he and Dr. Barbie could handle, with an emotional padlock of her own. From now on, any communication between Ben Carmichael and her would begin from his side of the hedge, while she put up a hedge of her own—through prayer.

And nothing more.

Because despite her deep faith in God, a true passion for prayer, and a belief in the Bible that went beyond bone deep ...

This was one time when "love thy neighbor" was just not going to work.

7. IDIOMS: Using idioms can be a fun way to piggyback on a phrase in order to drive a point home with humor or punch, such as in the clip below from *His Steadfast Love* with the idiom, "dead in the water." The hero attempts to save the heroine when she has a cramp while swimming in a lake, only to discover she's faking it in order to dunk him, resulting in a body-to-body moment when he kisses her against his better judgment.

They burst from the water as one, her body welded to his as she death-gripped his hair, obviously intent on one more plunge.

But the only thing that plunged was his gut when their eyes locked, the laughter in her face dissolving into something far softer and warm while her ragged breathing mated with his. Her gaze dropped to his mouth, and a tidal wave of want surged through his body, taking him down as easily as Cat had done with her well-placed dunking. She absently licked her lips, and his stomach cramped with need as he fought the pull of her parted mouth, her shallow breathing in dangerous sync with his own. His eyelids felt as heavy as if he were drugged, arms slowly curling around her waist like they had a mind of their own. And God help him, they did, because he had little control as they drew her close, luring his mouth to hers with a low, aching moan.

She tasted like sheer heaven as he nuzzled the lips he'd dreamed about since the night she had kissed him in her room. Forcing himself to take it slow, he caressed her mouth with all the tenderness that swirled inside for a lost little girl named Cat. But the moment a soft mew left her lips, he was a goner, his groan hoarse as he delved in to explore with a passion too long denied.

And that's when he knew.

He was dead in the water.

Literally.

8. INTERNAL MONOLOGUE: Heaven help me, internal monologue has to be my *favorite* way to either begin a scene or end one, so naturally I have quite a few examples. The reason I love it so much is because not only is it easy to come up with random thoughts, but those thoughts (internal monologue) also give you an invaluable glimpse into the character. And one thing I've learned as an author is that the more insight you can give into your characters through simple things like first lines or scene/chapter endings, the *more* your readers will invest in them *and* your novel! Here are some examples from *Love at Any Cost, A Passion Denied, A Heart Revealed,* and *Isle of Hope.*

"I'm sorry it had to come to this, Cassie, and I hope someday you'll find it in your heart to forgive us." With a stiff smile, she gave a short nod and made her way to the door, leaving Cassie to agonize alone.

Over a man she loved who betrayed her, a friend she trusted who deceived her, and a future deprived of them both. Tears slipped from her eyes and she pushed them away with a hard swipe, her anger surging like the waves on the shore. Forgive them? Maybe. But it would take time. And distance. She bowed her head as grief fisted her heart.

Oh, yes ... miles and miles of distance.

***

She drew in a deep breath and stood on tiptoe, cradling his face in her hands. "I forgive you, John, because I love you. Then and now."

He nodded and staggered toward the door, perversion leeching the life from his soul like a slow-bleeding death. I forgive you, John, she had whispered. But it didn't matter.

He could never forgive himself.

***

A heave shuddered from her throat and she put a hand to her eyes, numb over how her life had changed in just a few short hours. Yesterday she had been content to be alone, fear as foreign to her now as Rory's violent scorn. And yet, with one vile slap, her yesterday had shifted into a present steeped in fear, shame and guilt, all neatly laced with denial and despair.

"We *will* do this," Sean had said.

The memory of his mouth caressing hers burned in her thoughts, unleashing a flood of shame and guilt that caused her to quiver. Her hand trembled to her lips as tears slipped from her eyes.

No, God, we won't ...

***

"Marry me, Tess—please—and I'll even consider inviting your annoying friend to the wedding." He suddenly thought of Phillips touching her like this, and his jaw went to iron as he staked his claim with a possessive kiss.

Then again, maybe not.

9. ONE WORD: Okay, this is another of my favorite ways to end a scene because it's so powerful to see that final word lingering at the end of the page like a taunt, such as in the three samples below from *Love's Silver Lining*, the first of which is between an estranged married couple.

"Please don't let go ..." Her voice was a worried rasp when he tried to lay her down, panic rising within her at the prospect of his glorious warmth fading away.

"Never." His husky response carried a promise that set her free to curl against him when he lay down beside her. He drew her close, strong arms cocooning her in a heavenly warmth that soothed her into the peace and safety of sleep, taking her to a place she hadn't been in a very long time.

Home.

***

Maggie fought a gulp as he strolled toward the chute in his chaps with all the poise and confidence of a champion rider. No, when it came to women and winning, she suspected Clint Keller didn't need a whole lotta luck. He tipped his hat with an easy smile, and she twisted a strand of her hair in a nervous spiral that matched the one in her gut. Because she had a sneaking suspicion about somebody who just might. She gulped.

Me.

***

His nephew's eyelids lifted halfway. "No thanks, Uncle Finn. Even if I wanted to—which I don't—Maggie made it pretty clear she had no room for me in her life, so I need to move on." His lashes lowered once again, and Finn sensed a hopelessness he'd never seen in Blaze before. As if Maggie's departure had totally depleted him. There was no question Libby's departure had depleted Finn, too, but at least Finn had something to fill him back up again that Blaze didn't. He released a quiet sigh.

Faith.

10. PLAY ON WORDS: Another of my top ways to end a scene or chapter is to make a play on words, which is defined as "an expression that is worded in a distinctive way, especially one which is particularly memorable or artful."

In the first clip below from *His Steadfast Love*, the heroine's twin sister, Shannon, takes the pastor hero aside, telling him she's worried about her "wild" twin "falling apart" now that Shannon is married, so I played on that same phrase, "falling apart."

The second clip is from *A Passion Denied*, where the heroine is the "story lady" at a bookstore, so the concept of "fairytales" allowed me to impart a dual peek at the heroine's personality.

The final clip is from *A Heart Revealed*, where I used the phrase "tingles my tongue" to do double duty in order to give further insight into the hero.

***

He dropped his head back against the headrest with a loud groan. The memory of Cat's kiss branded his brain just like her mouth had branded his, stirring things he didn't want to feel.

Caring.

Attraction.

Desire.

Because just like Shannon had feared, her sister had **fallen apart**, getting so trashed, he'd had to get too close. Close enough to ache for her. And close enough to see the desire in her eyes and taste it on her lips. Slamming the steering wheel hard, he yanked his keys from the ignition and got out, hurling the door closed with more than a little temper.

Because at the moment, when it came to "**falling apart**," Shannon's sister had nothing on him.

***

The bell over the door jangled and she looked up, smiling at several children and mothers who entered the shop. She glanced at her watch. "Goodness, they're coming in early today. Could be a crowd."

Millie rolled her eyes. "Correction. Will be a crowd. Children and men—you have an uncanny knack for drawing them both, including Tom Weston. All, that is, except John Morrison Brady. I'd hold on to Plan C, Lizzie, if I were you. I think you're going to need it."

Lizzie scowled. "Maybe not."

Millie chuckled and headed for the front of the store, shooting a wicked grin over her shoulder. "**Fairytales**, my friend. **You read them so well. And live them even better.**"

***

"I do believe that nothing **tingles my tongue** quite like butter pecan. How about you?"

He slid her a sideways glance, and she looked up with a smile on those soft, pink lips. He swallowed hard. What **tingled his tongue?** His gaze jerked straight ahead, and his pulse pounded as if the bag over his shoulder was loaded with lead. None of your business, he thought with a grind of his jaw. But heaven help his sorry soul—it sure wasn't ice cream.

11. A QUESTION: Ending a scene or chapter with a question is probably the easiest way to add punch or tension, leaving the question lingering in the air along with the reader's curiosity. The example below is from *His Steadfast Love* and poses a question to the heroine, which also hopefully poses the same to the reader—will she or won't she?

The second example of a question is from *Surprised by Love* and is an internal-monologue question that is meant for both the heroine herself *and* for the reader, leaving a question in the balance in both of their minds.

"I *mean* the guy likes you, Cat, I can feel it."

Cat's mouth slid sideways. "Then how come all I can feel is acute frustration whenever he's around?"

"Because he doesn't want you to know it, sweetie." Tiffany sat back with a smug smile. "I've always had a sense about these things, and my gut tells me good ol' Pastor Chase is more vulnerable than you think."

Swallowing hard, Cat could only stare, heart picking up pace while her mouth parched as dry as the salt on her popcorn. "Are you serious?"

Tiffany's grin was positively decadent. "Completely," she said, grabbing more corn with a glint of trouble in her eyes. She pelted a piece in her mouth and chewed slowly, studying Cat through a shuttered gaze. "But the real question, Cat O'Bryen, is"—she jiggled her brows—"are you?"

***

He held on, gaze fused to hers. "Friends forever, Cait, yes." Her stomach fluttered at the graze of his thumb to her palm. "For now..." Lifting her hand to his mouth, he skimmed her knuckles with his lips. "Good night, Mrs. McClare." He gave a short bow, then turned and strode from the room, her eyes fixed on his broad back until he disappeared from view.

She heard the click of the front door, and with a shaky whoosh of air, she sank to the edge of her seat, her breathing as ragged as her nerves. Head bent, she put a hand to her eyes.

For now.

Her insides quivered at the memory of his lips on her skin, the caress of his thumb to her palm, and she knew Logan McClare was waging a battle she wasn't sure she could win. But the question that shivered her mind, her body, even more than his touch was one single thought.

Did she even want to?

12. REGRETS: When a character is sick inside over something they said or did, I don't know about you, but I'm sick inside, too, and I will actually continue reading just to try and alleviate that uneasy feeling. Which is what I tried to do in this scene from *A Hope Undaunted* following a heated fight between the hero and heroine after an even more heated kiss.

He turned and walked into his office, slamming the door hard.

Katie stared, her body still quivering from his rage. Closing her eyes, she sagged against the wall, too stunned to move and too shaken to care. She pressed a trembling hand to her mouth, her lips swollen from the taste of him. She was doomed, she realized, and the thought shivered through her like a cold chill. She wanted a man she didn't really want, and the very notion weakened her at the knees. He had called her one of the sorriest people alive. She grappled for her purse and put a hand to her eyes.

And God help her, she was.

13. RESPONSE: A short response to a question or comment can be very effective in wrapping a scene up nicely. It can bring it to an end that seals both the mood of the characters and the reader, hopefully prompting the latter to read on. The first clip below from *A Passion Redeemed* reflects the hero's regret, and the second from *A Hope Undaunted* instills an element of hope in a dire situation.

Charity blinked. The people she loved most in the world stood waving goodbye. A fresh wave of sobs choked from her lips. She pressed her head back against the seat and squeezed her eyes shut. Tears spilled with reckless abandon. Mitch nudged a handkerchief against her arm. She snatched it from his hand and wiped the wetness from her face. "I hate you, Mitch Dennehy."

She heard his long, weary sigh as the car picked up speed. "I know. So do I."

***

Luke started the car, and Katie finally broke into sobs—all of her hopes and dreams worthless in the face of losing her father.

Dear God, what can we do?

It came to her then—as soft as a whisper—the caliber of man that her father truly was. A man bent on serving God and family. And in one violent swell of hope, she suddenly realized.

They could pray.

14. REVEAL A DECISION MADE: When authors reveal a decision a character has made that changes the course of the story, my interest notches up. Which is what I was going for here in *A Passion Redeemed* to hook the reader in, using "anaphora" (repetition of the same word(s) at the beginning of successive clauses, sentences, or lines) to heighten impact and ramp up the stakes.

She closed her eyes and lifted her head, hands clasped to her chest. Yes! A completely workable solution. A situation where she could win, no matter the outcome. She hugged herself tightly in the sanctuary of her grandmother's kitchen, not even feeling the chill of the room from embers long since faded. No, she had **a plan** to keep her warm. **A plan** to stay in Ireland. **A plan** to be married. And at the moment, it didn't really matter to whom.

15. REVEAL A TRUTH: I love ending a scene revealing a truth that heats things up considerably, raising the stakes not only for the hero and heroine, but for the reader as well. Hopefully I accomplished that in this scene from *A Hope Undaunted*, where the heroine gets drunk and tells the hero she loves him—something he knows is not true.

At his touch, her lips tilted into a dreamy smile. "Mmm ... I love you, Luke McGee," she whispered, and then rolled to her side with a soft, little snort.

He rose to his feet and stared, his heart comatose in his chest. Drawing in a deep breath, he bent to tuck the sheet tightly to her chin, finally exhaling shaky air. What he wouldn't give to make it so. But he knew better. His lips tightened. Alcohol had a way of distorting the truth.

He bent to graze her cheek with his fingers one last time, then slowly lumbered to his feet. "I love you, too, Katie Rose," he whispered.

And he was stone-cold sober.

16. REVEAL SOMETHING ABOUT A CHARACTER: Another thing that keeps me reading is when an author gives me a little deeper glimpse into the character, almost surprising me with something I didn't expect. That's what I tried to do in the clip below from *A Passion Redeemed*, utilizing a short, punchy phrase at the end for impact.

She lifted her chin. Let her sister have her God. She didn't need Him. She would make Mitch Dennehy fall in love with her, and it wouldn't take prayer to do it. She turned and kicked her skirt across the room, then slumped on the edge of her bed. In the flickering shadows of her dark, cold room, she put her head in her hands. And cried.

17. ROMANTIC TEASE: Now as a die-hard romance lover, I will be the first to tell you that nothing gets me through a book like romance, especially when an author uses it to end a dreamy scene. But, I don't know ... maybe that's just me! In this scene from *A Passion Denied*, it was fun to wrap up a very serious bedroom scene with a little romance ...

Lizzie's gentle sigh merged with one of his own, and suddenly a rush of love flooded his heart. His eyes moistened at the touch of her warm body against his, carrying his child. He clutched her tightly in his arms, and when he spoke, his voice was rough with emotion. "What did I ever do to deserve you, Lizzie?"

He felt the curve of her lips against the stubble of his skin. "Oh, not much, Brady, just love God with all of your heart."

With a raspy groan, he kissed her hard, sweeping the curve of her body with his hands.

"And what did I do to deserve that?" she breathed, pulling back with a hint of a tease.

His palm stroked the full of her belly, then slid to her waist to gently shift her close. "Figure it out, Elizabeth," he whispered in her ear, and proceeded to kiss the hollow of her throat ... *this* time without interruption.

18. SARCASM: Sarcasm is one of those components that has a punch already built in, so to end a scene or chapter with it provides both added impact and insight into the character utilizing the sarcasm. That's what I was shooting for in the first scene from *His Steadfast Love* as well as the second from *Dare to Love Again*, illuminating further the state of mind for both characters.

"Everything will be okay, you'll see." Lacey patted Cat's knee. "Besides, you probably flattered Chase to no end."

"Sure. The operative word being 'end,'" Cat said with a wry twist of her lips. "End of friendship. End of relationship. End of story."

Shannon stood and kneaded her sister's shoulders. "No way. Chase is one of the most amazing human beings I've ever met, so trust me when I say he *will* forgive and forget if he hasn't already."

Cat couldn't help but grunt as she rose to her feet. Forgive, maybe. But forget? A shiver traveled her spine as she thought of the humiliating kiss that plagued her day and night.

Not a chance.

***

With a tic in his temple that belonged only to Caitlyn McClare, he rolled his sleeves and yanked a chair to the table, ignoring the gaping stares. "The deuce with Whist," he said, sweeping the table with his arm. He shuffled the cards into a ragged, little pile. "We're playing poker, so ante up."

"But Mama doesn't like us to play poker," Maddie said, tone innocent and blue eyes as wide as Caitlyn's would be if she were to walk in the room.

Logan shuffled and dealt the cards, sailing them hard to each player with a clamp of his jaw. Reaching into his pocket, he tossed a fistful of change onto the table along with a thick wad of bills. He slipped Maddie a wink before flashing a menacing smile. "Good."

19. SCENE PROPS: Oh my, do I love playing off scene props to end a scene! In fact, I'll often add props for this very purpose as a nice, clean way to wrap the scene up. In the two clips below—the first from *A Hope Undaunted* and the second from *Isle of Hope*, I utilize "cookies" to end both scenes with an element of humor and threat.

Lilly glanced at Gen, then shot Katie a crooked grin. "I don't know, I'd keep that spoon handy if I were you. Gotta feeling that hayseed lawyer knows his way around a stove—and a girl." She wriggled her brows as she bit into a cookie. "And something tells me he has a knack for turning up the heat."

Katie's lips flattened as she removed the cookie tray from the oven. "Well, I'll tell you one thing, Lil," she said with a threat in her tone. "*If* by some freak of nature he *does* manage to 'turn up the heat'"—she smirked while gripping the spatula like a weapon—"it sure won't be me who gets burned."

***

Monster cookies ... to tame the monster, no doubt.

Polishing off his fifth one, Ben snapped the lid back on and tossed them on the table with a grunt, determined to return the others when his neighbor wasn't home. Because whether Tess O'Bryen liked it or not, this was one monster with a nasty bite and a penchant for chewing. Aiming the remote, he jacked the volume up with a hard grind of his jaw.

And he sure wasn't talking cookies ...

20. SCRIPTURE: Ending a scene with a Scripture allows a great opportunity to play off that Scripture in any way you like—humor, insight, etc., enabling you to give an additional glimpse into the character, which is always a bonus. In the clip below from *A Passion Most Pure*, I felt the Scripture was a good way to reflect both the heroine's spirituality *and* her angst.

The brushing stopped. Slowly Charity turned, all smiles diminished. "I know what I'm doing, big sister, so I'll thank you to stay out of it. I love him. That's all there is to it." Tossing the brush on the bed, she turned to leave, but not before bestowing one final smile. "I trust you, Faith. We're sisters. And sisters love each other, right?"

Faith gritted her teeth. The Bible she read to Mrs. Gerson every Saturday night claimed "love never fails." She certainly hoped not.

21. SHOCK: Generally I only use shock endings towards the back of the book when tension is mounting, but you can use them anywhere because they are a tried-and-true way to keep the reader hooked. In fact, I have actually had readers email me funny stories about their reactions when they came to a shock ending, guaranteeing me that they could not stop reading from that point on. Kind of like Stephanie Meyer's first chapter of *New Moon!*

In the following scene from *His Steadfast Love*, the pastor hero knew that the heroine's anger at God was because her father—also a pastor—had had an affair. But this shock scene ending not only opened his eyes to the true trauma involved, but hopefully the reader's too.

"Well, at least you finally got your dad's trust."

A veneer seemed to settle over Cat's features as her lips compressed. "Yeah, right about the time he lost mine."

Chase glanced over again. "You mean when he had the affair?"

She didn't answer right away, eyelids closing while her mouth pursed tight. "Yeah," she said quietly, "when I found him in bed with Lacey's mom."

22. SHORT PUNCHY SENTENCE: One of the most effective chapter/scene endings—and admittedly, one of my favorites—is a one-, two-, or three-word sentence that wraps up the scene with a short and sweet conclusion such as in the two clips below. The first is from *His Steadfast Love* when a doctor gives the heroine good news, and the second is from *A Love Surrendered* when the hero finally turns to God.

Her pulse slammed to a stop ... then kicked back in when the breath she'd been holding whooshed out.

Luckier than most.

With a low groan, Chase crushed her in a powerful hug while saltwater burned beneath her lids. "Thank God," he whispered.

And for the first time in a long, long while.

Cat did.

***

The steady beat of the rain drummed on the roof while the cold air chilled Steven's body, the cool and damp of impending winter heavy in the air. And yet somehow, he felt warm, his breathing shallow as his eyes scanned the sky. There were no bolts of lightning to illuminate the dark nor peals of thunder to herald anything new. Only the still small voice of God in his heart, stirring a flame of hope that brought peace to his soul.

He leadeth me beside the still waters ... He restoreth my soul ... He leadeth me in the paths of righteousness...

"I don't understand," Steven rasped, eyes brimming with tears. "Why do You even care?

Because you are mine, the thought came, and Steven bowed his head and wept.

Because for the first time in his life, he finally understood.

He was.

23. SUSPENSE: Anything that prickles or unsettles is a surefire way to lure the reader into the next scene/chapter. Now, I'm not a suspense author, so I seldom use suspense. But hopefully the scene below from *His Steadfast Love* will give you the sense of urgency I was going for when the heroine's roommate tells the hero the heroine ingested a date-rape drug.

A new sense of fear quivered in her voice. "What s-should I d-do?"

"Fake a scream, pound on the door, whatever. Just get her out of that room—*now!*"

"Will you c-come by if I do?"

"I'm on my way, ten minutes tops." He flung his cell on the passenger seat and rammed his foot to the pedal, pretty sure his heart was pounding harder than Cat's on pure-grade ecstasy. "Please keep her safe," he whispered, practically taking the turn to the highway on two wheels. "And God?" He gunned it down the ramp, clocking close to ninety as he wove in and out of a slow stream of traffic. "Please don't let them stop me for speeding."

24. SUSPICION: Another excellent way to lead the reader on is by ending a chapter with questions that stir the pot of suspicion like this scene from *For Love of Liberty*, where the heroine overhears gossip about the hero who supposedly loves her. The suspicion I planted in the following excerpt alerts the reader that things are about to change for the worse, hopefully spurring them into the next chapter.

Body numb, Liberty slumped on the hay bale, head in her hands while tears stung in her eyes. Bettie had said Finn would be a fool not to propose to Jo Beth, and she was right. Finn McShane was a lot of things—a rogue, a tease, and a tyrant among them—but the man was definitely no fool. Her heart broke in two as a sob wrenched from her lips.

No, that title belonged to her.

25. THREATS: Let's face it, whenever somebody issues a threat, the tension ratchets up, whether it's romantic tension or the suspense kind, such as in the clips below from *Isle of Hope*.

Muscles bunched in his jaw, he wove his way through the parking lot toward the Intracoastal, determined to give her a piece of his mind—or what was left of it—about strolling a beach by herself at night.

Because Lacey Carmichael may have played him, tempted him, and left him for dead, but she didn't deserve some half-drunk cowboy or ballplayer giving her trouble.

He gritted his teeth, looking both ways before he strode toward the beach.

Not unless it was him.

***

Jack's mouth wrenched tight, memories of all the grief her father had given Lacey causing a sudden ache in his jaw. Yeah, he'd like to head in the right direction with her old man too, a direction his fist had been itching to take for a long, long time.

A hard right.

26. A TRIGGERED MEMORY: Triggering a memory is a good way to wrap a scene up with a punch, a technique I utilize a fair amount. For instance, in this scene below from *His Steadfast Love,* the secondary heroine is remembering something her first husband said to her before their marriage went south. Now when the scenario is repeated in her second marriage, it triggers a spur to action that clues the reader in that fireworks are coming …

The memory of Adam's words echoed in her brain. *"I'd say it's downright irresponsible for you to choose your job over your marriage, Tess, because that's what you're doing, leaving me vulnerable in the process."*

Vulnerable.

Just like Ben would be in the clutches of Dr. Barbie.

"Over my dead body!" Tess shouted as she vaulted from the bed, grateful that her son Davey was a sound sleeper. Jerking her travel valet from the closet, she rammed the hook over the towel rack and started throwing things in at random, determined to protect her interests. Oh, yeah, she would surprise her husband with a whole lot more than monster cookies. She grunted as she dragged her suitcase from the closet.

Like a wife in his bed.

27. A WITTICISM: A witticism is "a saying or observation that usually involves a clever turn of phrase or pun." As we all know, a pun is usually a humorous use of a word in such a way as to suggest other meanings. *Which* is what I attempted to do in the two examples below from *Love Everlasting* and *Love at Any Cost.*

"I can't tell you how much I appreciate you, Chase," Shannon said softly, the apology in her tone as telling as the gentle hand she laid on his arm. "Thank you." A hint of moisture glazed in her eyes when she stepped away, tossing him a soggy grin as she left with a wave. "You are a real **gem**, my friend, you know that?"

Oh yeah, he knew that. His smile went flat as he got in his Explorer and closed the door a little too hard.

Dumb as a **rock**.

***

"So far, it looks like you'll be buying your own Dr. Peppers for the rest of the year, Mac." Bram flashed some teeth. "The wager was 'love' as I recall, not friendship, so I'm not sure how you're going to pull that rabbit out of your hat."

A smug smile slid across Jamie's lips as he followed his friend into the reception area. "It's called the old MacKenna magic, old buddy, so I suggest you keep your pockets full." He opened the outer door, allowing Bram to go first. "Because first it's friendship where I woo..." He slapped him on the back and shot him a wide grin. "Then next it's lovestruck and I do."

28. WORD REPETITION: Being a drama queen, I LOVE to repeat words in the last line or last few paragraphs for extra pop and effect, which is why I have a ton of examples to share. I have found word repetition to be a surefire way to tease the reader with an alternate meaning, whether it's sarcasm, foreshadowing future obstacles, or a play on words. Note the repetition in each of the scenes below from *A Passion Redeemed, Love's Silver Lining, His Steadfast Love,* and *A Hope Undaunted,* which help to give the scene endings a real punch. BUT a word of warning ... do NOT overuse too many in one book!

In the last sample for *A Hope Undaunted,* the word repetition goes above and beyond with a deeper meaning since the scene is about the hero coercing his longtime best friend—who is pregnant via rape—to marry him despite the fact he's in love with the heroine.

She feathered his throat with soft, lingering kisses. "Really? I would have thought cold, cramped leather would have been the perfect bedding for a thick-skinned Irishman like you."

He skimmed his hand down the curve of her hip until flannel gave way to skin. Her soft moan matched his as his kisses became urgent. "No, darlin', not for sleeping ... or **otherwise.**" The silky warmth of her skin against his lips caused him to shudder. "And God knows how I've missed you, Marceline. *And* '**otherwise.**'"

***

In a ragged beat of his heart, she slipped inside, leaving him alone with a gloom in his soul darker than anything he'd ever known. He touched his hand to the ignition, then collapsed on the wheel, putting his hand to his eyes.

He'd had no choice. Not against her will of iron. No recourse but shame. And God willing, conviction. Tears stung his lids. **God help her.** He squeezed his eyes shut. **God help him.**

***

"Libby, where are you going?" Alarm edged Mama's voice as she took a step forward. "It's time for dinner."

"I don't need dinner," she shouted, hand on the knob. "I need **fresh** air—lots and lots of **fresh** air." Lashing the door open, she barreled out.

Right into a mountain of a man who smelled like leather, lime, and mint. Bouncing off a granite chest, she gasped while a whoosh of familiar air sucked right into her lungs.

And God help her—it was *anything* but "**fresh**."

***

Patrick lifted her chin with his finger. "We have to present a united front, my love, and you need to learn to say '**no**.' Or I'm afraid with Gabe, there will be a heavy price to pay."

Marcy nodded and sniffed again.

With a tight squeeze, he buried his head in her neck before pulling away with a lift of his brow. He stared at her new satin gown, then slowly fanned his hands down the sides of her waist. "And speaking of a price to pay—so you've taken to wearing perfume to bed, have you, Mrs. O'Connor?" He bent to caress the curve of her throat while his fingers grazed the strap of her gown. "And a new satin gown, surely not just for sleep." With a slow sweep of his thumb, the strap slithered from her shoulder. "Oh, I'm afraid this is going to cost you, darlin'."

He kissed her full on the mouth, and heat shivered through her. "I suppose this isn't one of those times when I need to say **no**," she whispered, her breathing ragged against his jaw.

"No, darlin', it's not." And clutching her close, he fisted the satin gown and moved in to deepen the kiss, his husky words melting in her mouth. "For all the good it would do."

***

Cat blinked, and then her face lit up in one of the most beautiful smiles he'd ever seen. "Now *that* I'd like to see—a pastor who **moans** over **dessert**." She tipped her head, approval sparkling in those deadly blue eyes. "You know, there may be hope for you yet, Griffin." And flipping a loose strand of hair over her shoulder, she marched to the café and disappeared inside.

He grinned, pretty sure his future held way more groans than **moans**. Shaking his head, he reached for the door, his smile refusing to wane.

And it sure wouldn't be over **dessert**.

***

Ignoring her comment, he eased her back to explore her throat with his mouth, finally nipping at her earlobe before whispering warm coercion in her ear. "Don't make me wait, Galetti—I need you *now*."

With a quivering hand to his chest, she studied his face a long, long time before a tentative nod finally signaled her consent. He watched as guilt worked its magic, dispelling her resistance with the soft exhale of a sigh. She caressed his scruffy jaw with the palm of her hand while a beautiful joy pooled in her eyes. "You're the love of my life, McGee— **yesterday,** today **and forever.**"

"Mine too, Bets," he whispered, then bent to kiss her again.

Yesterday and forever.

***

And we're done! Keep in mind that this list is certainly not exhaustive, but hopefully it will help trigger wonderful ideas and ways to write scene and chapter endings that are powerful, insightful, and entertaining. *And* ones that will lead your readers on with a "tease" they can't resist.

Find out more about Julie Lessman at the back of the book!

Chapter 13
Beyond Description – Write Like a Movie
By MaryLu Tyndall

Let's face it. We live in the age of video—phones, tablets, TV, movies, YouTube, Skype…I could go on. Everywhere you go, people are hunched over some screen. With the press of a button, we can watch our favorite movie, show, or video, or connect with loved ones. I admit it. I'm addicted to YouTube. I spend way too many hours there watching sermons and music videos, and even doing research for books. Yet doesn't it seem that the written word has dwindled into the background, at least for this new generation who seem to constantly demand visual stimulation and instant gratification.

I've been fortunate to receive many emails from readers over the years who have enjoyed my books. But the single most common comment I get from my fans goes something like this: "I felt like I was there with the character" or "I could smell the sea and feel the wind" or "I felt like I was in a movie!"

The strange thing is I never purposely set out to create that sensation. I didn't learn it from a writing instruction book. I didn't pick it up in a class. I had no idea why people were even saying such a thing. But they were. And it wasn't just one or two of them, either. It was so many people that I finally decided to try to figure out what, in particular, I was doing that was making my readers feel this way.

So I laid out a selection of other authors' novels on my desk beside one of mine and determined to discover the answer. I mean, what if someone asked me how I wrote like a movie? It certainly wouldn't bode well for a published author to shrug and admit she has no idea!

I read chapters from each book and then analyzed how I felt afterward. Was I engaged with the character? Did I visualize the scene? Did I feel like I was in a movie? I jotted down notes on each book, including my reactions and why I reacted that way. Then I read a chapter from one of my books and did the same.

Before I continue, let me say that I don't believe in comparing myself to other authors. Every author has his or her own unique voice and writing style. There really is no right or wrong style or voice. Some authors have a fast-paced, choppy style of writing, while others are more literary and move at a slower, more eloquent pace. Some authors add a lot of description; some barely give any. Some authors write dialog as if they were firing off a gun, while others add a lot of pauses and character movements. The good news is there are readers for every style. Some readers will not enjoy a certain author's style, while others will love it. So I am in no way comparing myself to other authors by way of saying one is better than another. I simply wanted to see what I was doing differently. As it turns out, even though other authors have similar styles to mine, my writing does bear some unique differences. Here are the general steps I take before writing a scene.

Step 1 - Visualize your surroundings

I have been blessed with a very vivid imagination. That's most likely true of every author. However, just before I write a scene, I close my eyes and visualize everything that surrounds the POV character—what they see, smell, hear, or even taste. Let's say character A is talking to character B on a street in Charleston in 1795. Now, close your eyes.

What do you see?

Do you see horses? Carriages? Are people walking around? What are they wearing, doing? What time of day is it? Where is the sun in the sky? Is it shining in the character's eyes? Do they have to squint? Are there buildings? What do they look like? Are they shops, hotels, taverns? What is the street paved with? Or is it paved? Are there trees around? Is water nearby—a lake, river, or harbor?

What do you hear?

Are the people talking, singing, shouting? Is there music coming from somewhere? Do you hear horses snorting and clomping along? Footsteps? Carriages creaking? If there's water nearby, do you hear the lap of waves, ship bells ringing, sails flapping, birds squawking?

What is the weather like? Are there clouds? Is it windy? If yes, is the wind fluttering leaves, stirring up dust on the street, blowing the character's clothing or hair? Is there thunder, rain, lightning?

What do you feel like physically?

Are you hot, cold, sweating, shivering? Are you wet, dry, have on too many clothes or too little? Do your feet hurt? Are you in pain? Hungry?

What do you smell?

Horse manure, sweat, tobacco, brine, pastry, flowers, perfume, rain, wood, tar, alcohol, lemonade, tea?

If you're eating, what do you taste? Is it sour, sweet, bitter, buttery, meaty, gamey…etc.?

You get the picture. Jot down the answers to each of these questions, then move on to step 2.

Step 2 - Decide which things to incorporate into the scene.

Description is a tricky thing. If you add too much description, write it as a laundry list, or choose a poor placement within the scene, your reader will be skimming. Or worse, he or she will close the book. Too little description and your reader gets lost. They hear what character A and character B are saying to each other, but they might as well be in a vacuum in outer space. Readers need to be grounded in space and time in order to feel a part of the story. Some authors keep their description to a bare minimum so the reader can use his or her imagination to fill in the blanks. They reason that this gives them more space to devote to the actual plot and story. I totally get that. Depending on the writing style, or if the location is a very common one, i.e., Times Square in New York, present day, it may work for some. However, how many of us have actually stood on a street in 1795 Charleston? Or sailed on a tall ship across the Caribbean? Or ridden across the Sahara on a camel's back? Readers typically read for two reasons:

- To experience other places, times, and even worlds
- To feel something deep within themselves—to be stirred emotionally.

As a reader, I need to experience what the character is experiencing in order for me to become fully engrossed in the book. When I'm reading a good book, everything around me fades away, and I'm right there in the character's shoes. If you can create that sensation in your readers, while adding great characters and a riveting plot, then I guarantee you'll never lose a reader.

Of course we can't put in every detail we listed above. Description overload will frustrate your reader. Too many details drive me crazy. For example, some historical novelists have a tendency to want to show off their many hours of research by adding in everything they learned on a specific topic. I've read pages of description on what the heroine is wearing from her beaded silk slippers to every article of underclothes--stockings, petticoats, chemise, stays, to the various overskirts and bodices, to her jewelry, hairstyle and finally what type of hat or bonnet she is wearing. Details include fabric, trim, color, pattern, lace, etc. Now, If I were an historical clothing expert who delighted in these particular details, that would be great. But let's face it, most readers are just looking for a good story. Endless lists of details will only bore your reader. Believe me, I know how hard it can be after spending hours, sometimes days, researching one particular detail not to be able to incorporate all the fascinating facts you learned. But you're not writing a history book, and your reader is not reading your book to learn history. Many people do enjoy learning some history, but if you add too many details, your novel soon reads like a textbook.

The trick is to choose certain details that do the following:

• Give your reader a general idea of the scene that involves most of the senses

• Reveal the mood of the protagonist. If you can tie the character's surroundings in with his or her mood or the mood you want to convey in the scene, then you've hit the jackpot!

Remember to choose details from all the senses. Many authors make the mistake of only choosing what the character sees and not including what they feel, hear, taste, or smell.

Step 3. Sprinkle your details carefully around dialog (both internal and external) and story.

Add in a small detail here, another one there, like sprinkling salt on a fine meal. Too much in one spot, and the reader will spit it out. Not enough, and the book will be bland. Very rarely do you put lots of these descriptive details all together.

That's it! Those are the three steps I go through when I write my scenes and chapters. You may think that it sounds like a lot of work, but with practice, it eventually comes so naturally that you won't have to stop and think about it.

I find the best way to learn is through example, so I'm placing a few scenes below from a couple of my books. The first one comes from my novel, *The Ransom*, chapter 1, scene 1. I've underlined the details that I feel help transform the scene into the movie in the reader's mind. Notice the attention to all the senses—what the character sees, hears, smells, and feels. Notice also how I don't just describe the scene, but I tie in those descriptions with the character's emotions.

MURK, MIRE, AND MAYHEM. 'Twas the only fitting description for the punch house in which Juliana Dutton found herself. No, not found herself. She had come here on purpose, passed through the display of debauchery once on her way to the brothel beyond, and now, yet again, on her way back to the street. Only this time, the room overflowed with patrons—if patrons was a fitting term for the slovenly-attired men and women guzzling their drinks amidst shouts and curses and a discordant fiddle. What had she been thinking?

But she had to make sure one last time that her friend Abilene was not among the dissolute cullions flooding the room—that the woman had not been hiding when Juliana had passed through before. Or worse, swallowed up in the arms of some foul ruffian. Yet, as Juliana peered from beneath the hood of her cloak, cringing at the visions that met her eyes, her friend was nowhere in sight.

What *was* apparently in sight was her. Dozens of glazed eyes fastened upon her as she wove through tables laden with mugs of Kill-Devil rum, card games, flickering lanterns, and plates brimming with roasted boar and fish pudding. The scent of food joined the odors of sweat, smoke, and bitter spirits, creating a stench that would keep the Devil himself away. Though, from the befouled language and equally befouled sights, it appeared he was already present.

The ensuing whistles and lewd invitations proved her assumption correct. Air fled her lungs. Gripping her throat, she hurried toward the door. A chair slid in her path. A man rose before her, brashly eyeing her from the hood of her cloak to the tips of her red mules. A brace of pistols crossed a chest the size of England and adorned with a red doublet trimmed in metallic lace. Two formidable swords hung from each hip. A scar on his neck disappeared behind a stained cravat that bubbled over his shirt like the ale foaming on his mustache.

Pirate.

With a jeweled finger that belied the crusted dirt beneath his nail, he yanked off her hood, releasing her golden waves.

One would think none of the men had ever seen flaxen hair on a woman before as groans of pleasure swept through the crowd.

Followed by vulgar suggestions that shocked her and caused her to tremble violently.

"That be a proper fine lady, says I," one man shouted. "Take 'er, Mad Dog."

"She be askin' fer it by comin' here," another man yelled, triggering an outburst of laughter.

Yet the man kept staring at her. Mad dog, indeed. A rabid one from the looks of him.

Juliana was not a timid sort, not a woman prone to hysterics or swooning, but when the rake clutched her arm and leered at her with teeth the color of dirt, her heart nigh burst through her chest.

"Leave her be!"

From behind the brute, a voice boomed like the crash of a massive wave. The pirate glanced over his shoulder, stiffened, then released her with a grunt. Wiping his mouth on his sleeve, he picked up the chair, shoved it beside a nearby table, and toppled onto it like a felled tree.

Moans of disappointment filtered through the mob before the music resumed and the men returned to their drink and games. Tugging her hood back atop her head, Juliana searched for her rescuer, unsure what price his chivalry bore. But no one came forward to claim his prize. Before the man revealed himself, or worse, before Mad Dog reconsidered, she dashed for the door, surprised when no one paid her any mind. No leers, bawdy comments, groping hands, lecherous grins. It was as if she'd disappeared. Mayhap God had made her invisible. She was, after all, on a mission of mercy.

Nearly at the entrance, her gaze latched upon a pair of startling blue eyes—so *piercingly blue*, they almost stopped her. They definitely slowed her. Mayhap it was the man's coal black hair, dark stubble on his jaw, and sun-bronzed face that made the color of his eyes so luminescent. But no, there was

something else within them. An intelligence, an intensity ...
and now a bit of humor as his gaze remained upon her. He
leaned against a thick post, calm, quiet, sturdy—a bastion of
control amidst the clamor surrounding him. Rounded, sinewy
arms folded over his leather jerkin, Hessian boots crossed at his
ankle. His lips lifted in a mocking grin.

Turning her face away, she shoved past a group of
inebriated patrons and fled down the stairs onto Thames Street.

Without even knowing the place or time period, could you
get a visual, a sense of the scene? Could you picture what the
character pictured? Feel what she felt? If so, then I've done my
job.

Here's some shorter scenes. This one is from my novel,
Veil of Pearls. I chose it because it's a rainy scene.

Her eyes flitted between his as if searching for his intent.
Rain transformed her hair into waves of dripping ebony. Water
beaded on her lashes, framing them in silver. He swallowed,
not wanting to move for fear she'd dash away and vanish. She
reached for him. Stopped. Hesitated. Bit her lip. But finally she
placed her hand on his arm. He hated that she seemed
frightened of him. Even now, as they started on their way, he
could feel her trembling.

The rain lessened to a sprinkle. A breeze whipped around
them, stirring the leaves of trees and loosening the raindrops
from their tips. Droplets fell to the ground in a *tap tap* that
accompanied the rhythm of their footsteps over the shiny
cobblestones.

Did you feel the rain, the wind? Notice how I connected
the sound of the droplets with their footsteps.

The following is also from *Veil of Pearls*. Notice how I
engage every sense, but I sprinkle those details around the

heroine's emotions and internal dialog. I'll forgo the underlining this time.

Morgan led her through the crush of men crowding the piazza, drinks and cigars clutched in their fingers. Feeling their gazes assail her as she passed, she held her breath against the sting of tobacco and alcohol, until finally they entered the house.

Light from dozens of glittering sconces and chandeliers blinded her. She blinked as they greeted the host and hostess, both of whom barely acknowledged her. A servant announced Mr. Morgan Rutledge and guest. *Guest.* She supposed that was as fitting a name as any, for with each step she took, she felt more and more like a temporary visitor—a peasant passing through a pageantry of opulence that would always be outside her reach. Perhaps announcing her as *stranger* or *foreigner* would have been more apropos.

The foyer was ten times the size of the doctor's and abuzz with chattering people who all glanced her way to see what strange oddity Morgan had brought to the party. From a room to their left, orchestra music drifted atop the beaded and jeweled coiffures. Before she could protest, a butler took her shawl and Morgan's cape and hat. She didn't plan on staying that long.

Morgan patted her hand as he led her into the massive ballroom. No doubt he knew how nervous she was. The first thing Adalia noticed was how large the room was, the second, the intricately carved crown molding lining the ceiling above Dutch floral paintings and crystalline chandeliers—such beauty and lavishness she'd never seen. The third thing she noticed was that once again everyone turned to stare at her. In fact, the chattering faded as ladies leaned together behind fans in clandestine whispers. This time, however, Adalia lifted her chin, took in a deep breath, and met their gazes with equal alacrity. If she was to endure their reproach, she would endure it with courage and pride.

And finally, here's a scene from a soon-to-be-released book, *Liberty Bride.*

Emerging from the companionway with Hannah on her heels, Emeline drew in a deep breath of fresh air, tainted with brine, moist wood, and a hint of earthy loam—the promise of home. She shifted her gaze to the left where she spotted land rising like a green cloud from the sea off the starboard railing. So close, she could almost reach out and grab it. Yet there might as well be an entire ocean between them.

Halting, she lifted her closed eyes to the sun. Warmth flooded her. It felt good to be on deck. She'd spent too much of the past two days in sick bay attending the injured or in the captain's cabin working on his portrait.

"I thank you, dear," Hannah said from beside her, drawing Emeline's gaze as they started their walk. "For takin' me on your walks. I 'ate bein' cooped up below like one of their pigs or chickens."

Emeline returned her smile. "The captain said I needed an escort, and who better than you?" Feeling uneasy, she looked up to see at least half the sailors staring their way...

....

Sails cracked above, and the deck slanted. Emeline stumbled to grip the railing. After nearly two months at sea, she should be used to the heaving and leaping by now. She should also be used to being stared at. She glanced over her shoulder once again to find Lieutenant Masters' eyes latched upon her. Instantly, he shifted them away.

The ship bucked again, this time showering them with sea spray. Hannah chuckled. Emeline joined her as the wind tore at her hair and cooled the droplets on her skin.

"Look lively men!" Lieutenant Masters shouted. "Lay aloft and unfurl topsails. Halt taut!"

Other shouts followed, and men scrambled to task. Backing against the railing, Emeline braced her feet on the teetering deck and watched as sailors flew into the shrouds and climbed aloft. Others remained on deck, hauling ropes, or *lines* as they called them, while other men busied themselves with repairs on lines and sailcloth, cleaning guns and weapons, and participating in drills. Every man had a duty and every man was busy at all times. Such an efficiently run ship. So different from the *Charlotte*.

Which made her swallow a lump of dread. How was America supposed to win against such power and expertise?

Did you feel like you were on a tall ship with the wind and sea spray and the shifting deck? I hope so!

I encourage you to give these three steps a try in your next writing project and see if it doesn't help your reader experience your book as if they were watching a movie.

Find out more about MaryLu Tyndall at the back of the book!

Chapter 14
Making Your Reader Cry
By Michelle Griep

I can write a fight scene like nobody's business. A slapstick slip-on-the-banana peel piece of humor? No problem. But when it comes to penning an emotional scene, whoa baby. Those are super hard. Why? Because the emotions I feel in relation to what's happening with my characters might not be the same emotions someone else would feel. Everyone reacts differently. The trick is to write the scene so that it appeals to readers across the board, so that the emotion of the scene hooks into the reader's heart. That's what readers want when they pick up a book. They want to "feel."

And that, dear writer, is a tall order to fill.

But there are ways to connect with your reader's emotions—and ways not to. Let's take a look at some of them.

Tugging on Heartstrings
Small children. Puppies. An old man sitting all alone in a wheelchair in a darkened room. These images instantly evoke an emotional response—and that's what you want to do with your story. Think about adding a character that garners sympathy just by merit of their age. Or add in a pet. Most people have a soft spot in their hearts for animals. It's not cheating to use these devices. It's a tool of the trade.

Skip the Melodrama

Emotional scenes are important, but don't focus too much time and energy on them. You don't want to overdo it and turn your characters into cartoonish buffoons. Instead, play up the action and the consequences because that will allow the reader to experience the situation without spelling out those emotions. Readers are smart. They'll know when a character's goal is thwarted and will automatically feel tense, or when a character's loved one is hurt in some way, they'll feel bad vicariously. Don't tell the reader how to feel. Just do your best job of describing the situation and allow the reader to live through the situation himself.

Keep it Tight

You don't write pages of small talk or unending descriptions, right? So why write great discourses on your character's emotions? Answer: don't. It's always the goal to keep the story moving forward. Don't slog it down in the mire of an emotional scene.

Word Choice is Everything

Broken and ruined. Light and hope. The first few words are dark, the second set uplifting. Words carry powerful connotations, so don't mix happy words into a sad scene or vice-versa. Keep your scene consistent by using specific words that correlate with the emotion.

Up the Stakes

For powerful emotions, you need to have powerful situations. There's got to be something at stake for the character in order to make your scene believably emotional. Give him a bad or worse choice to make. And don't forget to allow your character to fail or lose something dear to him. This is a powerful way to connect to your reader because as humans we all experience loss and failure.

Use Setting to Your Advantage

Tie your setting in to the emotion to ramp up the intensity. Going for fearful? Night's a good time for that. Lonely? Paint the walls of the room blue. Excited? Perhaps there's music playing in the background.

Do the Unexpected

So your story is going along, la-de-dah-de-dah, then wham! Put in something the reader—and your character—doesn't expect. This is a jarring experience for both. Maybe the baby gets sick. Or the heroine gets hurt. Or a lost dog is discovered and needs help. When the reader is thrown off kilter like that, you have the perfect opportunity for a poignant moment to unfold.

And last, but not least, *always* use the five senses to really tie your reader in to the moment.

Sight

Play up the emotion by showing your reader heart-wrenching sights. Example: The delight on a child's face as he's handed a big ice cream cone, the brightness of his eyes, his little mouth opened in a big *O* and then splat! The ice cream falls to the sidewalk. Tears shimmer in his eyes and spill onto his cheeks. See what I mean? The death of a dream, even a small one such as ice cream, can be shown in actions.

Sound

Sinister organ music. Ghostly strains of a hummed folk tune in a minor chord. Whispers in the dark. These are all sounds that raise the little hairs on the back of your neck, and all you did was read them, not actually hear them. Do that with your writing. Evoke emotion in your reader by adding in sounds.

Touch

Everyone longs to be held in strong arms. But what if your character is suddenly ripped away from those strong arms into the cold embrace of the villain? Don't forget to add in sensory cues so that your reader can feel right along with the character.

Taste

Isn't it strange how a bite of a juicy strawberry can instantly whisk you back to when you were five and first filled your mouth with sweetness? Describing tastes during an emotional scene can connect your character and your reader to bittersweet memories.

Smell

Just like taste, odors or fragrances are a strong tie to the past, and memories are rife with emotions. Sprinkle scents in your scenes that are universal so that your reader can relate to what your character is inhaling and experience the same emotions those smells create.

The best way to make your reader cry or laugh is to simply write about things that make you cry and laugh. It's the human condition we all share.

Find out more about Michelle Griep at the back of the book!

Chapter 15
Whose POV is it, Anyway?
Learning How to Write Deep
By Lynnette Bonner

First, I would be remiss in giving credit where it is due if I didn't tell you that I originally developed and taught the following material with fellow author Lesley Ann McDaniel. She was instrumental in forming much of this material, and I thank her for allowing me to share it with all of you.

In this chapter, I will cover two of the main elements of point of view (hereafter POV) and all the intricate details in between. First there will be a little bit of high school grammar review that we are going to cruise through fairly quickly because most of you will be very familiar with these tools. We will talk about first person, second person, and third person grammatical forms. Then we will cover character and how that relates to strong POV.

Some of you who are new to writing might be asking, "So, what is point of view anyway?" Well, the first thing to realize is that your POV choice determines and dictates what information the reader will receive. One definition of POV is "The perspective from which the reader experiences the action of the story. Sometimes known as Viewpoint, Voice (of the character, not the author), or Narrative Mode."

The reason you need to understand POV is that as authors it is our job to create an emotional experience for our readers. POV is a tool an author uses to allow their readers to see and hear what is happening in the story, thus creating that desired emotional response.

Let's talk about the elements of POV.

There are several grammatical forms of POV. The one you choose dictates the way the action of the story is told.

1. First Person

—First person uses the pronouns "I" and "We." Example: "I held my breath, listening intently for any indication that we might not be alone."

—Using this form means the narrator is also a character in the story, and they are almost always the protagonist. In fact, first person is a commonly used form of narration.

—Using first person is a very intimate level of writing (you have to know your character really well), which can be limiting. You limit the number of characters who can add to the story, which limits the amount of information you can convey.

—First person is usually written in past tense, like the example above, but could be present tense. Example: "I hold my breath, listening intently for any indication that someone else is here."

Exercise: Write in first person for 2 minutes.

2. Second Person

—Second person uses the pronoun "You." Example: "You hold your breath, listening intently for any indication that you might not be alone."

—In this form the narrator refers to one of the characters, possibly himself, as "you," making the reader feel as if they are a character within the story.

—Second person is rarely used, as it is hard to maintain for an entire novel. But it can be used to create intimacy with the reader while at the same time showing that the narrating character is distanced from himself.

—Second person is usually present tense but could be written in past tense under some circumstances.
Exercise: Rewrite the passage you wrote in the first exercise in second person.

3. Third Person

—Third person uses the pronouns "He," "She," and "They." Example: "She held her breath, listening intently for any indication that they might not be alone."

—With third person writing, the narrator is *not* a character in the story.

—Third person is the most common narrative form. It is also the most flexible form because it can be both intimate and detached.

—Third person is usually written in past tense but could be in present tense.

—**Types or Styles of Third Person:** Third person can be broken down even further into several types or styles of writing. Those are:

i. Objective: Think of this form as the author being a reporter behind a camera who merely observes without judgement and reports what they see.

ii. Omniscient: Think of this form as being reported from high above the story. This means the narrator can know things that none of the characters know, including future events. The narrator not only can know physical things that the characters don't know but can also know and report on the thoughts and feelings of any of the characters.

iii. Singular: Singular third person is told from the point of view of only one character.

iv. Multiple: Multiple third person is reported from the point of view of more than one character—but only one character's POV per scene. (As opposed to Omniscient, mentioned above, which can have more than one character's POV per scene.)

—**Levels of Third Person:** In addition to being broken down by type, third person also has several levels. Those are:

i. Distant. Distant third can be written in any of the four above styles. But there are some key requirements, the first being that the reader stays outside the POV character's head, and the second being that perceptions are reported as observations.

Example: Claire ran down the driveway. She thought she could hear a car coming, but as she skidded to a halt at the edge of the sidewalk, she saw nothing. She wondered if she was crazy.

She realized then that Ken wasn't coming tonight. With a sigh, she admitted to herself that he might not be coming at all.

ii. Deep. Deep third POV can only be written in the Singular Third Person or Multiple Third Person style. This level infuses third person with the intimacy of first person. It does away with almost all dialogue tags and verbs such as "see," "notice," "understand," "feel," "realize" and "think," which suggest *telling* as opposed to *showing*. And it is currently the most popular form of third person writing.

Example: Claire picked up her pace as the distinct hum of a motor reverberated in the distance. She skidded to a halt at the edge of the sidewalk. Nothing. Was she crazy?

Ken isn't coming tonight. It hit her like a rock. *He might not be coming at all.*

Exercise: Rewrite passage from first exercise in third person.

You knew all that already, right? I'm not teaching rocket science here. But keep reading, because here is where we start to get to the good stuff of writing in **deep POV**. Let's take deep POV even further by taking a closer look at character and how that relates to a deeply emotional, intimate story telling experience.

To truly achieve deep POV from the perspective of character, you need to ask yourself as a writer, "Whose head are we in?" We want to keep our characters authentic. This question is important because in deep POV the reader sees, feels, hears, and knows ONLY what the currently narrating character sees, feels, hears, and knows, and nothing more. So intimately knowing the character whose position you are telling the story from is key.

Ask yourself these key questions about your POV character.

—What are your character's perceptions?

—Think of their five senses. What can the character smell, hear, see, taste, touch?

—What is your character's temperament? Are they emotional? Rational? Easily discouraged? Psychologically damaged? Etc.

—What is their personality? Are they an extrovert? Introvert? Compassionate or hardened?

—What is their learning style? Do they learn visually, auditorily, or tactilely?

—Think about your character's introspection.

—What are they thinking?

—What are they feeling?

—Consider your character's voice.

—What is their diction like? Do they drop their Gs or have other lazy speech habits? Do they use unique pronunciations?

—What is their style? Do they dress formally or conservatively?

—Are they Conservative? Liberal?

—What kind of attitude do they have? This ties in with personality.

—Do they have regionalisms in dialect or mindset?

—What era do they live in?

—What is their background?

—What is their level of education?

All of that goes into how your character interacts with other characters in the book. Having a well-thought-out and well-fleshed-out character makes them believable, which helps the reader suspend their disbelief and get that powerful emotional experience that it is your job as the author to provide. Of course, you don't have to tell the readers the answers to all these questions, but knowing the answers will help you develop accurate, believable, and compelling dialogue, reactions, interactions, and choices for your character.

Once you have all that down, here are some more things to know about POV that will immerse your readers more deeply into the story.

—Remember that while your character can't know many things, they can guess or assume what others are thinking or feeling.

—This can feel limiting, but realize that being in one character's POV makes the reader's task easier because they don't need to know what everyone in the scene is thinking.

—This might lead you to ask what the right number of POV characters for a story is? The answer to that can vary. If you are a brand new author writing your first book, consider this comment from agent and author Noah Lukeman from his book *The First Five Pages*: "In general, I would strongly recommend beginning writers not employ multiple viewpoints. Developing one good viewpoint character can be hard enough, even for the most advanced writer."

—Once you've decided on the number of characters, you'll need to determine which character is the POV character for each scene.

—To determine that, ask yourself whose scene (story) is it? And which character offers the most compelling perspective (or has the most to lose)?

Consider these two examples of the same scene written from two perspectives. Depending on what you want to highlight for the story either of these could work.

— From Martha's POV:
"Martha?"
Kevin's voice sounded weak, like he'd been up all night again. The idiot.

"Will you drive me to Harry's?"

Martha groaned. What on earth was he thinking? "Not this time, honey." Anger rose in her throat, making speech all the more difficult. "You'll have to find another accomplice."

— From Kevin's POV:

"Martha." Kevin's voice sounded weak, even to himself. Why had he stayed up all night again? "Will you drive me to Harry's?"

Martha groaned as she tossed her gorgeous blonde hair over her shoulder. That move always got to him.

"Not this time, honey," she said, her gaze sharpening. "You'll have to find another accomplice."

You can see from those examples that you can use POV to highlight what you want the reader to know. Also, notice that Martha is likely not conscious of the fact that she tossed her hair over her shoulder, so in her POV that is not mentioned. Unless she is purposely tossing her hair over her shoulder with the intent of manipulating Kevin—in that case you would want to mention it. Kevin's weak voice can be mentioned from both characters' POV because Kevin can hear himself speak, thus can hear his own tone.

—You should always introduce your POV characters early on in the story. Usually within the first three chapters.

Let's talk about head-hopping for a moment. Head-hopping happens when an author jumps from the POV of one character into the POV of another character and then back in the same scene, paragraph, or even sentence. This technique should be avoided almost always but should never be employed in the following cases.

—Never in first person or deep POV

—Note that it is not currently acceptable by the majority of editors in the publishing industry, though it can be seen in many stories from past decades or from authors who have been publishing for a long time.

To clarify what I mean by head-hopping, here is a scene with head-hopping, followed by the same scene cleaned up and written in only Olivia's POV.

Head-hopping:

Olivia passed through the gate and scanned the garden party, dreading the afternoon that lay ahead. Bruce saw her from across the yard and smiled to himself. Today was his lucky day. From the corner of her eye, she saw him too.

"Olivia!" Grandma Lil swirled her lemonade, delighted to see her granddaughter arrive at her party, although Olivia had done her best to get out of it.

Pasting a smile on her face, Olivia crossed the lawn to Grandma. "I'm delighted to be here."

Grandma sensed a forced tone of happiness.

Bruce sidled up to Olivia, sliding one hand across the roughness of her lacey sleeve.

Olivia resisted the urge to gag.

Grandma's heart leapt with joy. It was about time those two got together.

"Hello, darling." Bruce waggled his brows in anticipation of winning fair Olivia's heart. He was certainly on top of his game today.

Pulling away her arm, Olivia lost all control and let fly the slap that she'd been longing to give him for weeks.

Horrified, Grandma fainted dead away. Her lemonade left a dark splotch down the front of her favorite lavender chiffon dress.

Do you see how the reader is jerked from the mind and thoughts of first one character and then the next in that scene? We are just settling in to realize we are going to be in Olivia's POV when we are jerked into Bruce's, then back to Olivia's, and then into Grandma's and back again. Let's take a look at the same passage cleaned up and written from the POV of only Olivia.

Deep 3rd:

Olivia passed through the gate and scanned the garden party, dreading the afternoon that lay ahead. And just as she had feared, there was Bruce standing by the potted cypress, smiling to himself. The jerk probably thought today was his lucky day.

"Olivia!" Grandma Lil waved a hand from her seat in the shade under the gazebo. She swirled her lemonade, obviously delighted to see Olivia arrive at her party. Little did Grandma know how hard Olivia had tried to find any reason not to be here. Not even her attempt to trade shifts with Sarah at work had panned out.

Pasting a smile on her face, Olivia crossed the lawn to Grandma. "Hi, Gran." She bent and kissed the soft leathery cheek that Gran lifted to her. "I'm delighted to be here." She hoped Grandma couldn't sense her forced tone of happiness.

Grandma pursed her lips and quirked one brow, revealing that Olivia's little lie had likely not gone unnoticed.

She started to apologize, but just then Bruce sidled up and slid one hand down her arm. "Hello, darling."

Olivia pulled her arm away and resisted the urge to gag.

Grandma glanced between them with a hopeful look, one hand going to her chest.

This was exactly why Olivia hadn't wanted to attend. Grandma never could take no for an answer. But inviting him here after what he'd done was a betrayal of the lowest kind.

Bruce waggled his brows—probably thinking he looked suave and debonair, but only managing to look like an idiot.

What had she ever seen in that two-timing—no make that *three*-timing!—low life? Olivia lost all control and let fly the slap that she'd been longing to give him for weeks.

Bruce grunted in surprise and leveled her with a shocked look, one hand going to the jaw he worked back and forth.

Good! Let him be shocked! Olivia glared, even as she shook the pain in her palm away.

Behind her, something thudded to the boards of the gazebo with a great *thwump*! Oliva spun around. "Grandma!" Grandma had fainted dead away! Her lemonade was now nothing but a dark splotch across the front of that hideous lavender chiffon dress she was so fond of wearing.

This is obviously a lighthearted story and overstated in a lot of ways for the purposes of this example, but I hope seeing these scenes side by side helps to expose that dreaded head-hopping that creeps unnecessarily into so many stories to the detriment of the reader's enjoyment. And also, that it highlights how writing in deep third can really pull your readers into the story.

I know this might feel like a lot to take in at first, but if all that feels overwhelming to you, don't stress about it. Go through your current project keeping one thing you learned from this chapter in mind. Then you can come back and read the chapter again and focus on the next thing. It doesn't all have to be done at once. Remember the oft' quoted saying, "Great writing is rewriting." I still have to remember that even with thirteen full-length projects and many other shorter works completed and published. If you have any questions about this material, I'm always happy to dialogue with people about writing. You can connect with me through my website at http://www.lynnettebonner.com.

Find out more about Lynnette Bonner at the back of the book!

Section 5

Finishing Touches

Chapter 16
Editing Your Manuscript: Can You Really do it all Yourself? The Whys and Hows of Self-Editing
By Louise M. Gouge

Why you should edit

You've finally done it! You've written that novel you always said you'd write. You love your characters, you've taken them on an exciting journey, and you've given them a satisfying resolution to their conflicts. Your critique partners applaud your unique storyline and call the book a real page-turner. Your gifted cover artist has designed the perfect cover that will attract a lot of attention from readers searching for a great book to read. Best of all, you've prepared a well-designed marketing plan. At last your book is ready to publish. So, because you're publishing independently, you're all set to put that puppy up on Amazon, Nook, Smashwords, and every other publisher in cyber-land…and wait for the money to roll into your bank account.

Hold on a minute. Before clicking "upload," maybe you should ask yourself a few questions.

Is my manuscript as perfect as I think it is? I've already taken the advice offered in previous chapters regarding research, plotting, characterization, POV, GMC, etc. But now I want to be sure it's polished to perfection, meaning there are no grammatical errors or typos. (I also want to avoid factual errors, but that's covered in our research chapters.)

Sure. No problem. Good to go.

Oh, wait. Do I really remember all of those basic grammar rules I learned in high school? Or do I simply write what sounds good? The problem with this latter approach is that most of us tend to talk in a casual way, tossing in clichés, using the latest slang, and ignoring those whispers in our ears from our long-ago high school English teachers. You know, terms such as dangling modifier, subject/verb agreement, pronoun antecedents, comma placement, and a bunch of other bothersome rules. But those rules have an important purpose: accurate communication to your readers of the story you've worked so hard to write.

Word choice

Take this little quiz to see if you know how to avoid some common word choice errors.

1. How will the weather (affect/effect) your trip?
2. If you don't have a map, you won't know where (your/you're) going.
3. During the hurricane, the house lost (it's/its) roof.
4. The difference between you and (me/myself/I) is obvious.
5. I'm going to (lie/lay) down for a nap.
6. It's necessary to know what (their/there/they're) contributing to our project.
7. I noticed that David and (me/myself/I) were on the list.
8. She did not know (whom/who) had called her.
9. There are some vitamins that you should take (everyday/every day).
10. How much (further/farther) do you plan to pursue your research for this book?
11. The bank has a (lean/lien) against my friend's house.
12. The soldier called out to (whoever/whomever) held the flag.
13. I will try (and/to) fix that broken fence.

Answers are at the end of this chapter. No peeking before you make your choices.

Grammar

Not only do you want to use the appropriate words, you also want to put them together in a way that accurately conveys to your readers the story of your heart. While your novel shouldn't sound like an academic paper, it also shouldn't have errors that might pull the reader out of the story. My purpose here is to help you be aware of some common grammatical mistakes you may wish to avoid. I used to tell my college English students this: In every sentence, each word has a job. The form that word takes depends on its job. This is especially true of pronouns such as who and whom, me and I. Make sure you use the right form of the word for its job in the sentence.

Here's another little quiz. In the following sentences, see if you can find a dangling modifier, a misplaced modifier, faulty parallelism, and errors in subject/verb agreement.

1. Are you a student, own a home, and need additional income?
2. As a doctor, this condition is a symptom of a serious disease.
3. Hiding from the sheriff, the woodshed was a poor option for the thief.
4. None of us are perfect.

Did you spot the errors? Learning proper sentence construction is essential. Again, you're not writing an academic paper, but you should know the grammar rules before you break them to accommodate your particular writing style or the slang your character may be using.

Caveat

As storytellers, we know the difference between narrative and dialogue. Depending on our writing style, we may choose to use Deep POV, in which the narrative will sound much the same as the dialogue. In this case, proper grammar isn't required unless your POV character is an English teacher. Otherwise, you can write narrative in the same style in which the POV character would talk. An excellent example of this is Mark Twain's novel *The Adventures of Huckleberry Finn*. The entire story is told in Huck's point of view, with both dialogue and narrative written just as if that rascally boy were speaking to us. Slang, improper grammar, and even some very offensive words fill the pages. Huck was, after all, a Mississippi "river rat" with no education except what he learned on the "mean streets" of his pre-Civil War home town.

Thus, in books such as *Huckleberry Finn*, narrative may contain many grammar errors. But the reader has been cleverly pulled into the story and doesn't object to them. Further, as you may have noticed, I'm writing this chapter just as though I were speaking to you. While my grammar may be generally correct, when I speak, you'll also hear this southern and Colorado raised gal say y'all or dropping the *g* in -ing words. I mean, who wants to be considered pedantic?

In traditional fiction, narrative passages will more likely be written in proper grammar, especially when the story is told from more than one POV. On the other hand, dialogue and thoughts will be written in whatever jargon the POV character uses. Whichever device you use, be sure you are consistent throughout the novel.

Now that we know the "why" of using proper grammar, let's move on to the "how."

How you can edit

So, let's get started. Let's assemble your grammar toolbox and, like an expert craftsman, know how to use your tools to hone a perfect story.

Although my mother (a one-time legal secretary) taught me to speak properly, although I made straight A's in English throughout my school years and earned a college degree in English, and although I taught college English classes for almost seventeen years, I still depend on the experts when editing either my own or a client's work.

My main go-to book is *Proofreading Secrets of Best-Selling Authors* by Kathy Ide. Based on *The Chicago Manual of Style*, which is the industry standard for fiction publishing, this book is a concise compilation of the most common concerns for fiction writers. It includes sections on proofreading, punctuation, usage, grammar, formatting, etc. It also provides space for you to write your own notes and reminders. If you have any doubts, check the rules.

Some tricky punctuation

In my work as a copyeditor, I see some common errors, especially regarding commas. Some writers seem to think a particular word signals a particular punctuation, especially commas. But remember it depends on that word's job in the sentence. The following are just a few such words I look for.

Now

Now, what was I doing before that interruption?
Now they tell me!

In the first example, *now* is used as an interjection and is optional. With or without it, the sentence means the same thing.

In the second example, *now* is an adverb telling when the action, *tell*, takes place. No comma is needed.

But

Another word that signals possible comma confusion is the conjunction *but*. In the following examples, observe where commas are used or not used. Do you know why all of these are correct? (By the way, it's all right to begin a sentence with *but*.)

Robert intended to focus on the game, but the children's antics kept diverting his attention.

(*But* joins two independent clauses and needs to be preceded by a comma.)

She shopped for the perfect set of tools but couldn't find any that pleased her.

(*But* joins two verb phrases and should not be preceded by a comma.)

But she refused to let go.

(*But* is part of the main clause.)

But, he now realized, his friends had already finished building the porch.

(The main clause is interrupted by a clause that provides additional information.)

Her tone was firm but gentle.

(*But* joins two adjectives.)

So

In the following cases, *so* is used as a conjunction.

They reinforced the bridge *so* heavier vehicles could use it.

(No comma before *so* because it's a subordinate clause. If you can put *that* in the sentence, omit the comma. *They reinforced the bridge so* that *heavier vehicles could use it.* In common usage, we omit *that* in this sentence.)

The bridge is now in place, so we're driving over it.

(This sentence has two main clauses, so a comma is necessary.)

Caveat

Like *now*, *so* can also be used as an interjection. In that case, it's followed by a comma.

So, what's the next step?

Then
The word *then* is most often used as an adverb. It is not a conjunction and therefore does not join two similar elements in a sentence. *The Chicago Manual of Style* and the *Merriam-Webster Dictionary* advise us to use a comma before *then* when *and* or *but* is omitted but implied.

I bought the seeds, then planted them in my garden.

The basic key to knowing when and where to place commas is found in knowing the differences between clauses (main and subordinate) and phrases.

One publishing house I wrote for didn't use the serial comma, which I found a bit disconcerting. This famous example shows why I prefer to use a comma before *and*. Perhaps it will bring you a chuckle.

I want to thank my parents, Mother Theresa and the pope. (Sounds like those two beloved and celibate religious leaders were my parents. Obviously not!)

I want to thank my parents, Mother Theresa, and the pope. (See how the serial comma makes it clear whom I'm thanking?)

I followed my publisher's rules, of course, but as an indie author, you get to make the choice of which form to use. Just be sure you're consistent.

Typos

Locating and fixing typos is just as important as editing for correct grammar. One of my common typing mistakes is *form* in place of *from*. My right hand seems to want to outrun my left hand. We need to be aware of any such finger patterns so we can remember to check them…not always easy when we're in the midst of writing an exciting story and the words just seem to flow. Sometimes it's the sneaky little typos, such as *is* for *it* or vice versa, *what* for *that*, etc., that get past our most diligent self-editing.

Advice from the experts

So how do you find your mistakes? After all, you don't know what you don't know, right? Also, after reading your story over a hundred times, your eyes may tend to skip over errors. Here are some tips from some bestselling authors. I'm sure you'll recognize their names.

James Scott Bell says: Print out a hard copy and put a "cover" on it that has your name and a made-up blurb from *Publishers Weekly* on how great it is. Then read the whole thing like a reader who wants to know if the blurb is right! James Scott Bell, International Thriller Writers Award Winner, www.jamesscottbell.com. Mr. Bell has also written a helpful book for self-editing you may want to add to your personal resources, *Revision and Self-Editing*, 2008.

C. J. Darlington says: What often helps me is to send my document to my Kindle and read it there as if I were reading any other author's book. It helps me to detach a bit from things and see the manuscript with new eyes. Visit Darlington's website at http://www.cjdarlington.com.

From multi-published, multi-award-winning author Deborah Raney (www.deborahraney.com): Two things:

■ Always print out your manuscript at least once. I'm amazed how many errors I find in print that I simply did not see on the screen.

■ Read your manuscript aloud—especially the dialogue and beats and tags surrounding dialogue. Again, I catch so much that I didn't see when reading on a computer screen.

Kerry Nietz, award-winning author of *Frayed* and *Amish Vampires in Space*, suggests: Read dialog out loud. That helps make it more natural. It doesn't hurt to read everything out loud, actually. Just make sure you're alone. (wink) Also, make sure to let the manuscript sit a while, maybe even a couple of weeks after finishing the first draft. Go back and read it for editing purposes as a reader. (http://www.kerrynietz.com)

From Stephanie Grace Whitson: Read it aloud to yourself. The ear will often hear syntax that doesn't flow as well as it might, repeated words, etc., things the eye misses with silent reading. Find Ms. Whitson at http://stephaniewhitson.com.

Steve Laube of the Steve Laube Literary Agency advises that Novelists should read *Self-Editing for Fiction Writers* by Browne and King. (https://stevelaube.com.)

Other tips

From Kim Vogel Sawyer: Staying in POV can be tricky. Color-coding your POV characters' scenes helps you stay in that character's head. You can also use the colors to see if you're giving equal voice to both hero and heroine in the story. (www.KimVogelSawyer.com)

Carolyne Aarsen suggests: Make a list of pet phrases or words and search for them when you're done editing. As well, double check that you don't use unusual words too often. I usually put an asterisk by them as I'm writing (yearned, flitted, etc.) Then, when it's time to edit, I do a search for the asterisks and I check to see how often I've used that word. (www.caarsen.com)

Louise here: I confess to having several pet words that keep popping up in my manuscripts. It can be hard to get rid of them but worth the effort.

Conclusion

It's not enough to create an exciting, compelling story. You also need to make sure it's presented to your readers in a professional manner so they are not pulled out of your story. If an author's mistakes are bad enough or frequent enough, some readers put the novel down for good and won't buy any more books from that author.

As you can see, self-editing is extremely important, but remember, in your quest for the perfect book, nothing beats hiring an experienced copyeditor to read your manuscript. Even though I work as a copyeditor for other authors, I always have a professional read my indie work before I publish. It's always worth the expense.

Checklist for your final self-edit

1. Set my manuscript aside for a week or more.
2. Review grammar and spelling rules I'm not sure of.
3. Print a copy of my novel and read it out loud.
4. Mark any typos and errors and correct them in the manuscript.
5. Have a professional copyeditor or at least a truly qualified critique partner read your manuscript.

When these tasks are completed, your novel truly will be ready to upload…and, hopefully, sell millions of copies!

Here are the answers to those quizzes. If you have any questions, be sure to check your dictionary.

1. How will the weather (affect/effect) your trip? **affect**
2. If you don't have a map, you won't know where (your/you're) going. **you're**
3. During the hurricane, the house lost (it's/its) roof. **its**
4. The difference between you and (me/myself/I) is obvious. **me**
5. I'm going to (lie/lay) down for a nap. **lie**
6. It's necessary to know what (their/there/they're) contributing to our project. **they're**
7. I noticed that David and (me/myself/I) were on the list. **I**
8. She did not know (whom/who) had called her. **who**
9. There are some vitamins that you should take (everyday/every day). **every day**
10. How much (further/farther) do you plan to pursue your research for this book? **further**
11. The bank has a (lean/lien) against my friend's house. **lien**
12. The soldier called out to (whoever/whomever) held the flag. **Whoever**
13. I will try (and/to) fix that broken fence. **to**

1. Are you a student, own a home, and need additional income? **faulty parallelism**
Corrected: Are you a student? Do you own a home and need additional income?
2. As a doctor, this condition is a symptom of a serious disease. **dangling modifier**
The condition is not the doctor!
Corrected: As I doctor, I can see this condition is a symptom of a serious disease.
3. Hiding from the sheriff, the woodshed was a poor option for the thief. **misplaced modifier**
The woodshed is not hiding from the sheriff!

Corrected: Hiding in the woodshed, the thief foolishly chose the woodshed.

4. None of us are perfect. **subject/verb agreement**
When none means no one, use the singular word: None of us *is* perfect.

How did you do? If you have any questions about these answers, check your dictionary.

Now, what's your plan for improving your self-editing?

Bonus

Here are a few errors I found recently in a self-published book. You don't want readers to hit these speed bumps in the middle of an otherwise exciting read! If you don't see what's wrong with these sentences, again, check your dictionary. These mistakes, which a reasonably priced copyeditor would have caught, just made me sad for the author, because I cannot recommend the book to other readers, nor will I waste my time on any other books he/she writes. These are just a few of the mistakes I found.

The borders (instead of boarders) sat around the table eating their supper.

When the sheriff uncovered the thief's plan, the gig (instead of the jig) was up.

I reigned (instead of reined) in my emotions.

The explosion didn't even phase (instead of faze) the old horse.

Its (instead of It's) got to be better than this.

The hat was to fancy (instead of too fancy) for me.

And finally:

His **paragons** did his dirty work for him.

(I assume the author meant minions, underlings, or henchmen. A paragon is a model of excellence, hardly the type of person to do someone's dirty work.

Such malaprops ruin story for the reader or, at the least, leave her scratching her head, wondering what the author meant.)

If your book is worth writing, worth spending money to research and market, it's surely worth the relatively small amount of money you will pay a copyeditor.

Find out more about Louise M. Gouge at the back of the book!

Chapter 17
Indie or Traditional Publishing?
Pros and Cons
By Louise M. Gouge, Julie
Lessman, and MaryLu Tyndall

Louise M. Gouge

When I sold my Ahab's Legacy series and later my Then Came series, I thought I was on my way to success as an author. But despite excellent reviews, I was dismayed twice when my two publishers closed the imprints through which my books had been published. Nothing I did or could have done caused those closings. They were just the way of the publishing industry. I went on to write fifteen more books for Harlequin's Love Inspired Historical line, but again, through no fault of mine, the publisher closed the imprint for which I wrote.

While still writing for LIH, I decided to self-publish my first two series as a backup plan, and I'm very glad I did. They were all out of print, and my rights had been returned. The publishers even sent the edited pdf files, so I didn't have much work to do to prepare them for republishing. I hired a cover artist to create new covers for the Ahab series and put them out in e-book form on Kindle, NOOK, and Smashwords. As for my Then Came series, I loved the covers so much that I bought them from the design company and put those titles up for sale, too. One extra detail about the third book in the series, *Then Came Love*, the publisher had not completed its publishing process. So I hired the very talented Jeff Gerke to design a cover that so closely matched those for *Then Came Faith* and *Then Came Hope* that no one would ever know they were not designed by the same artist. This is my bestselling series, in part I'm sure because of those beautiful covers.

While I continue to pursue traditional publishing by sending out proposals through my agent, at least now I have control over whether my books are published and put up for sale or hidden in a drawer (or computer file) never to see the light of day. And my indie books have been bringing in a steady, if modest, income every month. I have many other book ideas that were rejected by trad publishers, stories I believe in and want to make available for my readers. It's an ongoing process that fulfills my artist dreams, so you can be sure I'll keep on working on them.

MaryLu Tyndall

My first fourteen novels were traditionally published. Wow, what a great experience! I was very blessed to get into the business in 2003 when inspirational historicals were doing well and publishers were seeking new authors. Barbour, my publisher, was extremely good to me. They paid me well, sent me on book tours, brought me to conferences, hired the best editors, etc. It was a wonderful time, and I learned much about the publishing business, writing, and marketing. But times change. E-books began flooding the market—cheap e-books! Book stores closed. Authors began self-publishing their own books. Now readers had choices, many choices, and they got spoiled with low prices. Most publishers had a hard time keeping up with it all. So instead of trying new authors who had unique ideas, they gravitated toward their tried-and-true authors who were already making them money. Instead of taking risks, they tried to please readers who towed the middle ground. Hence, I was booted out! I laugh about it now, but it hurt at the time. Little did I know God had bigger plans for me.

Enter self-publishing. It was intimidating, scary, and completely unknown to me, but I took it step by step, learned the ropes, and published my first self-published novel, *The Ransom*, in 2014. I had a blast! I was finally in charge of my career. You see, when you are under contract with a publisher, they own your book. They can tell you what to write and what not to write. They have say over the cover, the editing, how much marketing they will do for you, when they release it and at what price. Now, with self-publishing, I could decide all those things. *The Ransom* did really well, and since its release, I've self-published five more books! They are all selling well, and I couldn't be happier. Since then, my publisher gave me back my rights to several more of my out-of-print books, so I slapped new covers on them and put them up for sale, too.

I currently have no agent, and I'm not seeking publication through traditional methods. Why? Actually, I don't see the point. The only thing a publisher can do for me is pay for the editor and book cover and invest money in marketing avenues that are not open to me as an individual. Marketing seems to be a huge reason many traditional authors give for staying with a publisher. I agree that publishers are able to do a much better job at marketing your books than you will be able to. However, from discussions I've had with many authors, that type of investment is not a guarantee by your publisher. They may prefer to place their marketing money with an established author and skimp on a new author they aren't sure of yet.

Having said all that, I'll list the pros and cons of self vs. traditional publishing below as I see them. I hope this helps you make the best choice for you.

Pros of self-publishing:
- You have complete control over your career and your book
- You keep your own profits. (Amazon pays you up to 70% royalty)
- You   can   write   whatever   you   want.

Cons of self-publishing:

- Expense. You pay for your own editor, book cover, and possibly formatting if you can't do it yourself. (I do my own with Scrivener. Easy.) Book covers are not expensive. I'm not paying more than $300 per cover. Editing can cost you close to $1000 or above, depending on the reputation of the editor.
- You don't have a marketing department backing you up or the contacts they have to advertise your book.
- You have to run your own business. Cover design, hire an editor, taxes, etc.
- Once you self-publish, if you don't sell well, it will be harder to break into traditional publishing. (Or so they say.)

Pros of Traditional publishing:
- Legitimacy (overrated)
- Your paperback is in physical book stores
- Marketing!
- All expenses are paid: Cover, Editor, marketing, etc.

Cons of Traditional publishing:
- Very hard to break into it, and even if you do, it's hard to stay.
- Advances and royalty rates are pretty low for new writers (and even for experienced).
- Once you sign over your rights, it can be hard to ever get them back.

As for me, I intend to continue self-publishing my books. I'm having a blast doing it, and I love being in control. However, if an opportunity comes up to publish traditionally again, I will consider it. But I will continue to self-publish, no matter what. I know it can be a tough decision for some writers, and I hope I've made it a little easier for you.

Julie Lessman

I am a hybrid author, which means I am both traditionally published by a top publisher and independently published on my own, which is the best of both worlds, in my humble opinion. My traditionally published books have garnered me a loyal readership that extends to my indie books, and then my indie books help sell my backlist from my traditional publisher.

See? Win-win!

No question that the rise of e-books has certainly changed the landscape of publishing over the last decade. According to author, columnist, blogger, and professor Jane Friedman, sales in "fiction alone are about half digital for traditionally published books. Once you factor in the nontraditional sales (self-published titles and Amazon Publishing titles), it would be within reason to expect about all fiction sales to be about 70% digital."

That's a lotta e-books, people!

Although I nervously dipped my toe in the indie waters with my first indie novel, *A Light in the Window*, I actually published it through my agent, who did all the work, so I don't really consider that my first truly independently published book. My first on-my-own indie book was *Isle of Hope*, and man, was I a nervous wreck, totally clueless about how to go about it. But I had an indie author friend who encouraged me and a God Who strengthened me, so I dove right in. And guess what? I discovered something really, really cool.

It's not that hard, people!

I've now published twelve indie books on my own in addition to my nine traditionally published books, and the final consensus is in.

I *love* indie publishing!

Don't get me wrong—my traditional publisher—Revell Publishing—is one of the best in the business and I absolutely LOVE my editor and everyone at Revell with whom I worked. Especially since a traditional publisher effortlessly and expertly handles the entire publishing process, from editing and cover design, to publishing and promotion, and everything in between. The only thing a traditionally published author has to do as far as publication goes is to write the book, make the edits requested, then promote it via their website and social media. Conversely, an indie author is responsible for everything from A to Z: writing, editing, proofing, cover design, e-formatting, paperback formatting, writing jacket blurbs and promo copy, uploading to Amazon and other online booksellers, and ALL promotion.

So, why go indie?

Well, for me, it was a personal decision that followed a sabbatical I took, when I told my editor I was taking time off to focus more on God, family, and writing for the sheer joy of writing. In those eight months I wrote *Isle of Hope*, which is a story based on my dysfunctional relationship with my estranged father and how God healed it. My publisher actually wanted the story but requested I cut it in half (it's 520 pages) and tone down the spirituality. Because of the powerful spiritual lesson involved in this personal story, both my agent and I felt I shouldn't cut it down but publish it myself instead.

And, yes, it was scary, but indie pubbing that series (four books) has been one of the most exciting and fulfilling things I've ever done as a writer. Suddenly I was in complete control of everything—from what I could say and do in the book and what the cover looked like, to deadlines and how to promote. I not only had all the say-so, I got all the royalties, too, although I will say that one's exposure is far more limited with indie publishing than that of a traditionally published author. After all, indie authors don't have a big publisher working on/promoting on their behalf or placing their books in libraries and bookstores.

In summation, it's my opinion that the best of both worlds is the hybrid author, but if traditional publication has eluded you, indie is certainly an excellent alternative and can be very profitable despite the glut of indie titles published over the last few years. How? Well, after careful observation, I have learned what I believe is the secret to the indie author's success. Mind you, this is not a scientific study, simply my opinion on the subject based on observation.

Ready for that tip?

I studied the amazing success of six top indie author friends of mine and discovered they all had one thing in common: they are speed writers who can put out three to five books a year. The formula for their success, therefore, has been to put out multiple books in a year and price them very low (usually 99 cents) to build a following. When they have several books out, they make the first one a freebie and promote it as such on BookBub or other discount-book promotion sites. Doing this for several years—literally feeding their readers' appetites with constant low-priced books—works like a breadcrumb trail to the point where they can slowly increase their prices. This seems to work well as long as the costs of their e-books don't exceed $4.99 and as long as they season their backlist with a lot of freebies and sales.

Personally, I am not a fast writer, so my chances for putting that many books out in a year are not great, but I have noticed that freebies and sales, when promoted, work wonders for one's profitability.

So, my final piece of advice? Don't let indie publishing intimidate you! It's not that hard, and if a technology-illiterate author like me can do it, anyone can! Just takes a little trial and error to get it right. Research it and go for it, because just the satisfaction and confidence one gets from actually doing it start to finish is well worth the experience.

Chapter 18
Marketing for those who hate Marketing
By Everyone

Michelle Griep

Just the word marketing makes me break out in hives. I want to be a writer, not a social media guru. But honestly, fellow writers, the truth is that you're going to have to master a few marketing skills in order to get the word out about your book.

One of my favorite ways to market is to do a giveaway. I know that it seems counterintuitive to hand out your work for free when it took you hours upon hours of slaving over a hot keyboard to get that novel finished, but it is a great way to garner new readers. In fact, some of my more rabid readers found out about me simply by me posting a giveaway on Facebook or Goodreads.

To do a giveaway, I recommend using Rafflecopter. It's a super easy site to use and gives you control over how people can sign up. You can have them tweet about your book. You can have them share on Facebook, like your Pinterest page, follow your blog or whatever it is you want them to do. And the best part about Rafflecopter is that it picks the winners for you totally at random.

Yeah, you'll lose out on the profits of one of your books by giving it away, but if you gain a reader who becomes a huge fan and buys all your future titles, then it's worth it.

Connie Almony

As I write this section, the United States Congress is holding hearings that could dramatically affect the practices of the tech companies most responsible for information dissemination in the United States. These hearings may have significant impact on the various avenues for marketing your book. Even if they do not affect change, many other factors will. We authors often discuss the shifting rules and algorithms of Amazon, Twitter, and Facebook, as well as the addition of "hot" new social media platforms and promotional sites. Today, information dissemination is as fluid as a swollen river in Noah's flood.

With that in mind, it is not only essential to be aware of a few methods of promoting your book today but to know how to keep up with the changing trends and be able to evaluate their effectiveness for your product. It is also important to understand that once a method of promotion is known to be effective, all sellers flock to it, making it harder to access due to competition (i.e., what we have seen with some book promotion newsletters), more expensive due to the effects of supply and demand, and crowded. How do you make your book stand out in that crowd? Given the multitude is continually shifting, the answer is not just about what I do *now* but how I stay in front of the herd.

Therefore, my advice to authors who want to have the most effective marketing plan is threefold:

■ Use a method that brings your readers to a platform which you control. For instance, it's a good practice to offer free and discounted material to those who sign up for your newsletter. By growing the number of recipients of your newsletter, you increase your permitted access to a ready audience. Not only can you promote directly to them, but you can also survey them in years to come on factors that will help you update your marketing strategy.

- Watch what bestselling authors in your genre are doing. Sign up for their newsletters, follow them on social media, and consider what they do in these places. Take note of where they advertise. It may even be more effective to shadow *newer* authors than it is established ones. Long-time bestselling authors may have an accumulated audience grown through promotions that were trendy—gasp!—a whole two years ago, but are not as effective for the newbie today.
- Do lots of A/B testing of your promotional activities. See which of two slightly different ads or activities bring the most Return-On-Investment (ROI). It is much easier to do this today, especially if you are an independent author, than it was many years ago. MailChimp, for instance, has an A/B model for evaluating subject headings for your newsletter. Most online advertising opportunities have stats that help the author assess the cost per click of comparable ads. And with the independent author's ability to access immediate sales information from the booksellers' dashboards, the author can calculate a fair estimate of the result of each ad.

So, make sure you stay well informed and are nimble enough to utilize the next best thing.

Lynnette Bonner

I will focus my marketing advice on two big things I've done that I feel have been beneficial. And then conclude my section with a few tips I hope you'll find helpful in a broad sense.

Newsletters: Many of the other gals in this book have spoken of the need for a newsletter. And I so agree with that. It is very important to have a marketing avenue that YOU as the author control. If social media sites suddenly start charging for the privilege of their use, you will still have a way of connecting with your most avid fans.

Ways that I've grown my list:

- Do a group giveaway with other authors in your same genre. You each give away one eBook and people can sign up for the newsletters of the authors they choose. Do this by using BookFunnel's group promotion option (you will have to be at least a mid-list level subscriber) so that the readers aren't batch subscribing to every author's newsletter, but only those they choose. With each author promoting the giveaway, it is easy to add hundreds or even thousands of readers to your list.
- Join a group promo hosted by Ryan Zee, Book Cave, or another author. Opportunities are out there. If you are part of some author groups via social media, chances are you'll come across some.
- Almost every month I do a giveaway of some sort on my newsletter. I collaborate with other businesses who might also want to gain some followers, and by doing this I add a few hundred subscribers each time. Just make sure people understand that they are subscribing to both lists.
- Put a link to your newsletter in the back of every single book you release. In between promotions I can tell these links are working by the few subscriptions that trickle in each week. These are actually probably your most valuable subscribers because they are the ones who truly, truly *want* to be subscribed to your list.
- For the content of your newsletter, remember that people want to know about you as the author. Sharing about my family and my life sometimes seems a bit

exposing, but since I started doing that, I've gotten a lot more interaction from readers.

Website: Think of your website as your base of operations. It should be beautiful and match up with the genre you write. It should be easy to navigate. It should be branded with your name brand in as many places as possible without being obnoxious.

What do I mean by your name brand? I encourage every author to develop a "logo" of sorts from their name. Every time someone sees your name, it should be in the same font-work, so that your name becomes as visually familiar as it does auditorily or conceptually.

Your website also gives you other distinct advantages over authors who do not have one. I hope it goes without saying that at the back of every one of your books there should be a link to another one of your books. If it is book one of a series, for instance, you would link to book two. The final book of a series can link to book one of your next series, etc.

None of the distributors will allow you to have a link to a different distributor in the books you list for sale with them. Amazon, for instance, doesn't want you to have links to a book for sale on Barnes and Noble and vice versa. But they will allow you to link to your own website. Early on in my career, when I only had a few books out, I would put only Barnes and Noble links into books I distributed via Barnes and Noble, and Amazon links into books distributed via Amazon. But this soon became too much of a burden. So now, I have all the links at the backs of my books point to my website. From my website I can then link out to all the distributors a book is available on. The website acts as a central hub. And I only have to create one eBook file for each of my books instead of one for each distributor.

Tips: Finally, for my section here, I'll leave you with just a few tips that I hope will be helpful.

-Nothing sells your writing like your writing. Your first and very best marketing practice is to write the absolute best story you possibly can and edit it so that it doesn't have any mistakes in it, both for plot and grammatical issues.

-After your writing, your cover is your next best marketing tool. Don't skimp on it. Don't try to do it yourself. Money spent for a quality cover will pay for itself many times over.

-It takes time to build a following. Don't get discouraged when things are slow.

-Focus more on connecting with readers than on making sales. Connecting means having conversations about things other than your book.

-Watch what successful authors are doing to market their books. You can usually tell what's working and what's not.

-Word-of-mouth is still the best form of advertising. Get people talking about your book. People are more likely to buy and talk about something that appeals to their emotions.

-Be sure you have your elevator pitch for your book. You should be able to answer in one or two concise and appealing sentences when someone asks "What do you write?" Focus more on the feelings you want to convey than on the actual plot of the story, yet the feel and the plot need to match. For instance, for my Shepherd's Heart series, which is an historical western romance series, the series' tagline is: "Step into a day when outlaws ran free, the land was wild, and guns blazed at the drop of a hat." It doesn't really tell much about the stories, but it gives a good feel of each of the plots in the series.

-Don't be afraid to try things. Whether something succeeds or not, it's a learning experience.

-Focus on learning one thing at a time.

-Plan marketing around events (holidays, the Super Bowl) Example: in May, ask people on your blog or FB page to comment about why their mom would enjoy a free copy of your book, then draw a winner.

-Be sure to keep all your marketing materials in a special file for reusing and revamping in the future.

-Keep track of what works and what doesn't work. As best you can.

-It's better to do a little marketing very well than a lot of marketing very poorly.

-Make it really easy for people to share your message. Always include a link. Make your Tweets clickable. More people will share with one click rather than copy and paste. If you write Tweets for people to share, be sure they're the right length. (www.clicktotweet.com)

-Consider time spent marketing for other authors as part of your marketing time.

-No matter what "they" say, nothing in marketing is a "have to." We all have limited time. Decide what YOU want to focus on and do those things well, while at the same time having an open mind to learning and trying new things to see if they work better than what you are currently doing.

-Most of all, try to have fun. This is part of our ministry as Christian writers. Remember that God gave you those stories and that He has people He wants to reach with them.

Elizabeth Ludwig

I've written for several different publishing houses since selling my first book, but one of the tips I heard repeated from the marketing teams at all of them was to market my books locally as much as possible. In fact, one of them told me explicitly to focus on establishing my name in my own hometown because they would take care of any marketing that needed to be done nationally. To do this, I focused on finding platforms where I could speak that might not even be a blip on someone else's radar. For my historical novels, I chose places like historical societies, DAR groups, libraries, and book clubs. As a former children's ministry sponsor and youth director, I also targeted audiences such as Women's Ministry Organizations, youth groups, Bible study groups, and mission teams. Community groups included Rotary Clubs, Lions Clubs, retirement homes, and public schools. For that last one, it helped that I'd also worked in public education for over twenty years.

The point is to focus on areas where I might have knowledge or information that will appeal to the group I am trying to reach. Of course, none of this would have done much good had I not taken the time to properly prepare and organize my material before speaking to each group. In fact, my best tip for promoting before a live studio audience is simply this: Understand that I am a *professional* author…and then act like it!

Louise M. Gouge

For me, the biggest issue with self-publishing is marketing. I'm not great at it, so to attain peace in that regard, I do what I can and let the Lord do the rest. Wise indie marketers always talk about ROI (return on investment), and this is an important factor to me. My modest indie sales don't provide the funds for me to go wide, so I have to be very careful and deliberate in each step I take. I literally can't afford to make mistakes.

So, taking the advice of some of the "big guns," I have a newsletter that I send out with the release of each new book and with each new season of the year. I love to read the newsletters I've subscribed to, and I try to make my own worthy of being read. I talk about other interesting topics beside my book, but I do mention my latest release or featured title and give a link where it can be purchased.

How did I build my reader list? I've taken part in several scavenger hunts with other authors. Not only are those fun, but the readers who participate are true fiction fans. They really do want to know about great books. In these events, each author offers special prizes beyond the grand prize. I always pick up a few new subscribers that way. I've also taken part in Ryan Zee's campaigns, adding even more to my list.

In an effort to catch the attention of as many people as possible, I announce my books through my Facebook author page. My only "friends" are people I know and/or people who have expressed interest in my books. While I don't post frequently and most of my posts are about my kitties, my "perfect" grandkids, or my favorite ice cream, I do mention my books when they're released. It's hard to gauge whether the ROI is worth the time I spend on FB, but I believe it's effective in getting my name out there.

Another method of getting noticed is joining a blog. I'm a member of a multi-author blog on which we can write about anything we want to. With only one post to write every other week, I can keep up with the schedule, which I wouldn't be able to do on a daily or weekly blog of my own.

Finally, I have a website to which I can send people who are interested in my books and my writing journey.

These are the methods of marketing I can manage without getting migraines or ulcers. And I have great admiration for those savvy authors who can go wide. We each must find what works for us.

Success-proven tips from 10 award-wining authors

Erica Vetsch

Cross-Pollinate. Gather with other authors and do a group promotion of like books. Get more bang for your buck by sharing the costs and multiplying the reach. Whether it's a group book signing, a Facebook Party, a hashtag party, or giveaway, you will spread the word faster and farther as a group than any author can do on his/her own.

Ane Mulligan

I'm not a prolific marketer. To be honest, like most writers, I hate marketing and would rather write. I have done Ryan Zee promotions to build my newsletter list, advertised in Book Bub, and did some e-Reader promotions. Those cost and while the ROI (return on investment) was good, I really like the Facebook reader groups. For one, they're free. They allow members to promote their books and the groups are filled with avid readers.

When I join a group, I add them to a spreadsheet. I have columns for:
- The group's URL
- The number of members
- Any posting specs
- The date I post

You do need to read their guidelines; a few only allow once a day, Fridays only, etc. When I first tried these, I checked my sales ranking on Amazon. Either that night or the next day, I checked again. In every instance, I found a significant jump in my sales ranking. Since those books promoted are traditionally published, I don't have exact numbers. But the corresponding months' royalties have always been excellent.

Here's a screen shot of my spreadsheet: note: some of the columns are hidden. I do that the next time I promote so it's easy to move to the check-off column. Also note there are several tabs across the bottom for different types of groups, i.e.: large, e-book, small, and paid promo.

Facebook Group	REACH	Joined	Posted CSS.HtC! 7/17	Posted BB 7/28	Posted CS 2 8/4	Posted BB 8/23	Posted LICS 9/5	Posted LICS 9/16	series 9/27	CSR 1-Oct	CSS 27-Oct
Kindle Book Market	40,888	x	x	x	x	x	x	x	x	x	x
Kindle Krazy	27,962	x	x	x	x	x	x	x	x	x	x
Amazon Kindle Goodreads	26,085	x	x	x	x	x	x	x	x	x	x
KINDLE PUBLISHERS	25,303	x	x	x	x	x	x	x	x	x	x
Nook & Kindle Readers	23,098	x	x	x	x	x	x	x	x	x	x
EbooksNBooksPromosGroup	21,429	x	x	x	x	x	x	x	x	x	x
There's an ebook in the room	18,573	x	x	x	x	x	x	x	x	x	x
The Kindle Hub	16,276	x	x	x	x		x	x	x	x	x
E books Rock.	15,086	x	x	x	x		x	x	x	x	x
Amazon Kindle	15,177	x	x	x	x		x	x	x	x	x
Kindle Readers & Kindle Writers	14,911	x	x	x	x		x	x	x	x	x
Free Kindle Book Promo	13,508	x	x	x							x

Tabs: Large Grps | E-book Grps | Sml Grps | $ Promo | CK OUT | +

Hallee Bridgeman

KNOWN AUTHOR

Goodreads did a survey of several thousand readers, asking them about the sources where they often find books. An overwhelming 96% of readers claimed they find books from a known author.

A known author means the reader is following this author in order to receive news about her, whatever that means. It could be that she interacts with her in social media or it could be that she waits for the next book display in the local bookstore.

What it means is that the author somehow gets the word out to her readers that her next book is available, or her backlist is available, or whatever.

NEWSLETTER

The best, number one way, to reach readers as a known author is through your newsletter. Better than social media, a newsletter is a reader intentionally clicking a box and saying, "Yes, I want to hear from you. I want you to tell me your news."

I cannot stress this enough: if you only have enough time or resources to do one single thing in the world of marketing yourself to readers, then pour all of your time and resources into developing your newsletter and growing your newsletter list with readers who want to hear from you.

When you set up your newsletter, it's important to use a newsletter service. Many of them are free up to a certain number of emails going out on a monthly basis. Do a web search for "newsletter services" and investigate the options. I used Mailchimp until I had too big a subscriber list. It was perfect for me to learn the art of newsletters, and it was really user friendly (and I still have it since that is the link in my backlist of books). But once I got over 2,000 subscribers, I had to switch because while it was free for a long time, the cost over 2,000 was way more than other services. I spent months investigating which one to go to next, and personally chose MailerLite. But I had Mailchimp for about four years.

The reason you need to use a service is because there are laws, nationally and internationally, about email marketing. The services keep up-to-date with those laws, making you in compliance with the FCC and other organizations.

One thing I didn't know early enough is to have a "double opt in" for your newsletter list. This keeps robots from signing up and flooding your list with fake emails. I honestly don't know what the purpose of that is and what they're able to do with receiving my newsletter; however, these same newsletter lists monitor how many people open your newsletter and interact with it, so you don't want to just be glutted with fake emails or your open rates will be low and you could potentially lose the ability to use that service in the future.

You are required by law to have a physical address listed on a newsletter that goes out to subscribers. I got a post office box for this purpose, so that my physical address wouldn't be listed. The cost of the P.O. Box is a normal business expense and tax deductible.

Once your newsletter service is set up, the link to subscribe to your newsletter should be everywhere your readers go. On your social media (there is a tab on my Facebook page titled, "Sign up for my newsletter, and on my Twitter, the pinned post is the sign up for my newsletter post), on your website (prominent), and in the back of every book or at the end of every article you write. Don't make it too difficult for a reader to connect with you, or you might lose the opportunity.

To see what my subscriber pages look like, here are the links:

Mailchimp: http://eepurl.com/sT4vn

MailerLite:
https://landing.mailerlite.com/webforms/landing/l6c2w0

Some authors like to offer an incentive for people to sign up for their newsletters. I offer three: every month I give away a $25 gift card from Amazon to one subscriber to my newsletter. I also offer a free ebook of my romantic suspense novella **On the Ropes** to every subscriber. I'll talk about how I do that in a few minutes. Finally, only newsletter subscribers can sign up to be part of my birthday club.

Once all of that is established and your mom and best friend have been the first people to sign up to receive all the news about you, then determine how often you'll send a newsletter out and what kind of information you're going to provide. I have friends who send out a newsletter quarterly, and friends who only send out a newsletter with a release or book special sales or whatever.

I send mine out monthly on the first Friday of every month, unless I have a release that week. Then, I send it on the second Friday, because I also send it out on release day. For the monthly newsletter, I use the same format for every newsletter:

My header is the same. It says, "Hallee's Happenings, the official newsletter of Hallee Bridgeman." My branded name style is used in the title (we'll talk about branded names later in this book).

As an introduction, I have some story about my personal life, especially as it pertains to the time of year. For instance, on the newsletter that will go out the first part of January, I'll talk about something at Christmas or New Year. I almost always include a personal picture of me or my children. Contained in the text of this personal story, I'll summarize some of the news contained inside the newsletter—either a preorder that's come up, a special sale I'm advertising, or if I'm speaking somewhere. Then I remind readers to keep reading to see who won the $25 Amazon gift card this month, because I don't notify my readers they won. They have to notify me that they're the winner.

Scattered among these normal sections are "find Hallee online" with all of the logos of the social media networks, "join the Fans of the Jewel Series Facebook group" (and all of my other series as well), and how to reach me.

Here is a link to one of my monthly newsletters if you want to look at it:

http://preview.mailerlite.com/c8h2v9/83832401348579057 4/o5y8/

NEWSLETTER ONBOARDING

Beyond my regular monthly newsletter, I also have what is called an "onboarding series". What this means is that whenever someone signs up for my newsletter, the very first thing that happens after they've confirmed they want to receive it is that an email automatically goes out with the subject line "Here's Your Free Book!" Inside it is the link to the free romantic suspense novella that I offer to all of my newsletter subscribers.

I am able to provide this book free through a site called Bookfunnel (http://www.bookfunnel.com), which watermarks the ebook that the reader receives so that the reader is unable to do anything with it but read it.

One day later, the subscriber receives and email with the subject line, "Welcome to the Family!". In this email, I tell the reader that I hope he or she is deep into reading **On The Ropes.** I then discuss, very briefly, how much I love romance and admit that my very first book hero crush was Almanzo Wilder from the *Little House on the Prairie* series. I casually mention my other series, but I don't put any purchase links or anything about buying my books in the body of the email in any way. The only information I provide is in a "p.s." with my website address and a link to email me.

Three days later, I send out an email with the subject line, "Do You Love Romance Like I Do?". I write about hoping the reader finished reading **On The Ropes**, and I talk about the German Shepherd who was prominent in the story. I tell the reader that if he or she enjoyed that story, then the first book of every series I've written is free, and provide the links to those books. I also mention the birthday club and say how much I hope that the reader will sign up for it so that I have the opportunity to pray for him or her as I write out the cards. Again, the only links are the ones to the free ebooks and the Birthday Club.

Two days later, I send an email with the subject line, "It All Began With a Dream." In this email, I give my writing testimony. I link to my website article about my own personal love at first sight story, link to a couple of the free ebooks, and thank the reader for being part of my family. Once again, there are no sales pitches.

Three days later, I send an email titled, "I Love You. Really." Here, I talk about how much I love my readers and love hearing from my readers. I encourage them to email me or write to me, because doing so gives me so much encouragement and keeps me writing. I talk about my YouTube channel and Monday Morning Coffee and Chats and thank them for reading my books. No sales pitches. Oh - and I include a picture of my two dogs. I often hear from readers in response to this email, and make sure I answer every single email in a timely fashion.

The final email is sent one week later. Here I title it, "I Wish I Could Be You" and lament about how I'll never be able to read my books for the first time like my readers can. And here, finally, I give brief descriptions of all of the series, list all of my books, provide book covers, and purchase links. For the first time, the reader is getting purchase links for books other than my free books.

The next email they'll get from me will be the normal monthly email, and other than the once-a-month, the only other email will be notifications of release days.

What is the purpose of this "onboarding series" and doesn't it feel spammy to me? Well, to be honest, it did feel a little spammy as I was setting it up and writing the emails. But the intent is not to sell anything, which is why I didn't try to with the first five emails. The intent is only to give the readers an impression of me that is personal, not some high and lofty unapproachable author. This way, they get to know me and start seeing me as a person. A friend. Someone who cares about them and about their birthday, and their romances, and their tastes, and their enjoyment of the books I provide them.

In the newsletter world, under the header of "author," the industry average open-rate for newsletters is 26.18%. Since this onboarding series began, I've sent over 20,000 onboarding emails, and the open rate is at 60%, even with the sixth email in 18 days. By the time the reader receives that sixth email, and the reader is opening them and reading them, he or she *wants* to know what else I have to say. The reader has become invested in me as a person.

I am now their "known author."

MaryLu Tyndall

I'm the worst marketer on the planet! It goes against everything I am. I'm serious. So, when I first got published, and later when I went Indie, I realized I had to do something or my readers would never know about my books! So, I forced myself to slog through a few ideas. The key is to choose something that you enjoy doing (or something that you hate the least). I'm going to keep this short and just list a couple marketing tactics that have worked best for me and a couple that have not done anything to help sell my books. Now, these things may work for others, so don't discount them altogether, but perhaps you'll find you are like me in this area.

<u>Two Best things</u> (okay, 3)

Newsletter - connecting with my readers on a personal level has been extremely helpful in establishing relationships with them and hence, gathering a group of loyal people who will always buy my next book.

Blog - If you're going to start a blog, post on it regularly, and post things of interest to your readers. In other words, don't just write about you and your books, write about what moves you, what interests you, give away free advice, devotions, stories, etc. Make it a gift to your reader.

Bookbub - expensive and hard to get into, but worth it if you can.

Two Worst things

Facebook/Twitter - I don't think I've ever sold more than one or two books from a facebook event. Others have great success here, but not me.

Purchasing expensive ads for online magazines.

Julie Lessman

Oh my goodness, how I *love* being an author! But God help me, if there's one thing I despise about it above all else (except 1-star reviews, of course!), it's marketing.

Brrrrr ... cold chills!

And I'm *pretty* sure I'm not alone. Most authors would rather write than promote, but unfortunately, it's a necessary evil if we want to sell books, which, of course, we all do. So, what have I found to be the path of least resistance and pain when it comes to marketing?

Well, I've pretty much tried it all—from Facebook parties, blog tours, and videos, to newsletters, e-blasts, and blogging, both independently and in a group. I've written articles for magazines, done video and radio interviews, Facebook Live, book signings, and even hired a publicist. I've gone perma-free and run 99-cent sales that I have promoted on BookBub and other e-discount sites, set up pre-orders on both Amazon and BookBub, and run review contests (before Amazon banned remuneration of any kind).

Out of all those mentioned above, there are a few tried-and-trues that I would always do, so I'm going to list those below, along with those I rarely utilize and/or have cut out altogether.

MY MOST EFFECTIVE MARKETING MUSTS:

1. **Set Up Pre-orders on Amazon and BookBub:** This is a must! But, of course, you have to set up both your Amazon and BookBub author pages first, which is also critically important, so I've included my author pages as examples.

2. **Send Out a Newsletter/e-Blast:** A personal touch and frequency are important here, as is a professional look utilizing newsletter services such as MailChimp, Vertical Response, Constant Contact, etc. Here's a link to a great blog by author Myra Johnson that appeared on Seekerville, which is a blog for writers: Author e-Newsletters for Dummies.
   Important Note: On May 25th, 2018 the European Union's new data privacy law—or General Data Protection Regulation or GDPR—went into effect and applies to any person or business operating or storing information of EU citizens. Any author with an international following, fan base, or email subscriber list must be GDPR-compliant or can be liable for up to millions of dollars in fines. Most companies who service emails on behalf of authors—i.e. MailChimp, Vertical Response, Constant Contact, etc.—have taken steps that will enable compliance to the GDPR. But ultimately, it's you—the author—who is responsible for implementing GDPR compliance for your subscriber lists, so I strongly suggest checking with your newsletter provider to determine what steps you need to take to protect yourself.

3. **Set Up Blog Tours:** On my traditionally published books, my publisher, Revell, set up extensive blog tours—anywhere from 60 to over 100 participating blogs—where Christian bloggers sign up to read and post a review for an author's latest release on their blog, Amazon, Goodreads, etc. during a specified time period. For my independently published (indie) books, I keep a list of blogger/reviewers

who I invite to participate in my personal blog tours, but on a much smaller basis. If you would prefer to utilize a blog-tour company to set up your blog tour, you'll want to make sure it's a Christian blog-tour company to insure the best exposure for your particular market. You can find a listing of Christian blog-tour companies on the Body and Soul Publishing blog that you may want to check out.

4. **Perma-Free Novella:** I think that one of most effective ways to promote a book or series is through a free prequel novella that kicks it off. I have done this with my Isle of Hope Series, where the prequel novella, A Glimmer of Hope, is permanently free, and it was a huge success when promoted on free/discount e-book sites like BookBub, Inspired Reads, etc.

   However, to make a book perma-free, one *does* have to jump through a few hoops as Amazon will not allow an author to make a book permanently free. The only way it can happen is if you and your friends contact Amazon to let them know the book is free on other sites like Barnes & Noble, Kobo, etc. Amazon will then match the free price per their policy. But there are a number of steps you'll need to take, and here is an excellent blog from author Holly Evans' blog on how to do just that.

5. **Sales and Free Books Promoted on BookBub, Inspired Reads, and Other e-Discount Sites:** There are a few sites where you can promote your books for free, but generally, the best success is through the bigger pay-to-promote sites like BookBub, E-Reader News Today (ENT), BargainBooksy, etc. There are a ton of free/discount book-promo sites out there, but here are the Best Book Promotion Sites 2018 from the Paid Author website. My advice would be to keep track of the sites you use and the success rate they generate for your book.

6. **Promote on Personal or Group Blogs:** For ten wonderful years, I was fortunate enough to be a part of the fabulous Seekerville blog, which "inspires, encourages, teaches, and informs aspiring writers on the road to publication and beyond." Although Seekerville has been listed on *Writers Digest* "Best 101 Websites for Writers" six years running now, it is also a blog devoted to readers as well, so I strongly recommend checking it out. As an original "Seeker," I was able to promote my books on a regular basis on the Seekerville blog, as well as on my own personal blog, Journal Jots, both of which have been a huge promotional help for me.

7. **Facebook Live:** Because Facebook Live is relatively new (as of 2017), Facebook wants to stimulate its usage, therefore, promoting the algorithms for anyone who *does* a Facebook Live in order to give them more exposure. Consequently, I quickly discovered that I generally get a book-sales boost every time I do a Facebook Live. Although doing a live broadcast on Facebook can be intimidating, I figure if someone as technically illiterate as moi can do it, anyone can, so here's a Seekerville blog entitled Facebook Live: A Guinea Pig's Perspective that I wrote on how I went about it.

8. **First Chapter Teasers of Next Book in Back of Prior Book:** Including a teaser chapter for your next book in the back of prior book is an absolute *must* for promotional value. As mentioned in Chapter 11, "The Tease: Scene/Chapter Endings to Lead Your Readers On," that's exactly what Stephanie Meyer did to me with her *New Moon* teaser at the end of *Twilight*.

Keep in mind that a teaser doesn't have to be the first chapter of your next book; it can be any excerpt you feel will reel your readers into the next book or another book.

For instance, after I finished my six-book Irish family saga published by Revell, The Daughters of Boston and Winds of Change series, I was sad to leave this close-knit family behind. As a result, I wrote a prequel novel to this saga which became my first indie book, *A Light in the Window*. Not only did *A Light in the Window* bring my beloved family saga full circle, allowing me enough closure to transition to my next series more comfortably, but it also helped me promote my backlist. How? My publisher, Revell, allowed me to include a teaser excerpt from Book One of my Irish family saga, *A Passion Most Pure*, showing the hero and heroine of *A Light in the Window* some twenty years into the future, when they are the proud parents of a large Irish family.

9. **Include Backlist and "Note to the Reader" in Back of Your Latest Book:** As indie authors responsible for our own promotion, we *must* take advantage of every bit of space in our e-books, so listing links to one's backlist is critical, as is a "Note to the Reader" that not only encourages readers to post a review for your book, but asks them to follow you on BookBub. Here's a sample of mine at the back of *For Love of Liberty*:

And now, I have a favor to ask. If you enjoyed *For Love of Liberty*, would you consider posting a brief review on Amazon and Goodreads? It can be as short as one or two lines stating why you liked the book. Good reviews are critical to book sales, so that's the best way to bless your favorite authors. **NOTE: Want to be notified of my new releases/deals? Follow me on** BookBub **by signing in or signing up, then searching for my name and clicking the "follow" button.**

Thank you again for your support and God bless!

MY LEAST-EFFECTIVE MARKETING PROMOS:

1. **Book Signings:** I used to do book signings all the time, sending out postcards to—are you ready for this?—my son's wedding-invitation list, to which I also added local names from my newsletter lists. Although I did sell some books, for me, it was never worth the time and effort. So I decided to forego on book signings altogether, a decision validated by my publisher, who stated that book signings were *not* the most effective use of time and funds.

2. **Blog Interviews/Giveaways:** Throughout the course of my career, I have done tons of blog interviews/giveaways—at least 30-35 per book release, answering over 2,600 questions that I keep in a master file. But you know what? I finally figured out that the excessive amount of time and money I spent to answer the interview questions, promote the interview, respond to comments on those blog interviews, and then mail the giveaway book *far* exceeded the promotional benefit, so I quit doing them.

3. **Magazine Ad Promotion:** I have advertised my books in a number of magazines, both digital and paper, but I don't believe the benefit warranted the cost of the ad, so I discontinued this practice.

4. **Facebook Parties:** As fun as Facebook parties seem and *can* be, for me they are not worth the time and effort expended. True, there is a fair amount of exposure because the giveaways always draw, but it's my opinion that the only people who attend are readers who already buy your books, friends who probably won't buy your books, or

people who are giveaway-driven rather than interested in your books.

All the points above are based on my own personal experiences in marketing, but I'd like to leave you with a truly excellent article entitled <u>100+ Places to Promote Christian Books</u> on the <u>TrainingAuthors</u> website that I hope is as big a blessing to you as it is to me.

Author Bios

Connie Almony

Connie Almony is trained as a mental health therapist and likes to mix a little fun with the serious stuff of life. She was a 2012 semi-finalist in the Genesis Contest for Women's Fiction and was awarded an Honorable Mention in the Winter 2012 WOW Flash Fiction Contest. She is the author of *At the Edge of a Dark Forest*, a modern-day re-telling of *Beauty and the Beast* about a war-vet, amputee struggling with PTSD. Other titles include, *One Among Men* and *An Insignificant Life* (the Maryland State University series), and *Flee from Evil* about a pastor with a past who uses his underworld connections to try and save the child of the woman he wronged years ago.

You can find her books and sign up for her newsletter at ConnieAlmony.com. And meet her on the following social media outlets:

https://twitter.com/ConnieAlmony
https://www.facebook.com/ConnieAlmony
https://www.pinterest.com/conniealmony/
https://www.bookbub.com/authors/connie-almony

Lynnette Bonner

Born and raised in Malawi, Africa. Lynnette Bonner spent the first years of her life reveling in warm equatorial sunshine and the late evening duets of cicadas and hyenas. The year she turned eight she was off to Rift Valley Academy, a boarding school in Kenya where she spent many joy-filled years, and graduated in 1990.

That fall, she traded to a new duet—one of traffic and rain—when she moved to Kirkland, Washington to attend Northwest University. It was there that she met her husband and a few years later they moved to the small town of Pierce, Idaho.

During the time they lived in Idaho, while studying the history of their little town, Lynnette was inspired to begin the Shepherd's Heart Series with Rocky Mountain Oasis.

Marty and Lynnette have four children, and currently live in Washington where Marty pastors a church.

Connect with Lynnette in the Following Places

Website: http://www.lynnettebonner.com

Facebook: www.facebook.com/authorlynnettebonner

Hallee Bridgeman

With over half a million sales, Hallee Bridgeman is a best-selling Christian author who writes action-packed romantic suspense focusing on realistic characters who face real world problems. Her work has been described as everything from refreshing to heart-stopping exciting and edgy. Hallee loves coffee, campy action movies, and regular date nights with her husband. Above all else, she loves God with all of her heart, soul, mind, and strength; has been redeemed by the blood of Christ; and relies on the presence of the Holy Spirit to guide her.

Please visit Hallee at her Website:
http://www.halleebridgeman.com

Louise M. Gouge

Florida author Louise M. Gouge writes historical romance fiction, receiving the prestigious IRCA in 2005, finaling in 2011, 2015, 2016, and 2017; and placed in the Laurel Wreath in 2012. A former college English and humanities professor, she and David, her husband of fifty-plus years, enjoy visiting historical sites and museums.

Please visit Louise at

Web site https://louisemgougeauthor.blogspot.com/
Facebook: https://www.facebook.com/LouiseMGougeAuthor
Twitter: @Louisemgouge

Michelle Griep

Michelle Griep's been writing since she first discovered blank wall space and Crayolas. She is the author of historical romances: *The Captured Bride, The Innkeeper's Daughter, 12 Days at Bleakly Manor, The Captive Heart, Brentwood's Ward, A Heart Deceived,* and *Gallimore,* but also leaped the historical fence into the realm of contemporary with the zany romantic mystery *Out of the Frying Pan.* If you'd like to keep up with her escapades, find her at www.michellegriep.com or stalk her on

Facebook
Instagram
Twitter
Pinterest. https://www.pinterest.com/michellegriep/

Julie Lessman

Julie Lessman is an award-winning author whose tagline of "Passion With a Purpose" underscores her intense passion for both God and romance. A lover of all things Irish, she enjoys writing close-knit Irish family sagas that evolve into 3-D love stories: the hero, the heroine, and the God that brings them together.

Author of The Daughters of Boston, Winds of Change, Heart of San Francisco, and Isle of Hope series, Julie was American Christian Fiction Writers 2009 Debut Author of the Year and has garnered over 18 Romance Writers of America and other awards. Voted #1 Romance Author in Family Fiction magazine's 2012 and 2011 Readers Choice Awards, Julie's novels also made *Family Fiction*magazine's Best of 2015, Best of 2014, and "Essential Christian Romance Authors" 2017, as well as Booklist's 2010 Top 10 Inspirational Fiction and Borders Best Fiction. Her independent novel *A Light in the Window* was an International Digital Awards winner, a 2013 Readers' Crown Award winner, and a 2013 Book Buyers Best Award winner. Julie has also written a self-help workbook for writers entitled *Romance-ology 101: Writing Romantic Tension for the Sweet and Inspirational Markets*. Contact Julie through her website and read excerpts from each of her books at www.julielessman.com.

Elizabeth Ludwig

Elizabeth Ludwig is an award-winning author whose work has been featured on Novel Rocket, More to Life Magazine, and Christian Fiction Online Magazine. In 2008, her first novel, *Where the Truth Lies* (co-authored with Janelle Mowery), earned her the **IWA Writer of the Year Award**.

In 2011, her second mystery, *Died in the Wool* (co-authored with Janelle Mowery) was nominated for a **Carol Award**. In 2012, the EDGE OF FREEDOM series released from Bethany House Publishers. Books one and two, *No Safe Harbor* and *Dark Road Home*, respectively, earned 4 Stars from RT Book Reviews. Book three in the series, *Tide and Tempest*, received top honors with 4½ Stars and was named a finalist for the **Gayle Wilson Award of Excellence**. Elizabeth was also named a finalist in the **2015 Selah Awards** for her novella "One Holy Night", part of the bestselling anthology collection, *Christmas Comes to Bethlehem, Maine*. Most recently, she was honored to be awarded a **HOLT Medallion** for her book, *A Tempting Taste of Mystery*, part of the SUGARCREEK AMISH MYSTERIES series from Guideposts. Her latest releases include *Don't Rock the Boat* and *Shifting Sands*, part of the MYSTERIES OF MARTHA'S VINEYARD series, also from Guideposts.

Elizabeth is an accomplished speaker and teacher, often attending conferences and seminars where she lectures on editing for fiction writers, crafting effective novel proposals, and conducting successful editor/agent interviews. Along with her husband and children, she makes her home in the great state of Texas. To learn more, sign up for her newsletter at ElizabethLudwig.com or visit her on Facebook at https://www.facebook.com/elizabethludwig102

Ane Mulligan

While a large, floppy straw hat is her favorite, award-winning author Ane Mulligan has worn many different ones: hairdresser, legislative affairs director (that's a fancy name for a lobbyist), business manager, and managing director of a community theatre troupe. Her lifetime experience provides a plethora of fodder for her Southern-fried fiction (try saying that three times fast). She's a multi-published novelist and playwright. She resides in Sugar Hill, GA, with her artist husband and a lovable, goofy dog. You can find Ane at her

You can find Ane at:
Her website: www.anemulligan.com
Facebook: www.facebook.com/anemulligansouthernfriedfiction
Twitter: @AneMulligan https://twitter.com/AneMulligan
Pinterest: www.pinterest.com/anemulligan/
Google+: https://plus.google.com/u/0/+AneMulligan
Instagram: @anemulligan

MaryLu Tyndall

Best-selling author MaryLu Tyndall dreamt of pirates and sea-faring adventures during her childhood days on Florida's Coast. With more than twenty books published, she makes no excuses for the spiritual themes embedded within her romantic adventures. Her hope is that readers will not only be entertained but will be brought closer to the Creator who loves them beyond measure. In a culture that accepts the occult, wizards, zombies, and vampires without batting an eye, MaryLu hopes to show the awesome present and powerful acts of God in a dying world. A Christy award nominee and Inspirational Readers' Choice Award winner, MaryLu makes her home with her husband, six children, four grandchildren and several stray cats on the California coast.

You can connect with MaryLu on

MEWE: https://mewe.com/i/marylutyndall
PARLER: https://parler.com/profile/Marylutyndall/posts
BLOG: http://crossandcutlass.blogspot.com/
PINTEREST: http://www.pinterest.com/mltyndall/
BOOKBUB:https://www.bookbub.com/authors/marylu-tyndall
AMAZON: https://www.amazon.com/MaryLu-Tyndall/e/B002BOG7JG

Or write her at marylu_tyndall@yahoo.com

For a list of Marylu's books, check out her website book page

Erica Vetsch

Best-selling, award-winning author **Erica Vetsch** loves Jesus, history, romance, and sports. She's a transplanted Kansan now living in Minnesota, and she married her total opposite and soul mate! When she's not writing fiction, she's planning her next trip to a history museum and cheering on her Kansas Jayhawks and New Zealand All Blacks. You can connect with her at her website, www.ericavetsch.com where you can read about her books and sign up for her newsletter, and you can find her online at https://www.facebook.com/EricaVetschAuthor/ where she spends way too much time!

Success-proven tips from 10 award-wining authors

www.ingramcontent.com/pod-product-compliance
Lightning Source LLC
Chambersburg PA
CBHW022350280326
41935CB00007B/140